VALUE OF PENSIONS
IN DIVORCE
THIRD EDITION

This new edition of *Value of Pensions in Divorce* replaces the previous edition. Please discard the previous edition and related cumulative supplements.

VALUE OF PENSIONS IN DIVORCE
THIRD EDITION

MARVIN SNYDER

A PANEL PUBLICATION
ASPEN PUBLISHERS, INC.

This publication is designed to provide accurate and authorative information in regard to the subject matter covered. It is sold with the understanding that the publisher is not engaged in rendering legal, accounting, or other professional services. If legal advice or other professional assistance is required, the services of a competent professional person should be sought.

—From a *Declaration of Principles* jointly adopted by
a Committee of the American Bar Association and
a Committee of Publishers and Associations

About Panel Publishers

Panel Publishers derives its name from a panel of business professionals who organized in 1964 to publish authoritative and timely books, information services, and journals written by specialists to assist business professionals in the areas of compensation and benefits management, pension planning and compliance, and human resources, as well as owners of small to medium-sized businesses and their legal and financial advisers. Our mission is to provide practical, solution-based "how-to" information to business professionals.

Titles available from Panel Publishers on related topics include:

Books and Manuals
Dividing Pensions in Divorce
Estate and Retirement Planning Answer Book*
401(k) Answer Book*
Handbook on ERISA Litigation
The Pension Answer Book*
Pension Distribution Answer Book*
Qualified Domestic Relations Order Answer Book*
Qualified Domestic Relations Order Handbook
Qualified Medical Child Support Order Handbook

Periodicals and Electronic Titles
ERISA Litigation Alert
The QDRO Report
Journal of Pension Planning & Compliance
Journal of Pension Benefits
Panel Pension Library on CD-ROM

Companion volume of Forms and Worksheets also available.

PANEL PUBLISHERS
A Division of Aspen Publishers, Inc.
Practical Solutions for Legal and Business Professionals

SUBSCRIPTION NOTICE

This Panel product is updated on a periodic basis with supplements to reflect important changes in the subject matter. If you purchased this product directly from Panel, we have already recorded your subscription for the update service.

If, however, you purchased this product from a bookstore and wish to receive future updates and revised or related volumes billed separately for a 30-day examination review, please contact our Customer Service Department at 1-800-234-1660 or send your name, company name (if applicable), address, and the title of the product to:

Panel Publishers
A Division of Aspen Publishers, Inc.
7201 McKinney Circle
Frederick, MD 21701

To the memory of B.Z.S., and for my loving wife of nearly 40 years, Sandy, and for my son, Randy, of whom I am very proud.

ABOUT THE AUTHOR

Marvin Snyder is Senior Actuary for Pension Analysis Consultants, Inc., in Elkins Park, Pennsylvania, and President of Marvin Snyder Associates, Inc., in Las Vegas, Nevada. He is a professional qualified pension actuary with more than 30 years of experience as a consultant for defined benefit pension plans, annuity plans, and profit sharing plans of all types and sizes. Mr. Snyder has prepared over 9,000 pension valuations for divorce cases, drafted hundreds of qualified domestic relations orders for counsel, and testified as expert witness on the equitable distribution of pension values on more than 100 occasions. Mr. Snyder has spoken at many seminars, including those sponsored by the American Academy of Matrimonial Lawyers and the National Judicial College, and has lectured at Temple University, Purdue University, and the Institute of Paralegal Training in Philadelphia. Mr. Snyder has authored numerous articles. He also writes a widely distributed newsletter on pension issues in marital dissolution. Mr. Snyder's professional designations include Enrolled Actuary (EA) and Certified Pension Consultant (CPC). He is a member of the International Actuarial Association, the American Academy of Actuaries, and the American Society of Pension Actuaries.

PREFACE

Value of Pensions in Divorce, Third Edition, is addressed to a wide audience—attorneys in family practice, mediators and conciliators, family therapists, actuaries, accountants, and business advisers. It provides the basic background and information needed by anyone working with pensions as marital property, explores in detail the structure of the basic federal law of pensions, and provides comprehensive coverage of other topics mentioned briefly or described only in a general way in prior editions.

The Third Edition contains discussions of pension benefit formulas, contributions, annuity contracts, and Social Security. It offers a chapter on pension court orders designed to help experienced as well as novice practitioners answer client's questions about qualified domestic relations orders.

Also of interest to the practitioner are discussions of what types of pensions are marital property, what is an appropriate valuation date, and mistakes to avoid in valuing pensions for a divorce.

Value of Pensions in Divorce, Third Edition, also contains numerous examples, diagrams and charts, sample plan documents and benefit statements, as well as pension valuation reports to guide readers through the complexities and interrelationships of laws, plan provisions, benefits, contributions, and other important factors affecting the value of pensions. This edition includes an expanded encyclopedia of pension terminology for divorce cases that readers will find handy for reference long after the basic text of the book has been read.

Las Vegas, Nevada   Marvin Snyder
January 1999

SUMMARY CONTENTS

CONTENTS

CONTENTS

CONTENTS

CONTENTS

CONTENTS

LIST OF ACRONYMS

AAA — American Academy of Actuaries

ASA — Associate of the Society of Actuaries

ASPA — American Society of Pension Actuaries

CAE — career average earnings

CEBS — Certified Employee Benefits Specialist

COBRA — Consolidated Omnibus Budget Reconciliation Act of 1985

CODA — cash or deferred arrangement

COLA — cost-of-living adjustment

CPC — Certified Pension Consultant

CPI — Consumer Price Index

CREF — College Retirement Equities Fund

CSRS — Civil Service Retirement System

CSRSEA — Civil Service Retirement Spouse Equity Act of 1984

DOL — Department of Labor
Pension and Welfare Benefit Administrator
200 Constitution Avenue, N.W.
Washington, D.C. 20210

DRO — domestic relations order

EA — Enrolled Actuary

ERISA — Employee Retirement Income Security Act of 1974

ESOP — employee stock ownership plan

FAE — final average earnings

LIST OF ACRONYMS

FASB	Financial Accounting Standards Board
FERS	Federal Employees Retirement System
401(k)	Section 401(k) of Internal Revenue Code for salary reduction, cash or deferred, profit-sharing plans
FSA	funding standard account
FY	fiscal year
GAM	group annuity mortality table
GATT	Pension Reform Act, General Agreement on Tariffs and Trade (1994)
IAA	International Actuarial Association
IRA	individual retirement account
IRC	Internal Revenue Code of 1986
IRS	Internal Revenue Service Employee Plans Division 1111 Constitution Avenue, N.W. Washington, D.C. 20224
J&S	joint-and-survivor
KEOGH	Self-Employed Individuals Tax Retirement Act [Keogh Smathers Act] of 1962
MAAA	Member of the American Academy of Actuaries
MO	military order (in lieu of QDRO)
MPPAA	Multiemployer Pension Plan Amendment Act of 1987
MPP/P	money-purchase pension plan
MSPA	Member of the American Society of Pension Actuaries
NRA	normal retirement age
NRD	normal retirement date
OBRA	Omnibus Budget Reconciliation Act of 1986

LIST OF ACRONYMS

OPM	Office of Personnel Management Allotment Section-Retirement P.O. Box 17 Washington, D.C. 20044
PBGC	Pension Benefit Guaranty Corporation 2020 K Street, N.W. Washington, D.C. 20044
PERS	Public Employees Retirement System
PIA	primary insurance amount (Social Security)
PSERS	Public School Employees' Retirement System
PVAB	present value of accrued benefit
QDRO	qualified domestic relations order
QJSA	qualified joint-and-survivor annuity
QMCO	qualifying military court order
QPSA	qualified pre-retirement survivor annuity
REA	Retirement Equity Act of 1984
RRA	Railroad Retirement Act of 1983
RRB	Railroad Retirement Board
SEP	simplified employee pension
SEPPA	Single Employer Pension Plan Amendment Act of 1987
SERS	State Employees' Retirement System
SPD	summary plan description
SSRA	Social Security retirement age
TAMRA	Technical and Miscellaneous Revenue Act of 1988
TEFRA	Tax Equity and Fiscal Responsibility Act of 1982
TIAA	Teachers Insurance Annuity Association

LIST OF ACRONYMS

TRA '86   Tax Reform Act of 1986

TV   terminated vested

USERRA   Uniformed Services Employment and Re-Employment Rights Act of
               1994

USFSPA   Uniformed Services Former Spouses Protection Act of 1982

W-2P   form for reporting annual pension payments (to IRS)

1099-R   form for reporting lump-sum payments (to IRS)

CHAPTER 1

PENSION ASSETS IN DIVORCE

§ 1.1   Divorce and Marital Property

When a marriage is breaking up, emotional and financial matters become entangled. For the divorcing couple, finding out what their marital assets are worth and determining the values and distribution procedures can be controversial. Typically, the divorce lawyer prepares a list of marital property with estimated values for each item: the house, the car, furniture, jewelry, stamp and coin collections, and so on. Although the house is usually worth the most, there is one asset that may have a value equal to or even greater than that of the house: the pension that either spouse (or both spouses) would receive at retirement.

In a divorce proceeding in an equitable distribution state, a nonemployee-spouse may lay claim to the employee-spouse's pension as community property or as marital property. A pension is marital property because it is a form of deferred wage of the employee. If there were no pension plan, in theory the worker would have received more take-home pay. All pay would be current, none deferred, and

1

the paycheck would go into the marital pot during the marriage. When the marriage ends by divorce and marital property is to be divided, the deferred wage aspect of a pension becomes important for consideration as an asset subject to allocation between the spouses.

Real estate appraisers can value the house. Bills of sale, records, or receipts may be available for the furniture, jewelry, and cars, or the worth of these items can be determined by comparison with similar items at current retail prices. The funded promise of a future payment of lifetime monthly pension benefits is a difficult item to place a value on.

When either party to a divorce is covered by a pension or retirement program of any type, or if both parties are so covered, their lawyers or financial planner may contact a pension actuary to assist in planning possible actions concerning the fair distribution of pension benefits or to help draft a qualified domestic relations order. Using mathematical procedure and assumptions as to interest rates and mortality tables, the actuary computes the present worth of the pension, which is placed on the inventory list as another item of marital property.

§ 1.2   What Are Pensions?

Employees of federal, state, county, and city governments, such as civil service workers, schoolteachers, police officers, and firefighters, are covered by generous pensions. Private employers may cover workers with pension plans of one type or another. A *pension* is a reward for long and faithful service. A good pension plan helps to attract and retain good employees. A well-designed pension plan offers tax benefits to both employer and employees. The employer receives a tax deduction for contributions made to the plan. The assets of the plan are tax-sheltered. There is no income tax on the investment income of the plan, earned or unearned, realized or unrealized. There is no capital gains tax on the plan funds and no income tax so long as the plan retains its tax-favored status under its Internal Revenue Code (IRC) section. Employees are not taxed on the monies put aside for them or on the benefits that accrue thereon.

§ 1.3   Types of Pension Plans

Pension plans come in many shapes and sizes, under various names, and with many different combinations of benefits, contributions, and values. The federal law of pensions, the Employee Retirement Income Security Act of 1974 (ERISA) distinguishes between two types of plans, pension plans and welfare plans. In ERISA the term ''pension plan'' encompasses both defined benefit plans and defined contribution plans, whereas in pension terminology a pension plan can only be a defined benefit pension plan, and a defined contribution plan has its own particular name depending on its type and contribution basis.

A pension plan subject to ERISA is either a *defined benefit pension plan* or a *defined contribution plan.* There are also hybrid plans, which represent a cross between defined benefit pension plans and defined contribution plans. Welfare plans—such as life insurance plans, medical, dental, and long-term disability plans, and so-called cafeteria plans that give the employee a choice of benefits—are not covered in this chapter. Pension plans are never part of a cafeteria arrangement.

§ 1.4   —Defined Benefit Pension Plans

A defined benefit pension plan employs a formula by which an employee's pension payout is determined at retirement, usually based on pay and service. There is one pooled fund of plan assets from which benefits are paid. The employer's contributions are not earmarked for individuals. An independent actuary advises the employer on the plan's assets and liabilities and recommends the amount of the total annual contribution.

A participant in the plan accrues pension benefits for each year of credited service in the plan, along with vesting rights to those benefits. At retirement the employee can choose between various forms of pension payment, all of which have equivalent actuarial value at that time. In a plan subject to ERISA, a married participant has limited pension choices at retirement. The plan must pay a form of pension known as a *50-percent joint-and-survivor* (J&S) pension unless the participant and the spouse each sign a waiver, properly witnessed. The waiver allows the participant to receive a lifetime pension, ending at death, leaving nothing to any survivor.

Although a J&S form of pension is required unless waived, it is not free. For example, assume Husband reaches age 65 under a pension plan formula that provides a monthly pension of $1,000 for the rest of his life. The plan's "normal form"—a lifetime pension—is computed under the plan's formula based on the employee's pay and length of service. To convert this form to a 50-percent J&S form of pension, the monthly payments must be reduced to maintain the plan in actuarial balance. It would cost the plan more to pay a pension over two lives instead of one. In this example, Husband would receive a monthly pension of $850 instead of $1,000. Assuming he gives up $150 a month to provide for a form of insurance for his wife, when he dies after retirement, she gets 50 percent of the reduced amount (.50 × $850), or $425. His widow would receive $425 a month for the rest of her life. But if Husband retires and survives Wife, he will continue to receive $850 a month for life. He cannot substitute a beneficiary. This "option" is a mortality risk that a husband and wife should consider carefully before deciding.

In a divorce where a form of deferred distribution is used to award a portion of the pension to a spouse, it is possible to include some form of death benefit

3

if the details are worked out correctly. A former spouse may be named as the beneficiary under a J&S option. Defined benefit pension plans are discussed in detail in **Chapter 2.**

§ 1.5 —Defined Contribution Plans

A defined contribution plan has a structure remarkably distinct from that of a defined benefit pension plan. A defined contribution plan maintains an individual account—often more than one account—for each participant. The employer's contribution and investment gains (and losses) are allocated to the individual accounts.

Some defined contribution plans allow the participant to make investment choices for his or her account, although the choices are generally limited to certain categories or subfunds. If a domestic court order (DRO) in a divorce affects a defined contribution plan, it is important to know whether the nonemployee-spouse may have the ability to make investment selections for the segregated account portion awarded by the court order.

The valuation of a defined contribution plan as an element of marital property does not necessarily require the services of an actuary. A knowledge of the workings of the type of plan, along with some financial or economic skills, is needed for the evaluator to report a reasonable and appropriate result.

The defined contribution plan reports the account status to each participant at least annually and often quarterly. The report usually shows the participant's opening account balance followed by the contribution allocated to the account, the share of investment gains or losses, and the year-end balance. Vesting is often more generous in defined contribution plans than it is in defined benefit pension plans.

A popular form of defined contribution plan is the 401(k) plan—a thrift or savings plan constructed in accordance with IRC Section 401(k). The most advantageous feature of a 401(k) plan for the employee is that the employee authorizes a contribution from his pay on a pretax basis. The employee's contribution is not subject to personal income tax when it is made, but is taxable when it is withdrawn or otherwise paid as a benefit distribution. Thrift and savings plans may or may not provide for employer contributions and are subject to valuation for immediate offset or for an award of all or part of the account by court order in deferred distribution. Defined contribution plans are discussed further in **Chapter 3.**

§ 1.6 —Keogh Plans

Keogh plans are sponsored and maintained by a sole proprietor or a partner; they are not corporate plans. These plans, named after the late Congressman Eugene

Keogh (D-NY), are also known as "HR-10 plans" because Congressman Keogh's bill was the tenth bill introduced in the House of Representatives in 1962. A Keogh plan may be either a defined benefit plan or a defined contribution plan. Most are the latter.

No new plans of this type are established any more, but there are many dormant plans that maintain tax-sheltered funds for the eventual retirement of the business owner or professional. No new contributions are made to these plans. If one party to the divorce was at one time a partner in a partnership or a sole proprietor of a business or profession, inquiry should be made as to whether an old Keogh plan is in effect. If so, the plan is subject to routine valuation for immediate offset and also subject to a court order for deferred distribution.

§ 1.7 —Individual Retirement Accounts and Simplified Employee Pension Plans

One type of retirement plan asset that may exist and should be investigated in a divorce is an *individual retirement account* (IRA). A person may have several such accounts, which may be with a bank, a stockbroker, a mutual fund, or an insurance company. Every IRA is of the defined contribution type; there is no such thing as a defined benefit IRA. Like any defined contribution plan, an IRA is subject to valuation for immediate offset. However, deferred distribution of an IRA differs from that of other types of plans.

A court order is not always needed to award a spouse an interest in an IRA. The IRC allows a tax-free transfer from the IRA of one spouse to that of the other spouse incident to divorce. The institution or entity holding the IRA funds may insist on a court order to satisfy its own administrative requirements.

An employer may establish IRAs for its employees for administrative convenience and as a goodwill gesture. Such an arrangement is known as a *simplified employee pension* (SEP) plan. A SEP is in every other respect the same as any IRA and may be valued or awarded in a divorce settlement.

Distributions from an IRA are taxable as ordinary personal income. If paid as a lump sum to an individual under age $59\frac{1}{2}$, there is an additional excise tax penalty of ten percent. Neither tax applies in an IRA transfer to another IRA in a divorce matter. However, a couple that is divorcing should be aware in contemplating a transfer that, if the original IRA must liquidate securities or redeem a certificate of deposit before maturity, a loss or penalty may apply that has nothing to do with taxation.

§ 1.8 —Non-ERISA Plans

In the discovery phase of a divorce case, counsel should ask whether either spouse is a participant in any pension or retirement program that is informal, supplemental, unfunded, or otherwise outside the normal range of plans covered by ERISA. For

5

example, an employer may offer an incentive retirement bonus program to selected key executives. Such a plan is sometimes known as a *"top-hat" plan.* Formally, it may be written as the executive supplemental deferred compensation plan. The plan may be a contract covering just one person, or it may be a group benefit. Valuation of a top-hat plan for divorce purposes is usually more difficult than it would be for an ERISA plan. A top-hat plan may have no vesting or it may have a complex vesting schedule. It may pay only a lump sum or only a pension, or it may pay a combination of a lump sum plus a pension. A top-hat plan will probably not accept a court order to distribute a portion to an employee's former spouse.

§ 1.9   Theory of Pensions in Divorce

Pensions are divided in a divorce settlement, or as ordered by a court, in three basic ways:

1. The working spouse keeps some or all of the rights to the pension by giving up an amount of money or property equal to the value of the pension.
2. The court retains jurisdiction of the pension until the working spouse retires, at which time the pension will be divided.
3. A special court order entered at the time of the divorce attaches or assigns some or all of the working spouse's pension as payments to be made the other spouse.

Under the first method, called *immediate offset,* the pension's present worth, or present value, is determined as a dollar amount and added to the inventory of all the assets of the divorcing couple. The second and third methods are known as *deferred distribution.* Deferred distribution is effected by a court order that makes a claim on the pension plan that will pay funds to the nonemployee-spouse. The court order, or DRO, becomes a qualified domestic relations order (QDRO), under the general category of deferred distribution. Deferred distribution is sometimes referred to as the ''if-as-and-when'' method, but the term is misleading. A court order may arrange for payment to be made to the nonemployee-spouse even before the employee-spouse receives a pension.

§ 1.10   —Immediate Offset

With immediate offset, the pension's worth is considered at the time of the divorce settlement and offset by comparison with other assets. This method commonly results in a division of assets characterized as ''she gets the house; he keeps his pension.'' The terms *present value* and *present worth* are used interchangeably. The word ''present'' causes some problems; it may refer to the time of marital dissolution, date of separation, filing date of the divorce complaint, date of hearing or trial, or date on which the final divorce decree is granted. Most often, ''present'' refers to the date on which the pension is valued.

Present value may be best understood as a sum of money today that will grow with investment results to provide an individual with a lifetime pension starting at a future date, provided the individual lives to the pension starting date. For example, individual A approaches a reputable life insurance company that sells annuity products and asks the current cost of an annuity contract. Assume the contract is a single-premium deferred annuity that provides a guaranteed income in a specified dollar amount, payable for as long A lives, backed by the assets of the insurance company and further backed by a state insurance solvency fund. If A dies before reaching the age at which the annuity is to start, A forfeits his payments; there is no refund before retirement. When the annuity payments start under the contract, the insurance company sends a check to A every month for as long as he lives. Payment stops when A dies. If A dies after receiving only a few payments, the insurance company has a *mortality gain* and adds to its profits. If A lives a very long time, collecting monthly payments, it is a *mortality loss* for the insurance company.

The insurance company prices its annuity products based on the determinations and recommendations of its actuaries. The insurance annuity actuary takes into account changing trends in mortality, the sex and age of the purchaser, and interest rates, as well as the company's allowance for overhead, expenses, commissions to the selling agent, and profits. The price the annuity purchaser pays on the day he buys his contract is the annuity's present value.

When an evaluator, who is usually a pension actuary, computes the present value of a pension as property for a divorce settlement, there is no need to consider overhead, expenses, and the like. The mathematical worth of a future series of payments is determined solely by the use of mortality tables and interest rates. The evaluator must select the mortality basis and interest rate to reflect the proper value of the employee-spouse's pension.

Even if the divorce case is settled so that the pension will be handled by deferred distribution instead of immediate offset, it is still important to know the pension's present value. How else will the parties know what value they are settling for? The future distribution of a portion of a pension by court order has a present value just as the pension itself has a value.

Many jurisdictions now accept a spouse's interest in a pension plan as marital property for equitable distribution in divorce. The value of the pension is determined and used as an immediate offset to other marital property. If the pension plan is of the defined contribution type with individual employee accounts, such as the popular 401(k) or thrift and savings plans, it is obvious that the value of the plan is equal to the value in the person's account.

§ 1.11 —Deferred Distribution

Defined benefit pension plans pose more of a conceptual problem because the promised pension benefit usually is expected many years in the future when the employee retires. The actuarial answer often seems frustratingly unsatisfactory to the family practice attorney, who knows that if the client—the employee—dies before retirement, then there is no pension. But the divorce settlement may give the present value of the pension to the client's former spouse.

The actuary includes in the computations of present value the probability of death at any time, either before or after retirement. But actuarial assumptions are not predictions. The employee may die the day after the present value of the pension has been distributed in a divorce settlement. Or the employee may live quite a long time. No one can say, but an actuary can provide a value that takes into account all possibilities of longevity.

The actuary's question may be formulated as follows: What would be a fair price to pay for the right to receive a fixed, guaranteed monthly payment, payable for as long as you live? There are three possible answers:

1.   I would pay nothing; that so-called right is in fact worthless because I could die tomorrow and lose the price that I foolishly paid.

2.   I would probably be willing to pay a lot; that sounds very valuable because I'll receive the monthly payments for the rest of my life.

3.   I would find out the actuarial present value of the guaranteed monthly payment, which would include the principles of mortality and interest, and I would be willing to pay a price equal to the present value.

Assuming that most lawyers and judges would find the third answer the most satisfactory, they must also consider whether it would still apply in two different time frames:

a.   During the active working lifetime of the employee, before retirement, when there is the chance that death may occur before any pension payments begin; and

b.   During the employee's retirement as a pensioner in pay status, when death at any time will end the pension payments.

The actuarial answer is that the appropriate present value does indeed equal the worth of the pension, whether it be a future pension to be paid or a pension now being received. The only difference is that there is a discount period for the active employee to represent the chance of death before retirement while also discounting the future prospective pension for interest during the period before payments begin.

A pension of whatever kind always has a calculable value. In some cases, the court may wish to modify the pure actuarial result by increasing or decreasing the present value based on the particular facts and circumstances of a situation. The starting point should always be the mathematically computed pension value using standard methods and reasonable actuarial assumptions of mortality and interest.

In a case in which present value would not be appropriate (for example, the parties do not have sufficient other assets to balance the pension value or, for personal or tax reasons, the parties do not wish to settle the case on a present value basis), the pension distribution issue may be deferred for future payment. This may be accomplished by the use of a QDRO or its equivalent.

§ 1.12   Basic Questions Concerning Pensions

Q. What precaution should be taken if the pension issue is unsettled pending or after the divorce?

A. If the financial settlement is postponed, obtain or maintain some form of life insurance with appropriate beneficiary in case death occurs before the final distribution is made.

Q. What is a COAP?

A. COAP stands for "court order acceptable for processing." The federal government accepts court orders to divide pensions of federal employees as property in divorce. There are two federal pension systems: the older Civil Service Retirement System and the newer Federal Employees Retirement System. Both accept proper court orders. A COAP is not the same as a QDRO.

Q. Is a disability benefit available?

A. In some jurisdictions disability benefits are not available property, but a disability award is usually larger than a pension would be and it may be considered that the pension benefit is subsumed by the disability amount. The "imbedded" pension may be separated by an actuary and valued, leaving the excess of the disability award alone. The pension amount would be computed using the regular pension benefit formula. This pension benefit is then compared with the disability benefit, in dollar amount and time and terms.

Q. How is life expectancy used?

A. If life expectancy is used in a valuation, ask the date on which the employee is expected to die to illustrate the problem of using life expectancy in mathematics. What should be used is a mortality probability table. All pension plans and insurance and annuity contracts are based on mortality tables and functions of probability, not on the average number of years of a person's expected remaining lifetime. However, wrongful death and personal injury cases properly may use life expectancy as a mathematical measure of expected lifespan.

Q. What is the "present" in present value?

A. It is the date of settlement.

Q. Who provides values for pensions, structured settlements, or lost wages in wrongful death or personal injury, and who drafts QDROs and COAPs?

A. Actuaries, economists, and pension or compensation specialists.

§ 1.13 Myths and Facts About Pensions in Divorce

Misconceptions about pensions abound. Set forth below are some of the more common misunderstandings—and corresponding facts.

MYTH: A future pension is too speculative for a value now.

FACT: All future economic events have a present value.

MYTH: The pension is not yet vested, so it's valueless.

FACT: All pensions have a present value regardless of vesting.

MYTH: The value of the pension is equal to the total of the employee's contributions.

FACT: In most cases, the pension value is far greater.

MYTH: The value can change every day, so what good is it?

FACT: The pension is valued as closely as possible to the relevant measurement date in the legal jurisdiction.

MYTH: Each spouse has a pension, so call it a ''wash'' and don't bother to get either one valued.

FACT: If the spouses work for different employers and their age and pay differ, their pension values are different.

MYTH: Fast case settlement is desired by all concerned, and neither side has raised the pension issue, so just forget it.

FACT: Fairness in settlement dictates examination of pensions. Furthermore, the divorce lawyer risks exposure to malpractice if marital assets are ignored or overlooked, especially an asset with as much potential value as a pension.

MYTH: It takes too long and costs too much to have the pension valued.

FACT: Time and costs are relative to the difficulty of a case and the information available to the evaluator.

MYTH: There is no authority for judging the quality of experts.

FACT: Ask one of the recognized actuarial professional organizations for a referral.

§ 1.13   MYTHS AND FACTS ABOUT PENSIONS IN DIVORCE

MYTH: The employee-spouse could die tomorrow, obviating any pension value.

FACT: The present actuarial value discounts for possible mortality before and after retirement.

MYTH: The employee-spouse could die soon after retiring, so the pension value is useless.

FACT: Actuarial values take into account the probability of death at any time.

MYTH: Immediate offset of the pension value is unfair; the employee does not receive a pension until retirement.

FACT: Pensions have current economic values determined by actuarial mathematics. The present value of a guarantee of a future payment has the same mathematical value as any other item of property.

MYTH: The pension should be valued at the date the couple separates and then brought forward with interest to the date of distribution.

FACT: The prior value was computed with death already discounted, so if the employee-spouse is still alive, adding only the accrued interest is not sufficient without an adjustment for mortality. Because the person is now living, the previously taken mortality discount must be added back.

CHAPTER 2

DEFINED BENEFIT PENSION PLANS

§ 2.1   Introduction

A defined benefit pension plan employs a formula, usually based on pay and service, to determine an employee's pension payout at retirement. There is one pooled fund of plan assets from which benefits are paid. The employer's contributions are not earmarked for individuals. An independent actuary advises the employer on the plan's assets and liabilities and recommends the amount of the total contribution to be made each year. A participant accrues a pension benefit for each year of credited service in the plan, along with vesting rights to that benefit. At retirement the employee has a choice of forms of pension payment, all of which have equivalent actuarial value at that time.

§ 2.2 Pay Basis

Most benefit plans are based on some form of the employee's compensation. When this applies, the plan defines what forms of pay are included and the period of time over which such pay is averaged for the pension benefit formula.

One type of defined benefit pension plan does not use any of the employee's pay in the determination of the pension benefit. In certain unit benefit plans, the benefits are based on service only. For example, a plan may provide a monthly pension benefit at retirement equal to $30 multiplied by the number of years and months of completed credited plan service. Under this plan, an employee retiring with 27 years and 4 months of credited plan service would be entitled to a monthly pension of $820 (27.33333 × $30).

When compensation is a component of the pension benefit formula, the plan spells out the details, the first of which would be the time period over which the person's pay is measured. The formal plan document, the plan booklet, or the summary plan description (SPD) specifies the basis of the year over which pay is counted for plan purposes

The time frame that most plans use to measure an employee's pay for benefit computation purposes is a calendar year (January 1 to December 31), but when the plan's accounting year is different from the calendar year, the plan year may be used as the pay time period. For example, a plan year may run from July 1 to June 30. With such a plan year, the employee's pay for plan purposes would most likely be counted over the 12-month period ending June 30; however, the employee's W-2 form would not report the same pay as is received over a July 1 to June 30 time frame, because W-2 forms always report a person's calendar-year pay.

The plan also defines exactly what items of pay are included in the year's compensation for benefit purposes. Certain aspects of compensation may be included in a plan's pension benefit formula using the following terms:

• Regular Pay	• Unused sick pay
• Base Pay	• Tips
• Salary	• Vacation allowance
• Wages	• Shift differentials
• Overtime	• Jury duty pay
• Sick pay	• Bonuses
• Sick pay allowance	• Commissions

Table 2–1 illustrates how the value of a pension is increased when future salary and/or cost-of-living increases are assumed. In Case 1, with no increases assumed in either item, the factor of 1.00 shows that there is no change in the normally calculated pension value. In Case 6, for example, for an employee age 40, the

assumptions are that pay increases at 3 percent per year, and that the benefits will increase 5 percent per year after retirement, resulting in a pension value that is 2.8 times larger than the normal value. Thus, if that employee's normal pay is assumed to be $100,000, then with these salary and cost-of-living assumptions the pension basis becomes $280,000.

Table 2–1

Sample Pension Factors

		Post-retirement	Present Age		
Case	Future Annual Salary Increases	Cost-of-Living Increases	35	40	50
1	0%	0%	1.00	1.00	1.00
2	0	3	1.20	1.20	1.20
3	0	5	1.40	1.40	140
4	3	0	2.40	2.00	1.50
5	3	3	2.80	2.40	2.00
6	3	5	3.25	2.80	2.20
7	5	0	4.00	3.00	2.00
8	5	3	4.75	3.75	2.50
9	5	5	5.50	4.30	3.00

Salary Scale and COLA Projections

Name: _____   Case #: _____

Valuation age: _____

Normal retirement age: _____

PVAB from divorce results: $_____

Pay averaging period
(circle applicable one)   3   5   ____

Salary scale rate (circle all applicable)   .03   .05   ____

COLA rate (circle all applicable)   0.0   .03   .05   ____

Standard GATT NRA annuity rate without COLA: _____

COLA GATT immediate annuity rates   .03: _____   .05: _____

Coverture fraction _____

	Results		
Case	Salary Scale	COLA	PVAB
1	0	0	—
2	0	3	—
3	3	0	—
4	3	3	—
5	3	5	—
6	5	0	—
7	5	3	—
8	5	5	—

§ 2.3 Benefit Formulas

Benefit formulations in defined benefit pension plans come in many and varied shapes. The formula may be as simple as one percent of five-year average pay multiplied by years of service. An older, larger plan may have a complex set of benefit formulas running to several pages of text, with minimums, maximums, alternatives, different classes, different locations and/or variable units. A number of different formulas are discussed in the following sections.

§ 2.4 —Based on Pay

The fundamental differential in benefits is whether the plan uses pay of any kind in its determination, or whether pay plays no part at all in the computation of the benefits. An example of a simple, straightforward pension benefit formula not based on pay is $30 per month per year of service. In this example, an employee with 20 years of service would have a pension benefit of $600 per month (20 years × $30).

§ 2.5 —Annual or Monthly

A pension benefit formula must be clear as to whether the unit of benefit multiplication is the month or the year. A plan may pay a pension derived as $360 per year of service. An employee with 20 years of service would have a pension of $7,200 (20 years × $360). It is safe to interpret this employee's pension as annual, with actual payment at the rate of $600 per month.

In some cases, the monthly/annual basis may not be as clear. Assume a benefit formula that pays a pension of $80 per year of service. If the plan means an *annual* benefit of $80 per year of service, an employee with 20 years of service would receive a pension of $1,600 annually ($80 × 20), or a monthly pension check of $133.33. But if the plan means a *monthly* benefit, then the same employee would receive a monthly pension check of $1,600, and a total of $19,200 annually.

One of the most common errors in pension work is confusing the monthly and annual bases of benefits. The preceding example illustrates how easy it is to fall into that kind of error. Some benchmarks exist to ensure the monthly or annual condition. One basic test is to compare the employee's current annual pay with the current accrued pension benefit. The average employee's pension is not going to be greater than his or her current annual salary.

Another benchmark is the language in the formal plan document; it will describe in detail the composition of the benefit structure, which should leave no doubt as to whether the pension is computed on a monthly or annual basis.

The plan booklet—technically, the summary plan description (SPD)—is useful as a guide, but should be read with caution because it is not as comprehensive as the actual plan document. Sometimes the error of confusing monthly and annual benefits even creeps into the plan booklet.

An individual employee's benefit statement may describe the pension benefit in either annual or monthly terms. The benefit statement may give the current accrued pension benefit amount, it may illustrate the estimated pension at retirement assuming service continues, or it may show both accrued and projected pension benefits. In any case, it is necessary to be sure of the basis on which the pension benefits are shown: annual or monthly.

The typical defined benefit pension plans pay annuity benefits monthly to retirees. Some plans pay semimonthly or even bimonthly, but few plans pay a pension annually—that is, only one payment a year. For administrative or computational convenience, a plan may describe a pension in annual terms, but not actually pay it annually.

§ 2.6   —Front Loading

A pension benefit is said to be "front-loaded" when an employee's earlier years of service are worth more than later years, but the benefit formula uses the identical pay basis. For example, a pension benefit formula may be one percent of the employee's final five-year average pay multiplied by years of service up to 10 years. After the first ten years of service, the pension benefit formula continues with one-half of one percent for service between 10 and 20 years, then one-quarter of one percent for service in excess of 20 years. This type of structure emphasizes the early years of service at the expense of later years. But this is true only if the pay basis used is the same exact pay no matter what service period is used in the benefit calculation. If the pay in earlier years is used in conjunction with the earlier service, and then later pay is used with later service, it may not be a front-loaded formula after all.

§ 2.7   —Back Loading

A pension benefit is said to be "back-loaded" when later years of service produce a larger benefit than earlier years, by reason of a formula using other than the mere passage of time or increase in pay in later years—for example, one-quarter percent of pay for each of the first 10 years, then one-half percent for each of the next 10 years, then one percent for service in excess of 10 years. The Internal Revenue Service (IRS) imposes limits on pension benefit formulas in which back loading unduly favors the executives of the employer company.

§ 2.8 —Minimum Benefits

A plan may be designed to provide a minimum benefit for employees with short service or low pay. A plan may contain more than one pension benefit formula to cover different groups or levels of employees.

Typically, an employee's data is run through all of the possibilities and the largest benefit is paid. Thus, the plan is providing a minimum benefit serving as a "floor." The minimum benefit structure, if there is one, may or may not be pay-based, or may have internal limits on service.

The caveat here is that when a benefit statement is provided by the plan, it may vary from year to year, if and when the individual becomes subject to the minimum benefit floor. The projected pension benefit at retirement may not be proportional to the current accrued pension benefit when a minimum floor basis is involved in the formula.

§ 2.9 —Maximum Benefits

A plan may impose maximum limits on the pension benefit in a number of ways, in addition to the requirements of the IRS. The years of service used in the pension benefit formula may be curtailed; there may be a maximum on the salary used in a pay-based formula; or there may be an actual dollar limit on the amount of the pension benefit no matter what the formula produces. All these details will be explained in the plan document and summarized in the plan booklet, but may not be revealed on an individual benefit statement.

§ 2.10 —Step-down Pension Benefit

A new feature in defined benefit pension plans introduces a layer of complexity to the valuation of a pension as a present value for immediate offset. Called the "step-down" pension benefit, this plan is also sometimes known as a Social Security supplement or bridge benefit or temporary bonus benefit. A step-down pension benefit plan is structured to pay a certain amount for a limited period of time to be replaced by a smaller amount thereafter.

Consider, for example, an employee who has the option to elect early retirement at age 58 with a lifetime pension of $1,200 per month starting right away. A typical step-down plan would pay instead, say, $1,500 per month to the employee retiring at age 58 until age 62 is reached. At age 62 the monthly pension would drop to a figure of perhaps $900 per month. That lower figure would then continue for the rest of the retiree's lifetime. The employee traded a level lifetime pension of $1,200 per month to obtain a larger payment for a smaller period of time, to be followed by a smaller payment as long as he or she lives thereafter. This is a good deal for a person with a short lifespan, but not for a long-lived person.

A pension of this type has the same actuarial value at the instant of retirement as does the unadjusted pension. But as time passes, the values change. As the retiree gets older and as the potential reduction in benefit approaches, the actuarial present value decreases.

A plan may provide this feature without the consent of the employee, or it may be an available option. It may be described as an advantageous feature benefiting the retiring employee, but of course that will not always be the case, especially for a retiree who lives long into the period of reduced benefits.

The step-down benefit, under any name, is subject to actuarial evaluation by the use of mathematical tools. It is also subject to distribution by the use of a qualified domestic relations order (QDRO). It presents both an opportunity and a challenge to the family law practitioner to be aware of occasions when such an arrangement is possible.

§ 2.11   Benefit Calculations

An active participant in a defined benefit pension plan accrues pension credits over time. In general, the longer the service, the larger the accrual of benefits. In theory, the dollar amount of the accrued pension benefit can be determined at any point in time, past or present. Also, a future pension amount may be estimated with or without factoring in future pay increases. In a divorce case where a pension is to be valued as marital property, the question arises as to which accrued pension benefit should be valued. There are four choices:

1. The pension accrued to date of marital separation;
2. The pension accrued to date of filing of complaint;
3. The pension accrued to date of hearing or trial; or
4. The pension to be paid at actual retirement.

Reasonable arguments have been advanced for each of these pensions to be considered marital property, at least in part. Basically, the issue is whether pension benefit increases should be counted past the cutoff date in a particular jurisdiction.

The argument for continuing to count the pension to the date of the hearing or trial is that a pension consists of a structure that must be based on a foundation of service and pay, and that the underlying framework was constructed during the marriage. The continuing increase in the benefit due to service and pay between the cutoff date and the date of distribution is justified because it would not exist without the base that was established during the marriage.

DEFINED BENEFIT PENSION PLANS

If the pension is considered up to date—that is, the current pension—then the method allocates the marital portion by use of a coverture fraction. The coverture fraction takes into account the cutoff date for marital property.

The opposing concept is that no pension credit should be considered as marital property based on service or pay past the cutoff date. The cutoff date is used to compute a fixed pension benefit only for pay and service counted to that date. If there is premarital benefit service, then a coverture fraction is used to back that out.

Whichever benefit is used, its value is determined currently. That is, one can use the present value of the current accrued pension multiplied by a coverture fraction to derive the marital portion *or* one can use the present value of the pension accrued only to the cutoff date. But in both cases it is the *present value* of the pension.

It has been suggested that the cutoff date accrued pension should be valued as of the cutoff date and then brought forward with interest. The problem with this is that these values are actuarially determined and they include a discount for mortality as well as for interest. To bring forward a prior "present value" with interest ignores the probability of death that was included in that prior value.

The following form is typically used in an actuary's office for a quick manual calculation of an estimated pension benefit.

BENEFIT CALCULATION FORM

Name _____

Plan _____

	Current	At Retirement

Date _____

Age _____

Service _____

Pay _____

Benefit Factor _____

Pension Benefit _____

§ 2.12   Anatomy of an Annuity

An annuity is a regular series of periodic payments, usually annually but in pension cases monthly, usually payable as of the first day of each period (month), usually in a fixed amount unless there is a cost-of-living adjustment (COLA), usually payable for the life of the recipient—a lifetime or straight life annuity. If the annuity is to begin right now, or if it has begun and is already in pay status, it is known as an *immediate annuity*. If it is to start at some future date it is a *deferred annuity*.

The *present value* of an annuity may be thought of as its current price. In the case of a deferred annuity, the value is the single premium paid now to an insurance company for a contract paying a future benefit—that is what the annuity is currently worth. If the annuity is in pay status, it is worth what it would cost now to purchase a contract to buy the remaining stream of future benefit payments.

The value of an annuity is based on the following factors: mortality, interest, age, sex, benefit, and the terms and conditions of benefit payments. The actual purchase price of an annuity will vary not only with these factors but also with the pricing philosophy of the insurance company—its commission schedule, loadings for future contingencies, allowances for overhead, and so forth. There may be hidden costs (such as surrender charges) if the annuity contract is terminated before it goes into pay status.

The concept of *interest* appears in annuities in two separate and distinct respects. First, the interest rates used in constructing the actuarial basis of the annuity play a prominent role in determining its present value. This is true of both deferred and immediate annuities: The lower the interest rate, the higher the present value. Conversely, the higher the interest rate, the lower the present value.

Second, a deferred annuity is often marketed as an *investment vehicle*. In this respect the future pension benefit is not as important as the internal investment yield credited to the individual who bought the contract. Banks compete with insurance companies in selling tax-deferred investment annuities, advertising high interest rates.

Investment contract annuities are not used to determine the value of pensions. The present value of a pension, payable now or in the future, is the current sum of money that would provide that future stream of payments, based on the assumptions and factors used by the actuary.

§ 2.13   Joint-and-Survivor Annuity

If one spouse in a divorce action is already retired and receiving monthly pension annuity benefits, one of the issues to be discussed is the form and type of the pension benefit payout. If the retiree is receiving ongoing pension benefits from an ERISA-defined benefit pension plan (and in some cases from a defined contribution plan), a form of pension had to be elected at retirement. The two most common available forms of pension (other than lump sum) are (1) straight-life and (2) joint-and-survivor. In a straight-life pension, all benefits end at the death of the retiree, with no survivorship benefits at all. In the joint-and-survivor pension, all or a portion of the retiree's pension continues to the named beneficiary. Generally, a plan does not allow a substitute beneficiary if the named beneficiary predeceases the retired participant because this would undermine the actuarial balance of the plan.

ERISA requires that when a married person retires from a covered plan, the pension must be in the form of a *qualified joint-and-survivor annuity* (QJSA), with the spouse as the named beneficiary, unless properly waived (see **§ 1.4**).

The QJSA is a pension benefit that continues in annuity form to the named beneficiary in an amount of at least 50 percent and up to 100 percent of the retiree's adjusted pension benefit. These are often labeled ''50% J&S'' and ''100% J&S'' annuities. Some plans allow percentages to be set at 66⅔ percent and 75 percent.

The plan may adjust the retiree's pension benefit downward to recognize the actuarial impact of this form of benefit. The plan may subsidize the joint-and-survivor benefit by not imposing a full actuarial reduction, or in a generous plan there may be no reduction at all. If the beneficiary is more than five years younger than the retiree, the actuarial cost grows significantly, reducing the retiree's benefit substantially.

A rule of thumb is that a 50-percent J&S reduces the retiree's pension by 12 to 15 percent, while a 100-percent J&S reduces the retiree's pension by as much as 25 percent, assuming the spouses' ages are within five years of each other.

A retiree and spouse may agree for any number of reasons that a straight-life pension benefit is preferable to a joint-and-survivor annuity. Perhaps both spouses are in excellent health, or perhaps there are other sources of income, so that they are not concerned about the potential financial impact of the cessation of the pension upon the death of the retiree. Or perhaps the plan's reduction for joint-and-survivor coverage is unpalatable because of its expense, and the couple would rather take the mortality gamble in order to receive the full, unreduced pension benefit.

Federal pension law has established a mechanism to allow a married couple to waive joint and survivor coverage, which would otherwise be mandatory. No reason need be given, but the waiver must be in writing, signed by both spouses, with both signatures witnessed by either an authorized plan representative or a notary public. Before the waiver form may be executed, the plan must make clear the details and consequences of the waiver.

The IRS requires that the waiver forms, or an accompanying distribution form, give the plan participant and spouse the material features and an explanation of the relative values of the optional forms of benefits available under the plan. This requirement applies only to benefits with a value of more than $5,000, but most plans issue the information to every retiring participant. In particular, the IRS is focusing on the specific disclosure of the dollar amount of the payments in the form of an immediate annuity at retirement. If the dollar amounts of alternative forms of benefits are not disclosed, the IRS may rule that the spousal waiver is not "informed" and is therefore invalid. This is a challenge to the plan as a defect that must be cured.

In the event of a divorce after retirement, however, the whole issue of J&S coverage takes on a new dimension. If J&S had been waived at retirement, counsel for the retiree's spouse may raise the issue of whether informed consent to the waiver was given under IRS specifications. The retiree's spouse may be able to assert that the required information was not sufficiently detailed or, alternatively, was too complex and confusing to be readily understandable. Counsel for the retiree should likewise be aware of this potential issue and should obtain from the plan copies of all information made available to the retiree and spouse and of all forms signed at retirement.

The existence of a proper J&S feature may affect the valuation of the parties' interests in the retiree's benefits under the plan, as well as create an issue to be explored if there is to be a settlement or adjudication that would use a QDRO.

§ 2.14   Benefit Statements

In determining the present value of a pension in a divorce case, it is vital to distinguish between contributions, benefits, and values. The contribution an employer makes to pensions in a defined benefit plan is the least important consideration. Defined benefit pension plans undergo routine actuarial valuations to determine the liabilities of the plan and the contribution levels for the employer.

The actuarial valuation method used for the plan is an aggregate prospective approach that pools experience in the application of group computations. Any attempt at an individual allocation of the employer's contribution in a defined benefit pension plan serves merely as a rough approximate measure of the relative relationships among the employees. The employer contributions provide the plan assets but do not directly concern the employee pension benefits.

There are no individual accounts in a defined benefit pension plan except in cases in which individual employee contributions are made to the plan. Even then an individual accounting is kept for the employee contributions, but not for pension benefits.

DEFINED BENEFIT PENSION PLANS

It is often difficult and time-consuming to obtain a pension plan benefit statement for an individual involved in a divorce action. The nonemployee-spouse's attorney is sometimes stymied by lack of information or cooperation. Many employees themselves do not know how to obtain a benefit statement from their employer.

Some plans provide annual statements routinely to employees. In such cases, it is up to the employee-spouse to find a copy of the statement, or to ask the employer for a duplicate copy. However, many plans do not routinely publish individual annual statements at all, and they are not required to do so. ERISA requires that a statement of accrued benefits in a qualified plan must be provided to a participant upon request. The request must come from the participant and not more often than once a year. This seeming contradiction is explained by the fact that the employer does not have to issue annual benefit statements routinely, but must honor, within a reasonable time, a written request for one from a plan participant.

Following is an excerpt from a statement of participant rights that should appear in every qualified plan's booklet or SPD:

As a participant in the Plan you are entitled to certain rights and protections under the Employee Retirement Income Security Act of 1974 (ERISA). All Plan participants shall be entitled to:

- Examine without charge at the plan administrator's office all plan documents, including insurance contracts and copies of all documents filed by the plan with the U.S. Department of Labor such as detailed annual reports and plan descriptions.

- Obtain copies of all plan documents and other plan information upon written request to the plan administrator. The administrator may make a reasonable charge for the copies.

- Receive a summary of the plan's annual financial report. The plan administrator is required by law to furnish each participant with a copy of this summary annual report.

- Obtain a statement telling you whether you have a right to receive a pension at normal retirement age and, if so, what your benefits would be at normal retirement age if you stop working under the plan now.

- If you do not have a right to a pension, the statement will tell you how many more years you have to work to get a right to a pension. This statement must be requested in writing and is not required to be given more than once a year. The plan must provide the statement free of charge.

The request to the plan for accrued pension benefit information may take the following form. It may be couched as a written communication from the plan participant or from counsel, either by cooperation with the employer or by subpoena.

24

§ 2.14 BENEFIT STATEMENTS

REQUEST FOR ACCRUED PENSION BENEFIT INFORMATION

Name: _____

Date of Determination: _____

As of the above-noted Date of Determination, or as of a date within sixty (60) days before or after that date for administrative convenience, what was the accrued monthly pension benefit under the plan as if employment had then terminated, as if fully vested, that would be deferred to be payable as a straight lifetime pension annuity beginning at normal retirement age as defined in the plan?

Please enter that age and the requested benefit amount below.

Normal retirement age: _____

Accrued monthly pension benefit
as of the date of determination
payable at normal retirement age: $ _____

This type of request, backed up by reference to ERISA, almost always provides the needed information. Then a competent evaluator should be engaged to compute the pension's present value for immediate offset in equitable distribution or for entering it as a dollar amount of marital property on the divorce inventory list.

Following are three hypothetical benefit statements, presented as typical annual statements given to participants in a defined benefit pension plan. The statements are for different employees employed by different corporations with similar, but not identical, pension plans. The plans are covered by ERISA and are subject to the Pension Benefit Guaranty Corporation (PBGC). Comments follow each sample benefit statement.

SAMPLE BENEFIT STATEMENT 1

Dear Loyal Employee WILLIAM NOBODY

This is Your Pension Benefit Statement as of DECEMBER 31, 1998, in The ABC COMPANY, INC. PENSION PLAN Based on Your Service and Three-Year Average Pay to Date.

AT Your Age 65 Your Monthly Pension Benefit	$2,250
YOUR Accrued Vested Monthly Pension Benefit to Date	$1,153

YOU are 100% vested

YOUR actual pension will be based on your three-year average pay when you retire or otherwise leave our service.

IF you retire early, between ages 55 and 65, your pension will be reduced at the rate of one-half percent per month.

Refer to your plan booklet for more details.

DEFINED BENEFIT PENSION PLANS

Comment. Example 1 concerns William Nobody, an employee of the ABC Company, Inc. The pension plan is administered on a calendar year basis, so the information contained in the benefit statement is as of December 31, 1998. The statement itself was prepared and promulgated in April of 1999 because it takes time to gather data and prepare the information to be reported.

According to the statement, Mr. Nobody's pension is based on three-year average pay, and the benefits shown use that average pay counted as of the statement date of December 31, 1998. The statement also tells us that the accrued benefit is based on his service up to December 31, 1998. A more comprehensive benefit statement would show the employee's date of birth and date of plan entry, but that has not been done for Mr. Nobody by the ABC Company, Inc.

When Mr. Nobody reaches age 65, his pension from this plan will be $2,250 per month assuming he continues in the employ of the ABC Company, Inc. and that his three-year average pay never changes. This benefit statement does not project nor illustrate any future pay increases. It assumes for the presentation of his pension information that he will continue to work to age 65, but that his pay will be level until then.

The statement shows his accrued pension benefit for service to December 31, 1998, and for his three-year average pay as of that date to be $1,153 per month. The way to read both benefit numbers together is to realize that as of December 31, 1998, he has attained $1,153 toward his potential $2,250 monthly pension at age 65. He is approximately halfway there. In reality, it is to be expected that his pay will increase. His actual pension at age 65 is likely to be much greater than $2,250 a month, but this statement does not attempt to predict the future payments.

Mr. Nobody is fully vested in his accrued benefit to date, but on that point the benefit statement could be clearer. It tells him: "You are 100 percent vested." But it does not specifically indicate that the benefit in which he is 100 percent vested is the accrued pension of $1,153, not the estimated age 65 pension of $2,250. He is not vested in the amount of $2,250 because, of course, he has not even accrued that yet.

The statement tells him that his actual pension will be based on his three-year average pay when he retires or otherwise terminates employment. It is not revealed what would happen if a future three-year average pay figure is, for some reason, smaller than the current three-year average pay. The plan booklet or the formal plan document will have the exact details on the definition of pay and on the measurement of average pay. A reasonable defined benefit pension plan would base its pension benefits on the employee's highest three-year average pay, which is not necessarily the same as the last or final series of annual pay amounts immediately before retirement or other termination of plan service.

If Mr. Nobody retires or otherwise terminates his employment before age 65, he will never lose his benefit, because he is 100 percent vested. But the amount of the benefit is not guaranteed under all conditions even though it is fully vested. A payout upon retirement prior to the plan's normal retirement age or a payout in an actuarially equivalent form other than a straight-life annuity would require a downward adjustment in the pension benefit. It is a paradox in pension semantics that a benefit can be fully vested and guaranteed but that the amount of it in the monthly check paid to the retiree can be much smaller than the guaranteed vested amount depending on the conditions of the payment.

The benefit statement gives Mr. Nobody an idea of the early retirement reduction in the pension. It informs him that his pension benefit will be reduced by one-half of one percent per month for each month that his pension begins prior to age 65—a reduction rate of 6 percent per year. If he retires three years early, he loses 18 percent of his pension forever. If he retires 10 years early, the permanent reduction is 60 percent, leaving him with only 40 percent of his fully vested and guaranteed pension. Is the employer being unfair? No, because when a person retires early, it is presumed that he will collect the pension over a longer period of time than would a person who retires later. If Mr. Nobody retires at age 60, he receives five more years of pension payments than he would if he had waited and retired at age 65.

Several considerations in early retirement are not disclosed on a benefit statement. Working to age 65 generally produces the largest benefit because presumably pay continues to increase and because the credited service counts until retirement at age 65. Earlier retirement reflects less service and most likely a lower average pay base for the pension benefit formula. The benefit at early retirement is reduced due to the longer period of time during which it is expected to be paid.

In addition, there are internal actuarial reasons why the early retirement pension is reduced. When the employee retires, he is no longer exposed to the mortality discount.

Usually, a pre-retirement death benefit is worth less than a full pension benefit. The plan discounts its costs for the anticipation of some deaths among the plan participants who may die before they retire. Once a person does retire, this particular statistical cost discount disappears. Further, the plan discounts its liabilities by anticipated investment interest and gains on the funds held in the pension trust before the monies have to be paid out. Upon retirement, payments commence so the plan assets are being paid out and are not held for continual investment increases. Thus, a combination of mortality and interest gains is actuarially lost when a person retires early. This contributes to the necessity for reduction in the pension benefit for early retirement.

The benefit statement ends by recommending that the employee refer to the plan booklet for details. Some benefit statements may refer to the formal plan document or give more guidance in how to elicit additional information, but this sample is satisfactory for its purpose.

Sample Benefit Statement 1 is an example of a basic, simple and straightforward communication of elementary benefit information to the employee.

DEFINED BENEFIT PENSION PLANS

SAMPLE BENEFIT STATEMENT 2

Dear Loyal Employee PAM SAMPLE

This is Your Pension Benefit Statement as of JUNE 30, 1998, in the ANYPLACE, INC. PENSION PLAN.

Based on Your Service and Three-Year Average Pay to Date

AT Your Age 65, Your Monthly Pension Benefit
if you complete 40 years of credited service $2,200

YOUR Accrued Vested Monthly Pension Benefit to Date
based upon your completion of 30.25 years of credited service $1,600

YOU are 100% vested

YOUR actual pension will be based on your three-year average pay when you retire or otherwise leave our service.

IF you retire early, between ages 55 and 65, your pension will be reduced at the rate of one-half percent per month, unless you have thirty years of credited service.

Refer to your plan booklet for more details.

Comment.   Sample Benefit Statement 2, which illustrates another layer of complexity, is for Pam Sample, who works for Anyplace, Inc. Her company's pension plan is administered on a June 30 fiscal year basis—i.e., the plan accounting year begins on July 1 and ends the following June 30. This benefit statement reports on the preceding June 30 plan year-end figures.

Ms. Sample has earned a fully vested, accrued monthly pension benefit of $1,600 as of June 30, 1998. This statement tells her that she has 30.25 years of credited service in the plan as of that date. This plan has a benefit formula that produces a full pension with 40 years of service. The statement shows that if she completes 40 years of service on or before she reaches age 65, she will receive a pension of $2,200 per month. As was the case in Sample Benefit Statement 1, the pension at age 65 is contingent on two assumptions: first, that Pam Sample continues to work for Anyplace, Inc. until she attains age 65 and, second, that her pay never changes. Pam Sample's actual pension at retirement will be larger than $2,200 per month if her pay increases between the date of this statement and her retirement date, but the employer is reluctant to predict any pay increases for employees.

§ 2.14   BENEFIT STATEMENTS

This plan has a special early retirement feature: It provides a full pension after 30 years of service with no reduction for retiring before age 65 if the 30-year period is completed. The benefit statement mentions this fact but does not emphasize it. Apparently, the employer does not encourage such subsidized early retirements because they are costly.

When an early retirement provision similar to the one in the sample is indicated on a benefit statement, the plan or its booklet should be reviewed to verify the terms and conditions. Early retirement may indeed be available after 30 years of service, regardless of age, but with the usual reduction for benefit commencement prior to normal retirement age. A true "30 and out" clause provides for a pension upon the completion of the service requirement without reduction for early retirement. The benefit statement itself may not provide the details.

SAMPLE BENEFIT STATEMENT 3

Dear Loyal Employee CHRIS GULL

This is Your Pension Benefit Statement as of DECEMBER 31, 1998, in the MISLED, INC. PENSION PLAN.

Based on Your Service and Estimated Average Pay

AT Your Age 65, Your Annual Pension Benefit
from your pension plan and Social Security $62,000

YOU are 100% vested as of the date of this statement.

YOUR pension will be based on your actual three-year average pay when you retire.

Refer to your plan booklet for more details.

Comment.   Sample Benefit Statement 3, provided for employee Chris Gull of the Misled, Inc. pension plan, is presented as an example of a communication to employees that misleads rather than informs, but is not erroneous nor unlawful. The statement shows a large benefit of $62,000. However, this is an annual benefit whereas the other sample statements showed monthly benefits.

This statement combines the plan's benefits with Social Security benefits without identifying the components separately. No details are given as to how the potential Social Security benefit is estimated, nor is its amount in dollars specified. There is no way for Mr. Gull to know from this statement what the plan's pension benefit is going to be. The statement refers to estimated average pay but does not describe the method by which future average pay is estimated for statement purposes.

The employer may consider this statement merely an intermediate benefit statement, which will report incremental estimates each year during the employee's service. If so, there is no need to be exact or detailed. However, because the statement fails to give many important details, it is misleading. This type of benefit statement is not recommended.

§ 2.15 —Questions to Ask of Employers

For a pension valuation in a divorce action, the employer should be queried about the amount of the accrued pension benefit based on plan definitions of pay and service as of whatever date is involved in that venue.

As for the rights granted to plan participants by ERISA, the parties to a divorce are entitled to obtain a statement showing the participant's total benefits accrued under the plan and the vested percentage, if any, or the date on which benefits will become vested. However, a pension plan is not automatically required to promulgate benefit statements. The employer has the option to routinely issue benefit statements periodically to participants or not to do so. But if a participant requests a statement in writing, it must be provided. The employer has wide latitude in the details and format of any benefit statement.

Listed below are questions to ask when reviewing a benefit statement:

1. What is the statement's date of issuance?
2. What is the date of information contained in the statement?
3. Do the names of the employer and the plan appear on the statement and does the statement identify the plan as a defined benefit pension plan?
4. Does the statement show the retirement age or retirement date?
5. Is an accrued benefit shown?
6. If so, what is the date of the accrued benefit?
7. Is there a projected benefit at retirement?
8. If so, what is the retirement age or date at which the future benefit becomes payable?
9. Are the benefits shown in monthly or annual terms?
10. Is a Social Security benefit illustrated?
11. If so, is the Social Security benefit included in the total or shown separately from the plan benefit?
12. Is the percentage or amount of vesting shown?
13. If the participant is not 100 percent vested as of the date of the statement, does the statement tell when 100 percent vesting will be attained?
14. Is the form of benefit (e.g., straight life, life with a guaranteed period, or joint and survivor) indicated?
15. Is a pre-retirement death benefit indicated?
16. Is early retirement mentioned?
17. Is the reduction for early retirement described?

18. Does the statement include the employee's basic data: full name, date of birth, date of plan entry, and, if applicable, name and date of birth of spouse?

Not every benefit statement contains the answers to all of the above questions, but the plan should be able to answer these questions if requested by the employee, or if the questions are listed in interrogatories or in a subpoena, as appropriate.

§ 2.16   —Aids to Obtaining a Benefit Statement

What if the employee-spouse cannot obtain a statement of retirement benefits from his or her employer, or if the employer is slow or unwilling to respond to counsel's request for benefit information? In this situation, counsel for the employee-spouse should remind the employer that ERISA requires that a statement of accrued benefits in a qualified plan be provided to a plan participant upon request.

Note 1. The employer is not required to issue benefit statements on an automatic basis. But a formal request from a plan participant must be honored within a reasonable time.

Note 2. It may be helpful to quote from the statement of participant rights that appears in every plan booklet (SPD) for a qualified ERISA plan:

> ERISA provides that a plan participant is entitled to . . . obtain a statement telling you whether you have a right to receive a pension at normal retirement age and, if so, what your benefits would be at normal retirement age if you stop working under the plan now. If you do not have a right to a pension, the statement will tell you how many more years you have to work to get a right to a pension. This statement must be requested in writing and is not required to be given more than once a year. The plan must provide the statement free of charge.

A typical form to send to an employer to request benefit information is set forth below.

REQUEST FOR ACCRUED PENSION BENEFIT INFORMATION

Name: _____

Date of determination: _____

As of the above-noted Date of Determination, or as of a date within sixty (60) days before or after that date for administrative convenience, what was the accrued monthly pension benefit under the plan as if employment had then terminated, as if fully vested, that would be deferred to be payable as a straight lifetime pension annuity beginning at normal retirement age as defined in the plan?

Please enter that age and the requested benefit amount below.

Normal retirement age: _____

Accrued monthly pension benefit
as of the date of determination,
payable at normal retirement age $ _____

31

CHAPTER 3

DEFINED CONTRIBUTION PLANS

§ 3.1   Introduction

A *defined contribution plan* maintains individual accounts for plan participants. The account consists of employer contributions and/or the employee's contributions and net investment income. The account value may fluctuate depending on the nature of the investments. The balance in the person's account is the value at any point in time.

At retirement the employee usually receives a lump-sum payment representing the total in his or her individual account balance. Occasionally the plan uses the account balance to purchase an annuity for the employee from an insurance company. The plan may provide for early retirement so that the employee who leaves service before the normal retirement age (NRA) may receive a payout of the account. For example, if NRA is 65, the plan may allow early retirement at any age between 55 and 64. This means that an employee retiring at, say, age 57 would be paid the account balance at that time as a distribution. There is no actuarial reduction for early payment, because the payment is in the form of a lump sum. If an annuity is purchased, the monthly pension amount provided by the annuity contract will be smaller because the employee is younger.

Typical defined contribution plans are profit-sharing plans, thrift and/or savings plans, and 401(k) plans.

§ 3.2   Account Balance

In most defined contribution plans, once the employee is vested, termination of employment will provide a payment of the account balance. Vesting in such plans is usually rapid, and a terminating employee normally receives a distribution within a reasonably short time following the termination of employment. No actuarial reduction occurs when a lump sum is paid upon vested termination of service.

How is the account balance in a defined contribution plan valued for equitable distribution in divorce? In a defined contribution plan, unlike in a defined benefit pension plan, it does not matter when the employee-spouse may retire or terminate employment; the account balance at the time of measurement is the account value. Once the account is vested, it is there, subject only to investment performance.

§ 3.3   Account Value

An employee's individual account in a defined contribution plan holds no promise of a guaranteed monthly pension at retirement. The account grows with employer contributions, employee contributions, and investment gains. If the employee's account has a substantial investment in equities, its value is subject to the vagaries of the stock market. Regardless of the potential of early or normal retirement or the possibility of termination of employment, the defined contribution plan has a current value for the employee, and thus for the marital pot, at the designated time of measurement.

The time of valuation varies by legal jurisdictional rules. Valuation may be required at the date of retirement, the date the divorce complaint is filed, or the date of the divorce decree. The account balance may fluctuate, depending on the plan—daily, monthly, quarterly, semiannually, or annually.

§ 3.4   Account Valuation Methods

The marital portion of an employee's account in a defined contribution plan can be ascertained if sufficient information is available. A coverture fraction may be used to separate out the marital portion of a defined contribution plan, similar to the approach in a defined benefit pension plan. (For a discussion of the coverture fraction, see § 13.4). However, a different method often applies in a defined contribution plan.

If the employee-spouse's individual account balance as of the date of marriage, as well as at the time of the divorce, is known, the marital property component is computed as the difference between the two account values. This method, known as the "subtraction method," provides results different from those obtained by the time rule coverture fraction method. The following example illustrates the two methods in a routine defined contribution plan.

Example: Employee *A* has participated in his company's 401(k) plan since 1975. He marries in 1985 and divorces in 1995. *A*'s account balance at the date of marriage in 1985 was $10,000. In 1995, at the date of marital dissolution, *A*'s account balance had grown to $50,000, including employee and employer contributions and investment gains.

If the time rule is used, the coverture fraction of 50 percent (10 years divided by 20 years) is multiplied by the current account balance of $50,000, resulting in $25,000 to be considered as marital property.

If the subtraction method is used, the account balance at the date of marriage is subtracted from the current account balance, resulting in $40,000 ($50,000 − $10,000) to be considered as marital property.

The difference between the marital property amounts developed by the two methods is substantial in this example. In practice, the difference may be more or less, whether by dollar amount or by percentage.

There is an argument in favor of using the subtraction method in a defined contribution plan when the information is available. It could be said that use of the time rule is not necessary, because the value of an individual account in a defined contribution plan is readily ascertainable.

The values of the employee-spouse's account in the plan as of the two dates—the date of marriage and the date of trial—were known and admitted as factual. The distinction between defined contribution plans and defined benefit pension plans is apparent; when the account values are available in a defined contribution plan, the subtraction method is the preferred method of determining the marital portion.

§ 3.5   Account Investments

Some defined contribution plans allow the participant to make investment choices for his or her account, although the choices are generally limited to certain categories. Table 3–1 illustrates the characteristics of various investment vehicles.

If a domestic relations order (DRO) in a divorce affects a defined contribution plan, it is important to learn whether the employee-spouse is permitted to make investment selections for the segregated account portion awarded by the court order.

§ 3.6   Guaranteed Investment Contracts

The guaranteed investment contract (GIC) is almost always one of the investment choices offered to participants in a defined contribution plan, especially a 401(k) plan. GICs are issued by insurance companies to hold and invest the assets of a defined contribution plan. They promise safety, nonspeculative growth, no exposure to the vagaries of the stock market, and peace of mind for the employee.

On the downside, insurance companies can experience difficulties; they are subject to failure, loss of assets, inability to stand behind their guarantees. The

DEFINED CONTRIBUTION PLANS

Table 3–1

Characteristics of Various Investment Vehicles

General Type of Investment Vehicle	Pays Interest or Dividends (cash or stock)	Realizes Gain/ Loss on Sale or at Maturity	Potential for Unrealized Appreciation
Cash and cash equivalents (e.g., money market accounts, savings accounts)	Yes	No	No
Government issues (but not zero coupon bonds)	Yes	Yes	Yes
Corporate bonds (but not zero coupon bonds)	Yes	Yes	Yes
Common and/or preferred stocks	Yes	Yes	Yes
Zero coupon bonds	No	Yes	Yes

only guarantee afforded by a GIC is the word of the insurance company. GICs are not federally insured as banks are. Some states maintain insurance protection funds, but most do not, and not all kinds of policies or contracts are covered.

Employees are learning that the balances reported in their annual benefit statements may be lower than expected—and in extreme cases accounts may become worthless. Retirees may find their annuity checks delayed, canceled, or reduced in amount.

Prior to these insurance company problems, defined contribution plans were generally considered very safe, convenient, easy to value as marital property in divorce, and good candidates for deferred distribution by way of a qualified domestic relations order (QDRO). But now new thinking is required.

Assume, for example, a wife is a participant in a profit-sharing plan and had $50,000 in her individual account at the end of last year, and the nonemployee-husband has been awarded 50 percent of the wife's 401(k) plan account in the divorce settlement. The payment is to be made by use of a QDRO when she retires. Is it equitable for him to share in the decrease in the account value due to GIC problems, or is he entitled to his share of the account at the time the issue was determined?

Consider an example in which the husband has been awarded the house with a net value of $50,000 at the time the wife's profit-sharing plan account had a balance of $50,000. For those two assets it was a fair settlement. But now the house still has a fair market value of $50,000 or more, while the plan account has decreased through no fault of the wife. It was never contemplated that her account balance could go down in value, especially because most, if not all, of her account was invested in a GIC.

No satisfactory answers may be available until insurance company problems are resolved. Family practice lawyers must consider these questions whenever an interest in a defined contribution plan is one of the marital assets to be allocated in a divorce.

§ 3.7   TIAA-CREF Plan

A special category of defined contribution plan is furnished in the Teachers Insurance Annuity Association-College Retirement Equities Fund (TIAA-CREF) program. The following form, available upon request from TIAA-CREF, may be used to transfer TIAA-CREF funds as community property in marital dissolution.

TEACHERS INSURANCE AND ANNUITY ASSOCIATION OF AMERICA
COLLEGE RETIREMENT EQUITIES FUND
730 THIRD AVENUE, NEW YORK, NEW YORK 10017

Marital Property Distribution
Authorization and Release

The following is given after I have had the advice of counsel, or the opportunity to seek such advice, to induce TIAA-CREF to accommodate the Marital Property Distribution of CREF annuity on the life of _____. I warrant that the time for appeal of the Divorce Decree and Property Settlement terminating my marriage to _____ has elapsed, and I waive any right I may have to appeal the terms as they relate to the TIAA-CREF annuity contract.

I understand and agree that:

1.   The exact value of $ _____ as of the date of withdrawal of the accumulation value** under CREF Certificate No. _____ shall be withdrawn and applied to my CREF Annuity Contract,* to be owned by me and on my life, upon receipt and acceptance of the necessary documentation by TIAA-CREF, and
2.   Should I die prior to the issuance of the CREF Annuity Contract, TIAA-CREF's only obligation will be to distribute said portion as a death benefit to my Estate, and
3.   I hereby release any and all rights or interest in the balance of the Annuities on the life of _____, and
4.   I acknowledge and understand that this authorization is irrevocable, and
5.   I understand and agree that TIAA-CREF accepts this authorization only as an accommodation to the parties.

_____

Signature

_____

Date

_____

Notary

---

* CREF Certificate No. Pxxxxxx-x.

** The CREF Certificate's current value is the dollar value of the number of accumulation units as of the date of withdrawal. The future value may be greater or lesser than the amount specified.

§ 3.8   Thrift Savings Plan for Federal Employees

One form of defined contribution plan is the Thrift Savings Plan (TSP) available to members of both the Civil Service Retirement System (CSRS) and the Federal Employees Retirement System (FERS). The TSP is a much more favorable, optional addition to the small FERS defined benefit pension plan than it is for members of CSRS. Each employee who participates in the TSP has an individual account that grows with employee and federal matching contributions and investment gains. There is no formula pension benefit and no formal normal retirement age in the federal TSP.

CHAPTER 4

SPECIAL TOPICS

§ 4.1   Teachers' Pensions

Teaching can be a stressful occupation, and teachers have not escaped the problems of divorce in our society. A teacher's pension plan may sometimes be the single most valuable asset in a marriage—possibly worth more than the house, even though the pension is a promise of future payments and a house is a solid piece of property that can be sold now.

Schoolteachers and school administrators in most states are covered by a public school employees retirement system (PSERS) or the state's public employees retirement system (PERS), which is usually a defined benefit pension plan. Defined benefit pension plans for employees of governmental or quasi-governmental organizations, particularly schoolteachers, provide both retirement pension benefits and death benefits.

Normally, the plan provides a routine annual pension account statement to all covered employees as of June 30 or December 31 of each year. A standard item often shown on this statement is the pension's "present value" or "present worth." In most cases this item is the dollar amount of the death benefit—not the actuarial present value of the pension benefit. This terminology may cause confusion in divorce cases involving the pension. The actuarial present value is the fair market value of the pension, the price that it could fetch as an annuity contract.

The death benefit in this type of pension plan is usually quite generous, a much larger amount than the value of the pension as a monthly pension benefit. On the usual individual annual statement of account, the death benefit may be referred to indirectly as the present value. Although this death benefit is a good employee benefit as life insurance, it does not indicate the pension benefit's worth as marital property. As used in a defined benefit pension plan, the term *present value* means the death benefit payable to the beneficiary of a covered member.

39

One way in which a generous death benefit is valued is to compute it using a low interest rate—say, 4 percent. A standard mathematical inverse relationship exists between the interest rate and the present value. The lower the interest rate, the higher the present value of a future payment. An interest rate of 4 percent, therefore, will produce a high death benefit.

The death benefit is *not* the value of the retirement pension. The present value of the retirement pension itself is probably not computed nor shown by the plan. In a divorce action, the amount of the death benefit labeled as present value may be given by the plan, which would be misleading.

Upon retirement, the plan participant has many options, some of which reduce or even eliminate a death benefit. A PERS frequently requires employee contributions, and credits the interest on employee contributions at the same low interest rate—for example, 4 percent. The rationale is that the low investment credit awarded on employee contributions is balanced by the high death benefit derived by using that very same low interest rate. In looking to the future for investment gains on present amounts, higher interest rates generate higher yields. But in determining the value now of money due in the future, higher interest rates mean a lower present value.

By using a low internal interest rate, the plan is able to provide a large death benefit but is not obligated to provide market-level interest earnings on employee contributions. Many more employees will leave service and withdraw their contributions with interest than will die in service.

The generous size of the death benefit may be considered to be balanced by the low level of investment earnings on the employee's own money. This does not mean that the plan or the political system is being deliberately misleading to communicate the death benefit as a "present value," but school employees may have been misled.

If a teacher's pension is determined to be marital property, it may be attached by court order in a divorce action, and a portion of the pension awarded to the teacher's spouse by an appropriate court order. The provisions for attachment and assignment of pensions parallel, but do not duplicate exactly, the federal rules for qualified domestic relations orders (QDROs). For further discussion of QDROs, see **Chapter 17.**

A typical set of provisions for a court order involving a schoolteacher's pension follows:

A *domestic relations order* (DRO) is any judgment, decree, or order, including approval of a property settlement agreement, relating to marital property rights to a pension.

An *approved domestic relations order* is a court order that has been accepted by the plan.

The *alternate payee* is any spouse, former spouse, child, or dependant of a member of a PSERS who is named in a DRO.

An *irrevocable beneficiary* is a person or persons designated in the order to receive all or part of a refund of employee contributions or lump-sum benefit upon the death of the member. Once established, such designation cannot be changed without approval by the court. If the designee dies first, the order may be amended to provide a substitute beneficiary.

An *irrevocable survivor annuitant* is an individual designated in the order to receive an annuity upon the death of the member. This designation, too, cannot be changed without court approval. Whether a substitute may be used if the designee predeceases the member is a matter for the plan to approve on an actuarially sound basis.

Cost-of-living increases and/or *supplemental annuities* may be awarded in part to the alternate payee as part of the pension division approved in the order. No cost-of-living or supplemental increases are payable to a beneficiary after the member's death.

This plan includes three kinds of pensions:

1. The regular retirement pension, payable when a member retires at normal retirement age, known as a *superannuation annuity*.
2. An early retirement pension, paid to a member retiring after 10 years of credited service but before attaining normal retirement age, known as a *withdrawal annuity*.
3. A *disability pension* payable upon the member's mental or physical incapacity.

The plan may offer different sets of pension increases. One type of increase may be a cost-of-living adjustment (COLA), which is sometimes called an *additional supplemental annuity*. The COLA applies a certain percentage increase to the annuity amount being received and may vary, depending on the member's retirement date.

The second type of increase, which recognizes length of service, is referred to as a *longevity supplemental annuity*, and covers distinct service periods.

Various legislated pension increases may be included as marital property by court order or by agreement of the spouses, and the benefits are subject to actuarial valuation to determine present value for immediate offset, as well as to attachment by court order.

§ 4.2 Lost Wages in Personal Injury

An important component in the financial aspect of many personal injury cases is the value of the wages lost by the injured individual. There are many parallel issues in pension and personal injury cases. Some injured individuals may never be able to work for any pay at all, and others may find work that is less well paid because of the injury. Disability or other compensation may be included in the derived lost wages value as a credit against the total amount otherwise lost, as illustrated in the following example.

Example: *B* was partially disabled at age 48 as a result of injuries suffered in an automobile accident. At the time of the accident, *B* was employed as a floor nurse in the intensive care unit of a major hospital, a job that required heavy lifting. After the accident, *B* was assigned to a light-duty position at the hospital, working 26 hours per week at a wage of $17 per hour, for a weekly pay of $442.

Had *B* not been injured in the accident, her hourly pay would have been $20.50 for a 26-hour weekly pay of $533. Therefore, on a 26-hour weekly basis, *B*'s current wage loss is $91 ($533 − $442).

Before the accident, *B* had intended to return to a 40-hours-per-week schedule after her youngest child graduated from high school, at which time *B* would have been 50. However, her physician testified that she cannot continue to perform even her current light duties and will be totally disabled by the time she is 60.

The consulting actuary's assignment was to evaluate seven basic scenarios, with and without inflationary increases, using certain work period assumptions. The actuary's report follows:

Data and Assumptions

Sex	Female
Current age	48
Payments end at death	Yes
Mortality basis	Disabled female mortality table
Interest rate	7% per annum, compounded annually
Inflation assumptions	(1) None or (2) Annual average 3%
Work period assumptions	(1) Continues part time to age 65 or
	(2) Changes to full time at age 50

Results

The results presented are the current actuarial present values of the individual's lost wages due to personal injury. Corresponding values may be generated for any other amounts of gross or net wage figures by reference to the posted results.

The values represent current actuarial present values based on the given data and selected actuarial assumptions for this case.

1. From age 48 to age 65
    a. Net weekly wage loss of $91
        (1) No inflation, present value $ 40,500
        (2) 3% inflation, present value   48,800
    b. Full weekly wage loss of $533
        (1) No inflation, present value   234,700
        (2) 3% inflation, present value   282,400

2. From age 48 to age 60
    Net weekly wage loss of $91
    (1)   No inflation, present value $ 34,600
    (2)   3% inflation, present value   39,900

3. From age 60 to age 65
    Weekly wage loss of $533
    (1)   No inflation, present value $ 34,400
    (2)   3% inflation, present value   51,600

4. From age 48 to age 50
    Weekly wage loss of $91
    (1)   No inflation, present value $ 8,800
    (2)   3% inflation, present value   9,000

5. From age 50 to age 65
    Weekly wage loss of $142*
    (1)   No inflation, present value $ 48,800
    (2)   3% inflation, present value   61,100

6. From age 50 to age 60
    Weekly wage loss of $142*
    (1)   No inflation, present value $ 39,700
    (2)   3% inflation, present value   47,400

7. From age 60 to age 65
    Weekly wage loss of $822
    (1)   No inflation, present value $ 52,900
    (2)   3% inflation, present value   79,400

*Full time regular (40 hours $\times$ $20.55)   = $822
 Full time light duty (40 hours $\times$ $17.00) = $680
                              Differential = $142

The foregoing sets of results satisfied *B*'s attorney's request for a lost wages report on his client. With this information, a reasonable and appropriate settlement was reached with the insurance carrier. All parties agreed to the data, facts, and assumptions, and all accepted the resulting versions of values. *B* was properly compensated. The analysis, methods, assumptions, and conclusions would be the same if the value of lost wages was due to wrongful termination of employment and similar to compensation for lost pension benefits.

§ 4.3   Welfare Plan Death Benefits

In *Metropolitan Life Insurance Co. v. Wheaton*, 42 F.3d 1080 (7th Cir. 1994), the court ruled that a divorce decree served as a QDRO to award welfare plan death benefits to the beneficiaries named in the divorce decree and not the beneficiary named on the plan beneficiary form.

Nowhere in the divorce decree was a QDRO mentioned. Nor was there mention of the legal and administrative details of a pension court order. The decree was neither communicated to nor served on the employer or the plan.

The court's problem was how to mold a just result after the former husband in the case violated the divorce decree. The husband had agreed to name the couple's sons as beneficiary of the life insurance provided by his employer, but after the divorce he remarried and named his new wife the beneficiary. Then he died, leaving disputing claimants to the life insurance proceeds.

The court said the Wisconsin divorce decree that gave the life insurance to the sons was equivalent to a court order and could serve as a QDRO. The husband's naming his new wife as beneficiary could not supersede a QDRO. The second wife (now widow) claimed the life insurance of some $60,000, as did the sons. The insurance carrier, Metropolitan Life, referred the problem to the court. The district court in Wisconsin entered judgment for the sons, and the widow appealed. The appeals court affirmed the judgment. The majority opinion covered the following points:

- A state law concerning spendthrift clauses may in general prohibit paying a benefit to a person other than named by the participant. Where this is the case, federal law (ERISA) preempts state law.
  (This reasoning seems to have been necessary for the court to allow the life insurance to be paid to someone not named as a beneficiary by the deceased. The court used ERISA and the QDRO concept to get around any spendthrift provision.)
- ERISA, in general, prohibits alienation, assignment, or attachment of pension benefits. The Retirement Equity Act of 1984 (REA) created the exemption, the QDRO.
  (To overcome the ERISA restriction that would otherwise prevent the insurance from being paid to the sons, the court found the exemption created under the REA.)
- QDROs were created to apply to qualified pension plans. A qualified pension plan is a plan subject to ERISA that meets IRS requirements for favorable tax treatment.
  (QDROs were extended to cover the life insurance provided by an employer through a welfare plan by this decision. This is an unusual interpretation of the intent of Congress, as it does not seem to have been contemplated that a QDRO would apply to a welfare plan.)
- QDRO requirements and ERISA details are too complex for lawyers and judges to use and follow literally. If flexibility is not granted, then the only recourse is to sue a lawyer for legal malpractice.
  (It seems a strange new idea that detailed rules and regulations can be flexible if they are too complicated to be followed correctly by lawyers.)

- The concurring judge's opinion held that reference to ERISA was not necessary—and the finding that the divorce decree was a QDRO also not needed—because the divorce decree itself was equivalent to a binding contract that precluded the divorced employee from changing his beneficiary.

  (The majority opinion dictated the meanings of commonly accepted practices and procedures in pensions in divorce. This conclusion exhibits clear thinking and offers a pragmatic solution.)

Conclusions

1. ERISA's preemption of state law with respect to employee benefit plans does not extend to divorce decrees;

2. The award of a welfare plan benefit in a divorce decree overrides the employee's beneficiary designation, because the decree is within the protection deemed to be provided by ERISA as formulated by the REA in terms of a QDRO;

3. The award of a plan benefit in a divorce decree may be the equivalent of a QDRO even when it is incomplete in details required of QDROs by the Retirement Equity Act of 1984.

The majority opinion in *Wheaton* created problems for practitioners, lawyers, and actuaries, as well as for administrators of all kinds of pension and welfare plans. The answers to the following questions about QDROs may be helpful.

Q. Is every divorce decree a QDRO?

A. No. A plan administrator should not blindly accept attachments of benefits just because they appear in a divorce decree. Plan officials should follow their best interpretation of the plain meaning of ERISA, REA, and the QDRO rules and regulations.

Q. May a divorce attorney plead ignorance, or difficulty in drafting a QDRO, as an excuse for incomplete or improper requests for a plan to pay benefits?

A. No, the plan is responsible to authorities other than a divorce court (the IRS, for example). Plan officials must preserve the integrity of the plan and remain responsible for the interests of all participants and beneficiaries, in compliance with prevailing law.

Q. May benefits from a welfare plan be subject to a QDRO?

A. Yes and no. The only benefits assignments or attachments authorized by federal law apply to qualified retirement plans. Either the *Wheaton* ruling is an anomaly that could be expected to be overruled or ignored, or more courts could adopt its reasoning so that welfare plan QDROs become set.

Q. If a plan accepts a QDRO with death benefit provisions, but the participant changes the beneficiary designation in defiance or ignorance of the QDRO, what should be done?

A. The plan should refuse to accept a beneficiary designation, or any other benefit selection from the participant, that is in conflict with the provisions of a QDRO.

Q. In the *Wheaton* case, who should have received the life insurance proceeds, and by what mechanism?

A. The persons named in the divorce decree should have been named by the participant in a plan beneficiary designation. The plan should have been put on notice, and the participant should have been subject to court sanctions that would have prohibited him from changing the beneficiary designation.

§ 4.4 Railroad Workers' Pensions

Members of the Railroad Retirement Board (RRB) pension system are employees of a particular railroad, not federal employees, but the retirement program is established by federal law. The RRB provides members with a two-tier benefit program. Tier I is equivalent to Social Security because all railroad workers are covered by Social Security. Tier II is a defined benefit pension plan, which provides benefits computed by the following formula:

0.7 percent (or .007) × covered average pay × credited railroad service.

The basic types of retirement ages in RRB are summarized in Table 4–1.

Table 4–1

Railroad Retirement Board Retirement Ages

Type of Retirement	Minimum Age	Minimum Service
Regular, normal	65	Fewer than 30 years
Regular, normal	60	30 years or more
Early*	62	Fewer than 30 years

* The RRB monthly pension benefit is available to employees with fewer than 30 years of service retiring at age 62, 63, or 64. The benefit is reduced 6 ⅔ percent for each year prior to attainment of age 65.

The Tier II provisions in the RRB defined benefit pension plan are quite restrictive with respect to death benefits in divorce situations. A former spouse has no right to be a beneficiary upon the death of the RRB member, before or after retirement, and the RRB will not honor any court order that attempts to award death benefits to a former spouse.

The RRB does not allow a current or former railroad employee to withdraw employee contributions, which actually are taxes. Like Social Security taxes, railroad retirement taxes are not refundable unless retirement tax withholding exceeds the annual maximum (e.g., if due to more than one employment in a year).

After retirement, a railroad worker's Tier I monthly pension check is generally increased each year at the same time and in the same percentage as his or her Social

Security benefits. Increases in Tier II monthly pensions are scheduled annually as an adjustment of 32.5 percent of the increase in the Consumer Price Index.

The RRB provides a disability pension to an employee with at least 10 years of credited railroad service who is found to be permanently disabled for all regular work. The disability benefit is intermixed with Social Security benefits in a complex arrangement, payable only if the worker is eligible for Social Security disability benefits.

CHAPTER 5

FEDERAL RETIREMENT SYSTEMS

§ 5.1   Pensions for Federal Employees

There are three nonmilitary retirement systems for employees of the federal government (apart from Social Security): the Thrift Savings Plan (TSP), the Civil Service Retirement System (CSRS), and the Federal Employees Retirement System (FERS).

Federal employees eligible for the retirement programs include members of the diplomatic corps, customs officers, agents of the Federal Bureau of Investigation and the Internal Revenue Service, federal marshals, air traffic controllers, postal workers, and others.

The TSP is a voluntary savings plan of the defined contribution type in which the balance in an individual's account is its value. Members' accounts grow with contributions and investment earnings, but there is no pension benefit formula and no actuarial computations are required. The CSRS and FERS are defined benefit pension plans. An employee may participate in the TSP and one of the defined benefit plans. An employee with credits in either the CSRS or FERS may be eligible under the other federal defined benefit pension plan with transferred credits.

49

The CSRS is the more generous plan, but its members are not covered by Social Security. The FERS pension benefit is far smaller than the CSRS pension benefit, but FERS members may join the TSP, and they are covered by Social Security, which is mandatory for members of FERS and transferred or reinstated members of CSRS.

The domestic relations lawyer must know in which federal pension system the client is a participant. When a federal employee is contemplating divorce, whether any or all of the increasing benefits after the dissolution of the marriage count as marital or community property depends on the jurisdiction and the circumstances of the case. Some jurisdictions permit the projection of a future pension with estimated future pay increases. The pension benefit—accrued or projected—has an actuarial present value, which may be computed and included in the totality of marital assets subject to equitable distribution. Alternatively, upon divorce there may be a deferred distribution of the pension share to become payable on an if-as-and-when basis by a QDRO or its equivalent.

§ 5.2 —The Civil Service Retirement System

The CSRS covers civilian employees of the federal government employed before December 31, 1983. Persons hired after that date are covered by the FERS. CSRS members may transfer to the FERS, but few have done so. If a person who was hired before December 31, 1983, and covered by the CSRS left service and was rehired after December 31, 1983, there are special conditions to become re-eligible for participation in the CSRS.

Members of the CSRS are not covered by Social Security. However, former CSRS members who have transferred to FERS or have been reinstated in the CSRS are covered by Social Security. A complex set of rules coordinates federal pensions with Social Security benefits to avoid a windfall, or "double dipping." An employee of the federal government who has federal pension credits may have previously worked in the private sector and had Social Security coverage. Such a person would not receive full benefits from both the federal pension program and Social Security. Part of the individual's Social Security benefits are offset against the individual's federal pension.

The CSRS is entirely a defined benefit pension plan. As such, it provides an accrued pension benefit for service to date, as well as a projected future pension if service is assumed to continue until retirement. The CSRS defined benefit formula is back-loaded because later years of service count more in the benefit computation than earlier years do, even though the same average pay is used. (For a discussion of back loading, see § 2.7.) As long as the employee works in federal service, the pension benefit increases by two factors: years of service and pay increases. Consequently, the three-year average by which the percentage is multiplied is larger, producing a larger pension benefit.

50

§ 5.3   —The Federal Employees Retirement System

The FERS pension benefit formula is simpler than the CSRS formula. The basic FERS formula is 1 percent of high three-year average pay multiplied by years of service. There is a small premium above that for employees who retire at age 62. For retirement at age 62, the FERS formula is 1.1 percent of high three-year average pay multiplied by years of service.

If a federal employee in FERS leaves service with a deferred vested pension benefit, before becoming eligible to collect retirement benefits, the actuarial present value is computed assuming payment at age 60. Because age 60 is the assumed payment date, the pension benefit formula is at the 1 percent level. However, if the FERS employee actually retires at age 62, the pension benefit formula is at the rate of 1.1 percent. The employee may continue to work and retire at age 62, with the larger pension, a fact to be carefully considered as an assumption for possible use in a valuation.

There are three elements in the FERS plan. One element is a defined benefit pension plan, which has a lower benefit formula than that of the CSRS plan. If only defined benefits are compared, CSRS is a better plan than FERS. Everyone in FERS is in the defined benefit plan.

The second FERS component is Social Security. Because all FERS participants are covered by Social Security, at retirement they are entitled to receive two pensions: the FERS defined benefit pension and the Social Security pension. Federal employees in CSRS either are not in Social Security or their benefits are offset, so it is equivalent to not being covered by Social Security.

The third component of FERS is the TSP. As previously noted, members of the CSRS may participate in the TSP as well but participation is more favorable for members of FERS.

In valuation of marital assets for a divorce, the spouse who is a participant in CSRS should be asked whether he or she is a member of the TSP. A participant in FERS is probably a member of the TSP, but not necessarily, so that should be checked.

For present values to work out a current settlement, the CSRS benefit is converted to a present lump-sum equivalent by an actuary retained by counsel; the FERS defined benefit is also reduced to present value. Then the TSP account, if any, is added in. At present, Social Security benefits are not available for equitable distribution in marital dissolution and cannot be assigned or attached by any QDRO-like procedure.

§ 5.4   Plan Provisions

CSRS and FERS have some similar provisions, but there are significant differences in the following areas:

51

- Normal and early retirement ages;
- Employee contributions, pretax, post-tax, mandatory, voluntary, matched by the government funds, with interest;
- Vesting upon termination of service;
- Disability pensions; and
- Cost-of-living increases.

At retirement from CSRS or FERS, the employee chooses a form of pension benefit from the defined benefit plan. The four general types of elections available are described below.

1. **Lifetime annuity with no death benefits.** This election pays the largest amount of pension, because the other elections require reductions. If the employee is married at retirement, consent of the current spouse is required for this election.

2. **Lifetime annuity with survivor benefits class A.** This election pays a death benefit to a named beneficiary if the pensioner predeceases the beneficiary. The choice of beneficiary is limited to the current or former spouse. (If the employee had divorced and remarried, and there is a current spouse at the time of death after retirement under this election, the current spouse must consent to the death benefit being paid to the former spouse.)

   The CSRS death benefit amount is 55 percent, and for FERS 50 percent, of a base annuity amount designated by the retiree-employee. The retiree-employee may designate all or a portion of the retirement pension for this purpose. There is an opportunity here for creative structuring of a settlement agreement to allow for remarriage of the retiree-employee. There is a small difference in the treatment of death benefits after retirement depending on whether the beneficiary is a widow or widower or a former spouse. In each case the death benefit pension continues until the death or remarriage of the beneficiary. However, remarriage after age 55 does not end the benefit; the penalty applies only if the beneficiary remarries before age 55. The difference occurs in the event of remarriage before age 55 and such remarriage ends by divorce or the beneficiary's death. If the beneficiary is the widow or widower of the retiree, then the death benefit pension is reinstated. However, if the beneficiary is a former spouse, there is no reinstatement.

   If the retiree-employee's divorce occurs after retirement, and the retiree's spouse at the time of retirement is dropped as a beneficiary, the retiree's pension is increased to reflect the absence of a death benefit. The retiree may choose whether to designate a former spouse as a beneficiary. For some retirees, this may be an important issue to be resolved in a divorce that occurs after retirement.

   If a pensioner remarries, a voluntary election is available within two years of the remarriage to provide a death benefit for the new spouse. Care must be taken if there is already an election to cover the former spouse. The cost of this class A death benefit is an approximate 10 percent reduction in the pension.

3. **Lifetime annuity with survivor benefits class B.** This election pays a death benefit to a named beneficiary if the pensioner predeceases the beneficiary. The choice of beneficiary is limited to an individual with an insurable interest (e.g., a relative or a former spouse). To elect the class B death benefit, the retiring employee must be in good health at retirement.

    Both CSRS and FERS pay a death benefit annuity of 55 percent of the pensioner's annuity, based on a reduced annuity the pensioner receives for choosing this option. The benefit reduction, which is based on the difference between the age of the retiree and the age of the beneficiary, ranges from 10 percent to 40 percent.

    The class B death benefit has no remarriage clause. If the named beneficiary predeceases the retiree, the pension is restored in full and there is no death benefit thereafter.

4. **Lump-sum payment with a reduced lifetime annuity**. This election pays an immediate cash lump sum to the retiring employee equal to the sum of the employee's contributions. The pension annuity is then reduced based on the amount of the lump-sum payment and the age of the retiree. A general rule of thumb is that if the pensioner lives 15 or more years after retirement collecting a pension, in the long run the total pension benefits received will exceed the lump sum plus the reduced benefits over the same period of time. If, on the other hand, the pensioner dies within 15 years of retiring, election of the lump sum would have been more advantageous for the pensioner. This election may be made in combination with any one of the three preceding elections.

In a divorce case involving a currently active federal employee, in which there may be a court order to pay future pensions to the employee's former spouse, it is important to recognize in advance the possibility that the employee's election of an option at retirement could defeat the purpose of the property settlement. For example, assuming Wife is awarded 50 percent of Husband's pension when he retires, the amount of pension may be radically altered if Husband elects lump-sum payment with a class B death benefit.

Also to be considered when property settlement in divorce involves a federal employee is the pre-retirement death benefit. Both the CSRS and FERS pay a death benefit to the retiree's named beneficiary, who must be either the spouse or an unmarried child under age 18. A former spouse is not eligible to be a beneficiary of the death benefit of a federal employee who dies while in active service. This could be an important consideration in divorce, a contingency that should be covered by some type of life insurance outside the retirement system.

A court order or its equivalent is required to provide for payment of a portion of the pension to a former spouse. The pension to the former spouse does not start until the employee-spouse actually retires. A court order cannot force a person to retire so that part of his or her pension can be paid to a former spouse, and there is no mandatory retirement age for federal employees.

Federal pensions are not subject either to ERISA or to the REA that established the concept of a QDRO. However, both the CSRS and FERS will divide a member's pension between the member and the member's former spouse subject to the proper receipt of a state court order, decree, or community property settlement agreement pertaining to child support, alimony, separate maintenance obligation, and/or equitable distribution pursuant to a divorce, legal separation, or annulment.

In the federal government, the Office of Personnel Management (OPM) is responsible for handling pensions. OPM receives and complies with proper orders and makes the payments directly to the former or separated spouse.

§ 5.5   Comparing CSRS to FERS

Table 5–1 compares features of the two federal retirement systems, based on the pension system change date of December 31, 1983.

Table 5–1

Comparison of CSRS and FERS Features

Feature	CSRS	FERS
Components	Defined benefit pension, no Social Security	Defined benefit, TSP, plus Social Security
Employee contributions	7% of pay	8/10% of pay plus Social Security tax
Pension pay base	High 3-year average	High 3-year average
Benefit formula	Varies from 1.5% to 2.0% of pension pay, base, by service	Basically only 1%, with additional 0.1% available
Unreduced pension benefits at age/service period, in years	55/30, 60/20, 62/5	62/5, 60/20, 30 years at ages 55–57 in future
Vesting in pension (without withdrawing employee contributions)	5 years of service	5 years of service
Refund of employee contributions	(1) At termination of employment, forfeit future pension; (2) at retirement, reduced pension	(1) At termination of employment, forfeit future pension; (2) at retirement, reduced pension

§ 5.6 Voluntary Employee Contributions

The CSRS Voluntary Contribution Program (VCP) is a little-known program for civilian employees of the federal government who are covered by CSRS. The VCP allows covered employees to make voluntary contributions virtually at any time and in any amount. The employee has no choice in how contributions are invested, but the investment is totally guaranteed. Members of FERS are not eligible to participate in the VCP.

Voluntary contributions are made by participating employees from personal after-tax monies. The employee makes a contribution by check or money order to the appropriate federal department. No payroll deduction is available. The interest earnings are tax-sheltered until withdrawn. The principal is always tax-free because it represents dollars that had already been taxed.

A participating employee may withdraw the total of personal contributions and interest at any time, before or at retirement, in a lump sum. The interest portion is taxable. If a withdrawal is made, it must be the total amount; no partial withdrawals are permitted.

At retirement, the participating employee may elect to have the CSRS apply the personal accumulated contributions and interest to increase the pension annuity benefit. This choice also includes an option for the employee to elect the increased pension annuity benefit with a survivorship feature. If survivorship is included, an actuarial charge reduces the monthly retirement benefit provided by the VCP. Thus, the basic CSRS retirement pension will be increased by the VCP account, but that increase will be less if there is an election of a survivor. No spousal consent is required for the election of an annuity or of a survivorship.

Neither the VCP account nor any elected annuity based on it is subject to garnishment or court action. Neither a QDRO nor a COAP applies. No spousal rights are attached to the VC account, which is solely for the benefit of the employee. When one spouse is a civilian employee of the federal government *and* a member of CSRS, inquiry should be made as to whether the employee maintains a VCP account. Even though the account is not subject to attachment or garnishment, it nevertheless has value as a potential community property asset and should not be overlooked.

§ 5.7 Postal Workers' Pensions

Employees of the U.S. Postal Service who were hired on or before December 31, 1983, and did not transfer out of the service are covered by the CSRS. Postal employees hired on or after January 1, 1984, are covered by the FERS. There was a transfer "window"—a period during which participants in CSRS were allowed to transfer to FERS—but few employees chose to take advantage of it.

In terms of benefits, CSRS offers far better pension benefits than FERS. However, FERS offers a generous thrift plan with better features than those of the old

CSRS thrift plan. Perhaps the single most important distinction between the two programs is coverage by Social Security, with consequent payment of taxes and eligibility for its benefit programs. Postal employees covered by CSRS are not covered by Social Security by virtue of that employment. If a person had other employment before or after CSRS service, or part-time employment, then there may be Social Security coverage from such employment. FERS participants are in mandatory Social Security coverage. They pay FICA and other Social Security related taxes and are covered for all Social Security benefit programs.

§ 5.8 —Postal Workers in CSRS

For postal workers whose employment started before1984, when only CSRS pensions and values were available, an allowance may be made for the absence of Social Security. The emphasis is on the defined benefit portion of CSRS, which by private industry standards is a generous pension plan. Funding is by mandatory contributions deducted from the pay of each participant, contributions by the employing agency, and the general taxing power of the federal government. The pension benefits are subject to valuation as marital property for equitable distribution in marital dissolution. Postal pension benefits are also subject to a form of attachment or assignment by court order acceptable for processing (COAP), a court order similar to a QDRO.

The CSRS will honor a COAP to pay a portion of the covered participant's pension to a former spouse on or after retirement. Unlike a corporate plan, the postal pension plan does not pay out benefits merely when the participant is eligible for retirement. The employee must first retire. Then the CSRS sends separate checks to the divorced spouses in the amount or percentage specified in the court order. The amount or percentage of pension benefit will have been previously negotiated, by settlement agreement, or by judicial determination.

Vesting in the CSRS occurs after five years of service. If termination of employment occurs prior to the completion of five years of service, the participant receives a refund of employee contributions and forfeits all potential pension benefits. The CSRS requires that a spouse be notified when this occurs. If the individual terminates employment after five years of service without being eligible for an immediate pension, there are two options: (1) the individual may withdraw employee contributions and forfeit all pension benefits, with notification to the spouse, or (2) the individual may leave the employee contributions in the system and eventually collect a lifetime pension. The second option is obviously financially advantageous because the pension is almost always worth more than the person's own contributions. In the rare case of a young worker who leaves the job after a short service period, the employee contributions may be worth more than the small pension accumulated over the short service period.

§ 5.9   —Normal Retirement Age

Normal retirement age in the CSRS, as in corporate pension plans, is the age at which an employee may voluntarily stop working and receive a full pension. In practice, the CSRS has three possible retirement ages, determined by years of service and certain special circumstances. But the special circumstances generally cover law enforcement officers, firefighters, and air traffic controllers, not postal workers.

Minimum Retirement Age	Minimum Service (Years)
62	5
60	20
55	30

There is no maximum retirement age and no requirement for a person to retire at the earliest possible normal retirement age. This may be a problem in valuing the pension of a postal worker who becomes eligible for two or all three of the possible retirement ages. For example, a postal worker hired at age 25 would have 30 years of service at age 55 and be eligible to retire with full benefits. If she continues to work, she could retire at any age beyond 55. The later she retires, the larger would be her pension because she would have more years of service and more pay in the pension benefit formula. However, if the postal worker is currently age 45, should we assume that she will retire at the earliest retirement opportunity, at age 55, or should we assume that she prefers to continue working for a larger eventual pension? One approach in valuing the postal worker's pension is to give it the highest value.

At whatever retirement age(s) the postal worker may become eligible, the age that produces the highest present value of the pension should be used in valuing the pension as a marital asset. Regardless of when the postal worker retires, this asset has that value, whether or not it is exercised. On the other hand, the employee may work to next higher retirement age, regardless of economic incentives, or may end employment for any reason before reaching the earliest possible retirement age.

The family law practitioner should ask the independent pension evaluator to prepare valuations to illustrate the financial differences between different termination and retirement scenarios.

§ 5.10   —Pension Benefit Formula

The pension benefit for postal workers in the CSRS is calculated using pay and length of service. The three-year average of pay is used in the following structure:

- 1.5 percent times pay times service up to five years, plus
- 1.75 percent times pay times service between 5 and 10 years, plus
- 2.0 percent times pay times service of more than 10 years.

Once pension benefits start, they are subject to annual cost-of-living increases in accordance with an inflation index. A QDRO-like court order may award cost-of-living increases to the former spouse but is not required to do so. A valuation of the present worth of the pension may or may not factor in future cost-of-living increases, depending on case law in a jurisdiction as to whether potential future pension increases may be considered as a current asset.

The CSRS has tabulated its pension benefit formula by years of service, a look-up table that quickly shows the pension evaluator the appropriate percentage. The percentage factor is multiplied by the retiree's three-year average pay to yield the pension benefit. An excerpt from the CSRS table is reproduced as Table 5–2.

Table 5–2

CSRS Pension Benefit Percentages by Service

Years of Service	Percent of Three-Year Pay
5	7.50
10	16.25
15	26.25
20	36.25
25	46.25
30	56.25
35	66.25
40	76.25

According to the percentages, an employee with 15 years of service and current three-year average pay of $30,000 would have an accrued monthly pension to date of $656 (.2625 $\times$ $30,000 $\div$ 12). If there were no further service or pay, $656 is all the pension would ever amount to. Depending on the jurisdiction in which the pension is being valued for marital property, the pension amount may be based on a prior or current amount of service and average pay. Note that employee contributions play no part in the pension benefit formula.

One school of thought holds that, because federal employees in CSRS are not covered by Social Security, an allowance should be made in the valuation of the pension as marital property. The reasoning is that Social Security itself is not valued as an asset in property distribution so that if a portion of a pension consists of a Social Security equivalent benefit, that portion should be deleted. Postal workers in the CSRS are not covered by Social Security and their CSRS pension benefit is generous by industry standards. The Social Security benefit could be computed and subtracted from the postal worker's CSRS pension benefit to arrive at a net pension benefit for valuation as marital property in equitable distribution.

§ 5.11   Information Sources

There are several sources of information on postal workers' pensions. A comprehensive list of service credits and salary history, along with pension benefit figures, may be obtained free of charge from the National Retirement Counseling Service, at the following address:

> Retirement Branch
> Minneapolis Postal Data Center
> One Federal Drive
> Ft. Snelling, MN 55111-9620

To request an annuity estimate, it is necessary to provide the employee's full name, date of birth, and Social Security number. If the request is made by someone other than the employee, a consent form signed by the employee is required. When this or any other CSRS pension statement is received, one item to be checked is the pension credited service. The service credit date should be compared to the date of employment. If the dates are different, inquire as to the reason. It may be that prior military service has been credited. The marital component must be determined in the total service credited for pension purposes.

Biweekly pay stubs of a postal service employee show an item in the lower right-hand corner labeled "USPS Retirement." "USPS" refers to the United States Postal Service, but "Retirement" does not mean the pension benefit. It is the employee's total contributions to date that have been deducted from pay.

The pay stub also shows the employee's contribution for that particular two-week period on a line labeled "Retire." The stub also indicates that the individual is not covered by Social Security, because there is no FICA or OASDI tax withholding. Every employee, whether covered by Social Security or not, has a Social Security number.

Upon request, the U.S. Postal Service provides to an employee a document called the Personal Statement of Benefits, which shows the employee's name, date of birth, and Social Security number. It indicates whether the employee is in the CSRS or the FERS. It also shows the benefit credit starting date, labeled "Retirement Computation Date." The statement shows the current year's pay (but not the pay history) and the current year's contributions (but not the total for all years of service). The statement does not show any pension benefit amounts, but does indicate the person's normal retirement age.

The annuity estimate from the Minneapolis Postal Data Center is a more useful document than the Personal Statement of Benefits for purposes of valuing the pension benefit as marital property.

CHAPTER 6

STATUTORY FRAMEWORK OF RETIREMENT SYSTEMS

§ 6.1   Introduction

All retirement systems, pensions, and savings plans of whatever nature are established, maintained, and operated under one or more statutory frameworks. The umbrella structure for most plans is ERISA, the federal law of pensions. ERISA significantly affected the nature and design of most pension and welfare plans. It also established the professional designation "Enrolled Actuary" (EA).

Retirement plans for employees of federal, state, and local governments and retirement plans for the armed forces are not covered by the Employee Retirement Income Security Act of 1974 (ERISA) or its progeny. A non-ERISA plan is governed by its own laws, rules, and procedures. For example, the Railroad Retirement Act of 1983 (RRA) covers railroad employees with a pension arrangement under the Railroad Retirement Board (RRB)—a federal non-ERISA structure.

Plans that are covered by ERISA are also covered by the Retirement Equity Act of 1984 (REA), which allows pensions to be attached as marital property. Certain plans covered by ERISA are also covered by the Pension Benefit Guaranty Corporation (PBGC), which acts as an insurance fund should a plan terminate with insufficient assets to meet its pension obligations.

Federal laws pertaining to pensions include the Internal Revenue Code (Code; IRC), the Tax Equity and Fiscal Responsibility Act of 1982 (TEFRA), the Consolidated Omnibus Budget Reconciliation Act of 1985 (COBRA), the Taxpayer Relief Act of 1997 (TRA '97), and many others. The 1994 General Agreement on Tariffs and Trade (GATT) plays an important role in pension issues, as it includes a pension reform act that sets the criteria for the mortality tables and interest rates in ERISA defined benefit pension plans.

Each law has sets of rules, regulations, interpretations, and case law opinions. The IRC has numerous regulations, revenue rulings, revenue procedures, and letter rulings in place, with new ones being continually issued. The statutory structure may be viewed as a skeleton fleshed out by continuing additions, large and small.

In all cases, for purposes of determining the worth of marital or community property, every pension or retirement plan may be valued by an actuary. However, the use of a court order to award all or some of the pension to a spouse varies according to the auspices under which the plan operates. Virtually all ERISA plans are subject to a qualified domestic relations order (QDRO), and many non-ERISA plans will accept similar court orders. Before a divorce matter is adjudicated or settled, inquiry should always be made concerning the type of plan, its governance, and whether it is subject to a QDRO or similar order.

Figure 6–1 shows the interaction between ERISA, the PBGC, the IRS, the GATT, and the EA regarding rules for lump-sum cash-outs in defined benefit

Figure 6–1

Lump-Sum Rules in ERISA Defined Benefit Pension Plans

ERISA	IRS	GATT
Basic law of pensions	Prescribes minimum and maximum limits for lump-sum distributions; now conforms with GATT.	Establishes mortality table and interest rates for plan liabilities and for lump-sum distributions with interest at smoothed average of 30-year U.S. bonds, changing monthly.

PBGC

Establishes benefits and liabilities for terminated pension plans (rates changed November 1993). Used for lump-sum amounts before GATT.

EA

Helps defined benefit pension plans to maintain conformance with the IRS, the PBGC, and the GATT.

pension plans. Each box in the diagram contains a brief description of an item under its appropriate heading. The boxes flow downward from top to bottom in order, and lines connecting the boxes show their interrelationship.

§ 6.2   Internal Revenue Code

The Internal Revenue Code of 1954 was amended periodically through the years until it underwent a major overhaul in 1986. References to the Code or to IRC are with respect to the 1986 law. Table 6–1 is a selected list of IRC sections relevant to pension-related matters.

Table 6–1

Selected List of IRC Sections

Code Section	Subject Matter
72	Taxation of annuity payments
401(a)	Basic rules for qualified plans
401(k)	Salary reduction plans, with cash or deferred arrangements (CODAs)
402	Lump-sum distributions
403(b)	Tax-sheltered annuity plans and/or tax-deferred annuity plans
404	Employee stock ownership plans (ESOPs)
408	Individual retirement accounts (IRAs)
411	Vesting
412	Funding requirements
413	Multiemployer plans
414	Plan administrator
415	Benefit and contribution limits
416	Top-heavy plans
457	Deferred compensation plans
501	Tax-free trust fund of qualified plans
501(c)(3)	Nonprofit tax-exempt organizations

Many more somewhat obscure and arcane references to pensions are scattered throughout the IRC, as well as in voluminous published regulations and rulings and in proposed, temporary, and final regulations of various federal departments and agencies.

§ 6.3   Employee Retirement Income Security Act

ERISA was signed into law on Labor Day, September 2, 1974. The law is codified in four titles, each designed for a specific purpose in the governance of pension plans over which the federal government has jurisdiction. Responsibility for administering its provisions is spread among four governmental bodies: the Department of Labor (DOL), the Department of the Treasury, the Internal Revenue Service (IRS), and the PBGC.

Title I of ERISA, administered by the DOL, deals with the protection of employee benefit rights and contains definitions of terms and requirements of a qualified plan. Title II deals with amendments to the IRC to implement the details established by Title I. Title III deals with the division of responsibility between the agencies administering the law. Title IV deals with the termination of defined benefit pension plans and the establishment of the PBGC.

ERISA places plans into one of two broad categories: pension plans and welfare plans. Welfare plans encompass medical and dental insurance plans, group life insurance, severance pay plans, and any others that are not pre-funded to provide retirement type benefits. Welfare plans may provide sickness, accident, disability, death, or unemployment benefits, as well as vacation benefits, apprenticeships or other training programs, day care centers, scholarship funds, or prepaid legal services.

The pension plan category under ERISA includes all pension, retirement, and savings plans. All ERISA pension plans are then divided into two types: defined benefit plans and defined contribution plans.

Defined contribution plans always establish and maintain individual accounts for plan participants. Defined benefit plans typically establish a pooled fund of assets from which benefits are paid. Both types of plans may allow contributions by employees as well as by employers. If a defined benefit plan permits employee contributions, it must maintain an individual account for each employee.

The following types of plans are *defined contribution plans:*

- Profit-sharing plans
- 401(k) plans
- Thrift plans
- Savings plans
- Money-purchase pension plans
- Target benefit plans
- Assumed benefit plans
- Keogh profit-sharing plans
- Employee stock ownership plans

The following types of plans are *defined benefit plans:*

- Cash-balance pension plans
- Keogh defined benefit plans

Some versions of the following types of plans are known as *hybrid plans*; they are a cross between a defined contribution plan and a defined benefit plan:

- Multiemployer union plans
- TIAA-CREF plans

The law does not require any employer to establish a pension plan. Nor does it guarantee benefits to every worker, specify amounts of benefits or contributions, or provide automatic transfers of benefits. The law also does not provide PBGC coverage for all employees or all plans. The following employees and/or plans may not be covered by ERISA:

- Foreign Service officers and Coast Guard members
- Members of the Armed Forces and the National Guard
- Police officers, firefighters, schoolteachers, and postal workers
- Railroad workers
- Faculty and staff of colleges and universities
- Hospital workers
- Federal, state, county, and municipal government pension plans
- TIAA-CREF plans, depending on the sponsoring institution
- Individual retirement accounts (IRAs)
- Simplified employee pension plans (SEPs)
- Excess-benefit ("top-hat") plans
- Non-U.S. plans (plans established for employees outside the United States)

§ 6.4   Pension Benefit Guaranty Corporation

The PBGC was established by ERISA as a nonprofit corporation under the aegis of the federal government. It covers the defined benefit pension plans of private businesses with 25 or more employees. Covered plans pay an annual premium to the PBGC based on their actuarial liabilities. If a covered plan does not have enough assets available to meet its accrued benefit amounts, the PBGC takes over as the plan trustee. The PBGC guarantees covered employees' accrued monthly pension annuity benefits up to annually adjusted maximums. In a divorce action, the benefits guaranteed by the PBGC may be valued and/or made subject to a QDRO to the extent funded by the PBGC.

Before 1995, the PBGC was the primary source for interest rates used in the valuation of a pension when a marriage ends in divorce. Since 1995, PBGC rates are no longer recommended for the valuation of pensions as marital property in a divorce case. For such purpose pension evaluators use the prevailing interest rate of 30-year U.S. Treasury bonds (see § **6.6**).

§ 6.5   Retirement Equity Act

After ERISA was enacted in 1974, the alienation or attachment of pension benefits was prohibited. This created a dilemma for state domestic relations courts attempting to award a portion of a spouse's pension as marital property. Federal law and state law conflicted in this area.

The solution came with the passage of Public Law 98-317, the Retirement Equity Act of 1984 (REA), which created the concept of domestic relations orders (DROs) and QDROs. Another new term introduced by the REA is *alternate payee*, the person designated to receive all or a portion of the employee's pension benefits as awarded by the QDRO. The alternate payee is usually the employee's spouse (or former spouse), but it may be a child or other dependant of the employee.

The REA applies only to ERISA plans, but many non-ERISA plans have established procedures to accept similar court orders in marital dissolution cases. The federal government accepts a court order acceptable for processing (COAP) instead of a QDRO. The Armed Forces prefers to use a qualifying military court order (QMCO). When one spouse has a non-ERISA plan, the divorce lawyer should inquire as to the name of the order to be used and the limits, terms, and conditions allowed by the particular retirement program.

§ 6.6   General Agreement on Tariffs and Trade

Public Law 103-465, which Congress passed in December 1994 to implement the international negotiations culminating in the Uruguay Round of the General Agreement on Tariffs and Trade (GATT), included pension provisions that originally had been drafted as a separate bill. These pension provisions in GATT apply only to United States pension plans, under the theory that such plans will produce a net revenue gain to offset anticipated losses due to GATT's trade provisions.

The pension provisions are found in Title VII, Subtitle F, Part I of Subpart C, Section 767. The provisions are labeled "The Retirement Protection Act of 1994." The mortality table prescribed therein is the 1983 Group Annuity Mortality (GAM) Table as spelled out by the IRS in Revenue Ruling 95-6.

GATT prescribes the interest rates to be used in defined benefit pension plans as the smoothed average of 30-year U.S. Treasury bonds; that is, the 30-year constant maturity extrapolated from the daily yield curve, which relates the yield on a security to the security's time to maturity and is based on the closing market bid yields on actively traded Treasury securities in the over-the-counter market.

Rates thus derived are reported weekly in a Federal Reserve Statistical Release known as Selected Interest Rates, with yields shown in percent per annum. The release lists 39 different interest rates each week, ranging from the federal funds overnight rate to the 30-year constant maturity rate. Only one of the 38 listed rates is of concern to pension practitioners: the 30-year constant maturity rate. The GATT rate has replaced the PBGC rates to become the preferred rate for the determination of pension values.

Table 6–2 shows the history of GATT interest rates through May 1998 and the sample pension values determined for a male, currently aged 45, for a monthly pension of $1,000 payable upon retirement at age 65.

Table 6–2

Sample Pension Values Derived from GATT Annuity Interest Rates

Month and Year of Valuation	Nominal Interest Rate (%)	Effective Interest Rate (%)	Sample Value Male age 45 Retirement age 65 $1,000/month
09/94	7.71	7.58	$21,500
10/94	7.94	7.49	22,000
11/94	8.08	7.71	21,000
12/94	7.87	7.94	20,000
01/95	7.85	8.08	19,000
02/95	7.61	7.87	20,000
03/95	7.45	7.85	20,000
04/95	7.36	7.61	21,500
05/95	6.95	7.45	22,500
06/95	6.57	7.36	23,000
07/95	6.72	6.95	25,500
08/95	6.86	6.57	28,000
09/95	6.55	6.72	27,000
10/95	6.37	6.86	26,000
11/95	6.26	6.55	28,200
12/95	6.06	6.37	29,600
01/96	6.05	6.26	30,500
02/96	6.24	6.06	32,000
03/96	6.60	6.05	32,100
04/96	6.79	6.24	30,600
05/96	6.93	6.60	27,850
06/96	7.06	6.79	26,500
07/96	7.03	6.93	25,600
08/96	6.84	7.06	24,800
09/96	7.03	7.03	24,900
10/96	6.81	6.84	26,200
11/96	6.48	7.03	24,900
12/96	6.55	6.81	26,400
01/97	6.83	6.48	28,730
02/97	6.69	6.55	28,216
03/97	6.93	6.83	26,256
04/97	7.09	6.69	27,217

(continued)

67

Table 6–2 (*continued*)

Month and Year of Valuation	Nominal Interest Rate (%)	Effective Interest Rate (%)	Sample Value Male age 45 Retirement age 65 $1,000/month
05/97	6.94	6.93	25,592
06/97	6.77	7.09	24,568
07/97	6.51	6.94	25,526
08/97	6.58	6.77	26,663
09/97	6.50	6.51	28,508
10/97	6.33	6.58	27,998
11/97	6.11	6.50	28,583
12/97	5.99	6.33	29,868
01/98	5.81	6.11	31,625
02/98	5.89	5.99	32,630
03/98	5.95	5.81	34,205
04/98	5.92	5.89	33,496
05/98	5.93	5.95	32,974

As may be seen from Table 6–2, the effective rate for a value in a given month is derived from the published or nominal rate of the second preceding month. For example, the table shows that the effective rate for a pension value in March 1996 is 6.05 percent, which was the published rate two months earlier, in January 1996. The federal regulations for pension plans using GATT rates allow plan administrators considerable flexibility in choosing the ''look-back'' period a plan may use for valuations. Plan administrators commonly use the two-month look-back period illustrated in the table. That allows time for receipt of the published GATT rate, entering the rate into computer programs, recording it in files, and preparing for administrative processing. The Federal Reserve Board publishes the nominal GATT interest rate at the end of the first week of each month. Generally, this date makes it too late for any advance planning, estimates or value computations for a valuation date in a given month.

The plan's pension evaluator must decide which month's rate to use and then apply it consistently in valuations performed for all covered employees. In some situations, upon request, a pension evaluator may illustrate the different values that would result if a different prior month's GATT rates were used. If this is done, the reported values should be labeled clearly so that interested parties can refer back to the GATT rates and check the computations, and perhaps discuss the appropriateness of using a particular month's rates in a particular case.

CHAPTER 7

PLAN ADMINISTRATION

§ 7.1   Introduction

When a party to a divorce is (or has been) a participant in a pension program of any kind, one of the first things to determine as part of the initial discovery is the status of the plan with respect to ERISA and its administrative framework. Whether the determination is sought for purposes of valuing the pension for immediate offset or for developing a court order for deferred distribution, the following items of information are needed:

1. Type of employer (which may be one or a combination of the following)
   A. Corporation
      (1) Regular business C corporation
      (2) Small business S corporation
      (3) Professional corporation
      (4) Limited liability corporation
   B. Partnership
      (1) Individual partners
      (2) Partnership of corporations
   C. Sole proprietor
   D. Parent company or subsidiary
   E. In common control with another entity

  F. Government (e.g., federal, state, county, or municipal; railroad; government agency or department)

  G. Armed Forces (e.g., active duty or reserves, National Guard)

  H. Nonprofit association

  I. Labor union (national, regional, local)

2. Type of plan (which may be one of the following)

  A. Defined benefit pension plan

  B. Defined contribution plan

   (1) 401(k) plan

   (2) Profit-sharing plan

   (3) Thrift or savings plan

   (4) Money-purchase pension plan

   (5) Target benefit or assumed benefit plan

   (6) Employee stock ownership plan

  C. Hybrid plan

   (1) Cash-balance pension plan

   (2) TIAA-CREF (Teachers Insurance Annuity Association-College Retirement Equities Fund)

   (3) Multiemployer (Taft-Hartley) plan

  D. Plan Compliance

   (1) ERISA

   (2) PBGC

   (3) QDRO

   (4) Other court order attaching benefits for spouse.

Once the type of employer and the type of plan are known, the case may proceed. Always check to see if the individual has a vested benefit in previous employment.

§ 7.2 Importance of ERISA Status

There are two reasons why it is important to determine whether the retirement plan of a divorcing spouse is an ERISA plan.

First, ERISA plans must provide certain information on request, with penalties for failure to properly and promptly respond. The plan must provide a statement of accrued benefits upon request of the plan participant and must automatically send certain general plan financial information to all participants annually. The plan must have a summary plan description (SPD) available for participants at no charge (usually in the form of a booklet), must make the full plan document available for inspection, and must make copies of the full plan document available upon request for a reasonable copying charge. Non-ERISA plans are not required to provide plan booklets or documents, to issue benefit statements, or to release any financial information.

Second, the basic legal way to obtain payment from a plan to the non-participant spouse in a divorce proceeding is by using a qualified domestic relations order (QDRO). All ERISA plans must honor a QDRO, but such is not the case with non-ERISA plans. Federal pension plans will honor a court order, as will military pension plans. However, plans of state, municipal, and other nonfederal entities may or may not honor a court order.

§ 7.3   Plan Qualification

A plan is said to be qualified when it has applied for and received an approval letter (known as a favorable determination letter) from the Internal Revenue Service (IRS). When a plan is amended, an updated approval letter is generally sought. If the divorce lawyer or pension actuary has any doubt as to the plan's IRS status, the basic and amended approval letters should be requested. For example, it may be appropriate to inquire about the status of a one-person plan where the only employee is the owner, who is the party to the divorce.

Continued IRS qualification of the plan provides three basic tax-favored elements. First, the employer contributions are tax-deductible within prescribed limits. Second, the invested plan funds are held in a tax-exempt trust. Third, the employee is not taxed on the accruing benefits until payment occurs.

Plans that are not subject to ERISA are not subject to IRS qualification. The following are examples of non-qualified plans:

- Retirement plans of federal, state, and local governments, including plans for postal service employees and railroad employees
- Retirement plans for military personnel on active duty, in the reserves, or in the National Guard
- Deferred compensation plans
- Executive plans for key employees (''top-hat'' plans)
- Special partnership plans (e.g., supplemental plans)
- Excess-benefit plans (providing benefits greater than ERISA maximums).

Often, there are valid business reasons for an employer to establish and maintain a nonqualified plan. Some entities nevertheless apply for and receive IRS approval letters for the trust fund that holds and invests the plan's assets even though the plan itself is not qualified. In a divorce proceeding, a court order to attach pension benefits from an ERISA plan must be qualified.

§ 7.4   Plan Documentation

Every ERISA plan has a formal plan document, which may run to over 100 pages for the more complicated plans. In addition, all ERISA plans are required to provide a description of the plan written in plain language capable of being understood by the typical plan participant. This description, often found in the plan booklet, is the SPD. The plan may charge for photocopying or otherwise reproducing the formal plan document, but copies of the SPD must be made available at no charge.

Plans not subject to ERISA may not have a plan summary in the form of an SPD, but they usually have some type of booklet for the covered employees. Another source of the plan summary might be the plan's actuarial or accountants' reports.

§ 7.5   The Plan Administrator

An ERISA plan is required to have a plan administrator, who may be a named individual, a corporate officer, a committee, or the employer itself. The plan administrator is charged with such duties as determining eligibility for benefits, calculating plan benefits, and bestowing on domestic relations orders (DROs) the necessary degree of qualification to make them QDROs. The formal plan document designates the plan administrator; by default, the employer is deemed to be the plan administrator.

A plan often contracts with consultants (actuaries, attorneys, or accountants) or an insurance company to perform the routine administrative chores. The consultants may advise on eligibility, benefit options, calculations, and the determination of the qualification of DROs, but the performance of these duties ultimately rests with the plan administrator.

§ 7.6   The Enrolled Actuary

An ERISA defined benefit pension plan must be certified every year by an enrolled actuary (EA), an actuary approved by the Joint Board for the Enrollment of Actuaries, a federal agency qualified for this purpose. Similarly, when a plan covered by the Pension Benefit Guaranty Corporation (PBGC) terminates, its benefits and liabilities must be certified by an EA.

Enrolled actuaries are automatically qualified to appear before the IRS with respect to pension issues. They also serve in the family practice area, computing the present value of pensions and providing advice and assistance to counsel in the preparation of QDROs.

§ 7.7   Required Disclosures

A qualified plan faces both mandatory and optional disclosure requirements. The plan is required to distribute to an employee a copy of the SPD when the person becomes eligible to enter the plan. The plan is required to distribute to all plan participants each year a general report of the plan's assets, known as the summary annual report (SAR). (See, for example, **Appendix G**.) The SAR is usually not useful in the preparation of an actuarial valuation of a person's benefits or in drafting a QDRO, but it may provide helpful information when a very small plan—such as a one-person owner plan—is involved.

A qualified plan is required to provide a benefit or account status report to a plan participant upon request. The plan need not furnish annual or other periodic benefit or account statements automatically, but many plans do so. Individual account plans almost always furnish statements to participants, annually or even quarterly or monthly. Defined benefit pension plans usually furnish benefit statements only once a year.

A plan may charge a fee for computing an account balance or an accrued pension benefit for a specific date—if the plan is willing to do so at all—when such information is requested by the employee or with the consent of the employee. ERISA, however, prohibits a plan from charging a fee with respect to reviewing or processing a QDRO. This means that, although the plan cannot charge a fee for the QDRO, it may charge to do calculations for the QDRO.

§ 7.8   Required Filings

A qualified plan must file certain forms with government agencies, primarily the IRS. The basic requirement is the annual filing of a form in the 5500 series. Depending on its size and other technical criteria, a plan must file either Form 5500, Form 5500-C, Form 5500-R, or another form in the series.

In addition, a qualified plan may be required to file attachments and schedules. For example, a defined benefit pension plan is required to file Schedule B, which must be signed by an enrolled actuary. Schedule B lists the actuarial assumptions used in funding a plan, but is not determinative in valuation of the pension as marital property. The funding assumptions for the plan are generally more involved and complicated than those used to ascertain the value of an individual's particular pension benefit, so in most cases plan assumptions are not used in computing the value of the benefit as a marital asset.

§ 7.9   Plan Assets

The assets of a qualified plan are held in trust, as established by the plan documents. The trustees may be the owners and officers of the company, individually named. Alternatively, a bank or trust company may be designated. Non-qualified plans are often not funded, because benefits as they come due are paid from the general assets of the employer.

Governmental plans may or may not have separate funding arrangements with assets put aside for benefits. Deferred compensation plans may be partially or fully arranged through insurance company policies or contracts. In a small plan, if the company owner is the trustee as well as the employee, close attention should be paid to the assets of the plan when valuing the pension for property rights.

Plan trustees have the duty of holding, preserving, and investing the assets of the plan. In individual account plans, such as a 401(k) plan, the participants may be given full or limited investment rights over their accounts. In rare cases, unusual but legal investments—for example, artwork, coin collections, real estate, or other property—may be found with title held in the name of the plan. These investments may be made by the trustees, but they are not available as assets in the individual accounts of plan participants. Assets of this nature are usually held in the trust fund of a small defined benefit pension plan.

Neither pension valuations nor QDROs should be undertaken without some knowledge and understanding of the underlying assets available in a plan.

§ 7.10 —Overfunding and Underfunding

If a defined benefit pension plan has insufficient assets to meet its accrued pension benefits, but has enough funds to meet at least the value of a plan participant's own pension benefit, it is not an issue of concern in a marital dissolution. Similarly, in a QDRO situation, if the plan can meet the obligation to pay the benefit awarded to the non-participant spouse, it should not matter that the overall plan is underfunded.

On the other hand, if the plan is severely underfunded and demonstrates on a reliable basis that it cannot meet its benefit obligations as presently accrued, that may be cause to modify the valuation or the QDRO.

At the other extreme, an overfunded plan may provide an opportunity for viewing the benefits of an individual as more than just the computed actuarial value of the accrued pension benefit. In a plan with more assets than liabilities, the surplus may be used to fund an increase in benefits by plan amendment. Consideration should be given to the possibility of a plan termination, with a consequent reallocation of surplus assets to plan participants. A surplus of assets in a one-person plan indicates that the employee's benefits may be worth more than the computed benefit alone.

For example, assume the actuarial present value of the lone participant's current pension benefit is calculated to be $45,000. A review of the plan's balance sheet shows the plan assets have a market value of $60,000. If the plan were to be terminated instantly, there would be an asset surplus of $15,000. Such a surplus could be handled in various ways upon plan termination. For purposes of valuing community property, however, this could be a case in which the benefit is worth more than the value calculated by the actuary. Whether or not that is appropriate depends on the facts and circumstances of the situation. Maybe other liabilities or taxes would preclude any of the perceived surplus from being available ultimately. In any event, the assets of a plan may deserve a review, subject to the judgment of the actuary, the client, and counsel.

TERMINATION AND RETIREMENT

§ 8.1   Introduction

In most divorces, at least one spouse is currently employed. In some cases, the employee may already be retired and drawing a monthly pension check—in pay status—or may have retired and received a lump-sum cash-out with no further benefit payments due. Alternatively, the person may have left the job with vested benefits on a deferred payment basis—that is, a terminated vested (TV) participant. Benefits are usually frozen for a TV participant, to be paid when the person reaches a stated age.

§ 8.2   Vesting

Vesting is the nonforfeitable right to receive a benefit. ERISA plans have vesting schedules, based on credited vesting service (usually defined as 1,000 hours worked in a consecutive 12-month period). The common ERISA vesting schedule provides 100 percent vesting after five years of service, with zero vesting before the fifth year is attained.

Non-ERISA plans have various vesting schedules, or none at all. Members of the U.S. Armed Forces, for example, must complete 20 years of service to be eligible for a pension. This could be considered a 20-year absolute vesting schedule, or no vesting at all. In other words, there is no benefit for military service, active or reserves, short of 20 years.

In some cases, a vested benefit otherwise deemed nonforfeitable may be lost or reduced. A defined benefit pension plan could terminate without sufficient assets to pay for all vested benefits. If the plan is covered by the PBGC, that agency guarantees some, but not all, of the plan's vested benefits. If a vested benefit exceeds a given maximum (with annual cost-of-living increases), or if the plan was amended within the last five years to increase benefits, not all of the vested amounts are protected.

§ 8.3   Termination

Upon termination of employment, a participant in an ERISA plan must be informed by the plan of his or her vesting status, potential benefit payment dates, amount of benefits vested, and available options. In a defined contribution plan with individual accounts, the departing employee is given choices. One available selection is a lump-sum cash-out, subject to mandatory IRS withholding. For a person under age $59\frac{1}{2}$, this option is also subject to a 10 percent excise tax. Alternatively, the departing employee may request a full or partial transfer of the account balance to an IRA so as to defer taxes. Another choice, not usually elected, is for the plan to purchase for the employee an annuity that will pay a monthly pension benefit.

In any case, inquiry should be made as to whether a spouse in a divorce case has one or more vested benefits from previous employers.

§ 8.4   Deferred Payment

If payment of the vested benefit from a defined benefit pension plan is deferred to retirement age, there are choices as to when that will be. Typical retirement age is 65. If an employee leaves service at age 45 with a vested benefit, it will be paid 20 years later if the employee is alive and claims it. A plan may allow a TV participant to elect early payment of the vested benefit, at the plan's early retirement age, subject to reductions for early commencement of monthly pension benefits.

The actuary should pay special attention to the early retirement reduction. It is not uncommon for a defined benefit pension plan to have two different sets of reduction factors for early pension payments: (1) the standard set for employees who retire early and (2) a separate set for TV employees who apply for early benefit commencement.

For example, Joe works to age 60, which is the plan's early retirement age. At that time, he has a vested, accrued monthly pension benefit of $1,000, payable at age 65. Age 60 is five years earlier than the plan's normal retirement age (NRA) of 65, so a reduction is imposed on Joe's monthly pension benefit because the payments are starting five years early. An average reduction for a five-year early pension would be 30 percent, so Joe would receive 70 percent of his pension. His benefit drops from $1,000 per month to $700 per month. Joe gets a smaller monthly—$700 instead of $1,000—but he gets it for the extra five years between age 60 and age 65, and it continues at the same fixed amount for the rest of his life.

Bill, on the other hand, terminates employment at age 50, too young to receive an early retirement pension. Bill's vested accrued monthly pension when he leaves service is $800 per month, payable at age 65. Because Bill is vested, if he lives to age 65, his monthly pension will start at $800 and continue during his lifetime. At age 60, Bill may ask to have early retirement pension start. However, because 60 is five years earlier than the plan's NRA, early retirement would subject Bill's pension to a reduction factor of 40 percent. It would leave Bill with 60 percent of his $800 pension, or $480 per month.

The plan's reduction factors for a vested, former employee such as Bill, are different from those for an employee who has worked up to the early retirement age, such a Joe. Bill's monthly pension benefit for commencement five years early, instead of waiting until age 65, is reduced 40 percent. Joe's pension was reduced 30 percent. The reduction factors are different even though each retiree is receiving a pension five years before NRA.

The difference in early retirement factors give employers a way of recognizing and rewarding employees who continue in service to at least early retirement age. For employees who leave service earlier than that, their vested benefit is worth less if collected any time sooner than the plan's NRA.

§ 8.5   Normal Retirement Age

NRA usually is not an important consideration in a defined contribution plan with individual accounts, because once the employee is vested, the benefit can be paid at any time upon termination of employment. In a defined benefit pension plan, however, the normal retirement age is often a factor in determining the plan's basic benefit structure, amount, and value.

In an ERISA plan, when an employee reaches NRA, automatic full vesting occurs regardless of the plan's vesting schedule. Also, the benefit matures at NRA, making it available for payment in full at the option of the employee. If the employee continues to work beyond NRA, the benefit must continue to accrue and, in a defined benefit pension plan, to bear an actuarial increase for the delay in payment.

In some cases involving a pension as marital or community property, the employee may delay a contemplated benefit award to his or her former spouse by continuing in employment beyond NRA. A court cannot order a person to retire, but it may—as part of a property settlement award—order the employee to make personal payments to the former spouse until the retirement pension begins.

A plan's NRA need not be a fixed age. A plan may have a combination of age and service requirements—for example, age 60 with 20 years of service—in which case both conditions must be met. Whatever age at which the conditions are satisfied becomes the individual's NRA. Some plans use a "magic number" to define the NRA. Unlike the situation where conditions of age and service each must be met, the magic number is a fixed number that represents the *total* of the employee's age plus years of service.

If the magic number is 80, for example, an employee could attain NRA at age 52 with 28 years of service. Another employee, after 23 years of service, could reach NRA at 57 as the years of age and service add up to 80.

The plan with a magic number differs from a plan with a combined age and service requirement. If, for example, the combined requirement is age 60 with 20 years of service, and the employee has only 18 years of service at age 60, the NRA for that employee is age 62.

§ 8.6   Early Retirement Age

No plan is required to have an early retirement age, but most do have such a feature. It is attractive for employees, and it is a means for the employer to move out older employees legally to make room for younger ones to move up in the ranks. Moreover, older employees with long service tend to be more highly paid, so employers find it economically desirable to pension them off.

§ 8.7   Pension Values at Early Retirement

In the valuation of a spouse's interest in a defined benefit pension plan as marital property, a very important assumption is the spouse's future retirement age. Most pension plans allow for retirement with a pension at an age earlier than the plan's stated NRA, usually with a reduced benefit to offset its early start. Early retirement pensions are common and should be considered when the pension is included as marital property for equitable distribution.

A defined benefit pension plan has a fixed NRA at which the full accrued pension is payable. However, the plan may establish earlier ages for pension in reduced amounts. If so, the plan specifies the amount of the reduction for early retirement. The penalty may range between two extremes: no reduction at all or 100 percent reduction (no benefit at all). The latter occurs only if a plan has no early retirement feature—as is the case of the pension plan for members of the armed forces.

An actuary prefers to see the benefit provided by any defined benefit pension plan for early retirement reduced by actuarial factors so that the early pension is equivalent in value to the normal retirement benefit. The plan would be in actuarial balance and there would be no cost to the plan or the employer when a worker retires early. Actuarial factors are difficult to compute for early retirement, however, and difficult to communicate to employees. They often pose an administrative burden that the employer prefers to avoid.

A plan should have a set of simplified factors to provide for early retirement pensions that are convenient to administer and easily understood by employees. For example, a pension might be reduced by 0.5 percent for each month that the employee retires before NRA. This translates into a reduction of 6 percent per year for early retirement for each year preceding the employee's normal retirement.

Example 1:   Employee A has an accrued pension benefit of $1,000 per month based on pay and service at her present age, 55, payable as an annuity commencing at age 65. The plan uses early retirement reduction factors of 0.5 percent per month before normal retirement. The reduction is 60 percent (6 percent per year × 10 years), so the pension benefit is 40 percent, or $400, for immediate early retirement payment starting at age 55. Employee A receives a smaller dollar amount every month for life but, assuming a normal life span, will receive it for 10 years more than if she had waited until age 65 for the payments to start.

A typical situation would put normal retirement at age 65, at which time the employee retires and receives the full pension amount. The amount by which the pension is reduced for early retirement is set forth in the plan. The full pension may be paid at age 55 without adjustment for early retirement. Typical reductions for retiring 10 years early (at age 55 as opposed to age 65) range between 40 and 60 percent. The rule of thumb estimate is 50 percent reduction in the pension benefit for retiring 10 years early.

Example 2:   Employee B is a 50-year-old man in a pension plan in which the NRA is 65. Assume that, at age 50, B has accrued a monthly pension for service to date of $2,000 and that he is fully vested. If B leaves work as a deferred terminated vested participant and lives to at least age 65, B will then start receiving his earned pension of $2,000 a month for the rest of his life. The actuarial present value of the pension, at age 50, under these circumstances is approximately $65,000. But suppose the plan allows B to apply for his pension when he reaches age 55 instead of 65. Suppose further that the benefit reduction factor for retiring 10 years early is 60 percent. By electing to have his pension start at age 55 he gets 40 percent of it—that is, $800 a month—every month for the rest of his life (0.40 × $2,000). B loses $1,200 a month forever.

The actuarial present value at age 50 for a monthly pension of $800 starting at age 55 for life is about $65,000. It is no coincidence that the actuarial value in this example is the same. The plan's adjustment for early benefit payment is an exact actuarial equivalence. However, such an adjustment need not be exactly an actuarial equivalent figure. A plan may subsidize early payment of benefits either by charging less than the true actuarial reduction or by imposing no reduction at all. For example, if the adjustment for early retirement at age 55 is 50 percent, the monthly benefit in Example 2 would be $1,000 (0.50 × $2,000) instead of $800. This is a better pension for employee B, but it costs the plan more.

The actuarial present value at age 50 for a monthly pension of $1,000 starting at age 55 is approximately $81,000. In a divorce case, the property interest would have increased from $65,000 (representing $800 per month) to $81,000.

Next, consider a situation in which no reduction is made for pension commencement at age 55. The full pension of $2,000 a month starts at age 55 and is paid for life. At the employee's current age, 50, the pension has an approximate actuarial present value of $162,000. In this case, the marital interest in the pension would increase dramatically.

For a divorce in which the present value of a pension is needed for immediate offset in equitable distribution, the question may arise as to the value of an early retirement pension. One argument would be to ignore any possibility of early retirement if the person has not elected such retirement.

No one knows when retirement will occur. It is sometimes argued, therefore, that one cannot place a value on a speculative potential early retirement pension. The counter argument is that a pension is a benefit that is or will be available, one that has a presently determinable value.

Set forth in Table 8–1 are examples of typical early retirement reduction factors in defined benefit pension plans for a male now aged 45, with an NRA of 65. The present values are all equal because the early retirement pensions have been reduced by true actuarial factors to be equivalent. The monthly pension amounts are obviously different, but they all have the same value.

Another plan may penalize the employee for retiring early by providing a pension that is less than the actuarial equivalent, as shown in Table 8–2. On the other hand, some plans encourage early retirement by offering a subsidized pension that is larger than the actuarial equivalent would be, as shown in Table 8–3.

In every divorce case involving a pension as a marital asset, the various contingencies of early and normal retirement should be explored, so that the values may be fully and fairly presented for adjudication. The early retirement benefit should

Table 8–1

Actuarial Equivalent Early Retirement Factors

Age at Retirement	Monthly Pension	Pension's Present Value
Normal at 65	$2,000	$65,000
Early at 62	1,550	65,000
Early at 60	1,300	65,000
Early at 55	900	65,000

§ 8.7 PENSION VALUES AT EARLY RETIREMENT

Table 8–2

Non-Equivalent Early Retirement Factors

Age at Retirement	Monthly Pension	Pension's Present Value
Normal at 65	$2,000	$65,000
Early at 62	1,400	60,000
Early at 60	1,200	60,000
Early at 55	800	59,000

Table 8–3

Subsidized Early Retirement Factors

Age at Retirement	Monthly Pension	Pension's Present Value
Normal at 65	$2,000	$65,000
Early at 62	1,700	73,000
Early at 60	1,470	74,000
Early at 55	1,015	75,000

not be overlooked as a possibility when a defined benefit pension plan is a marital asset.

When early retirement incentives are offered, the effect on marital property should be considered. Corporate downsizing has resulted in opportunities for employees to elect early retirement with generous subsidies. A defined benefit pension plan may be modified for a temporary period, known as "the window," during which eligible groups of employees may elect to participate in an early-out program.

The typical special limited early retirement program increases an employee's pension by adjusting the pension benefit formula with respect to age, service, and benefit percentage. For example, five years are added to the individual's age and five years are added to his credited service, and then his pension is figured based on these artificial adjustments. The reduction factors normally applied in the event of early retirement may be minimized or eliminated.

In some plans an employee who retires at age 55 suffers an approximate 50 percent loss of benefits. But in an incentive program, the employee is considered to be age 60 for purposes of eligibility and computation, and his benefit is computed in the plan's formula with an additional five years of service factored in. Then his special early retirement pension would be up to 75 or 80 percent of his accrued pension, instead of only 50 percent. If the enhancement is so generous so as to temporarily waive the early retirement reduction factors, the resulting early pension benefit could be larger than the actual accrued benefit.

How much, if any, of an early retirement incentive should be considered for the purpose of property distribution in a divorce? If it can be demonstrated absolutely to the satisfaction of the court that the spouse eligible for an enhanced early retirement situation will not use it, then the issue is moot.

If the spouse is eligible and elects enhanced early retirement, and retires during the marriage, then the pension benefits derived therefrom are considered marital property, subject to the length of the marriage and any other factors the court may wish to consider. If the early retirement program is announced after the date of marital dissolution but before the marital property issues are settled, it is debatable whether any portion of the increased early retirement benefits should be counted and valued.

If the employed spouse is not eligible for early retirement incentives at the time the marital property is valued, the special program probably should not be included. The possibility to allow for marital participation in an early retirement incentive program should at least be considered, based on deferred distribution, instead of immediate offset using the present value. A QDRO would serve the purpose if the issue is not clear.

The trial court must determine whether an asset is marital property or separate property for purposes of distribution of the marital estate in accordance with prevailing statute and case law in the particular jurisdiction.

§ 8.8   Retiree in Pay Status

Even after the employee has retired, the issue of marital property does not necessarily end. If the retiree properly received a lump-sum cash-out and the money is gone, there may be no action available against the plan. What may be reviewed in such an event is whether the distribution was properly made. Were the required formalities of law followed and were the plan's own administrative procedures followed? Was disclosure full and complete, and were the details and consequences understood by the retiring employee and his or her spouse? Was a QDRO pending at the time that should have acted on the payout?

For a retiree in a defined benefit pension plan, the benefit in pay status as a monthly annuity may be valued actuarially to determine its value at the time of marital dissolution. A valuation does not assume that the person will survive to retire, and has no interest discount for the period of time remaining to retirement and—especially—no estimate of when retirement will occur.

An annuity form of pension in pay status may be attached in full or in part by a QDRO. If the plan purchased an annuity contract from an insurance company, that can be valued as well and is also subject to a QDRO. One issue for review when a spouse is already retired is the form and type of pension benefit. If a post-retirement survivorship benefit is in place, it is important to identify the beneficiary and ascertain whether the plan will allow the named beneficiary (or the optional death benefit) to be changed by a QDRO.

§ 8.9   Disability Pensions vs. Retirement Pensions

Disability pensions are not marital property in most jurisdictions. However, as a disability award is usually larger than the typical pension benefit, the pension amount may be subsumed in the disability award. When a pension is embedded in a disability award, an actuary may separate it out and value it as marital property, leaving the rest of the disability award as nonmarital property. The pension value would be computed based on pay and service using the regular pension benefit formula. This value would be compared to the disability award, in terms of dollar amount as well as time and conditions of payment.

A plan may (but is not required to) provide for retirement due to disability. A benefit labeled as a disability benefit may be no more than the vested benefit that the employee would receive anyway. A pension plan may have no disability benefit, but the employer may provide disability insurance for its employees. A plan may have a provision whereby service credit for a participant continues while the person is on disability and is replaced by a pension when the employee attains the NRA stipulated by the plan. Any of these conditions can be valued by an actuary. Whether a disability benefit can be awarded by a QDRO depends on the definition and nature of the benefit in the plan.

The differences between disability insurance benefits and pensions are as follows:

1. A pension represents deferred wages; a disability policy is not present compensation for foregone pay.

2. Insurance disability payments are made from a separate fund of the insurance company, not a pension fund.

3. Disability payments are not based on the recipient's statistical life expectancy as a pension would be, but usually end at a stated age in the contract or policy.

4. Disability payments are compensation for loss of future earning capacity; there is no such feature in pensions.

5. Disability payments may be compensation for pain and suffering; there is no such feature in pensions.

6. Disability payments are seldom based on age and service; pension benefits almost always depend on age and service.

7. Disability payments are uniquely personal to the injured person; a pension plan applies to all participants.

8. An employee who reaches retirement age without becoming disabled never receives any benefits under a disability program.

9. Disability programs have neither cash value nor accrued or redemption value.

10. Disability payments from an insurance policy are separate and distinct from pension plan benefits; the employee cannot elect one or the other.

11. Pension benefits are promised and funded for eligible participants; disability payments occur only when there has been an accident or medical condition that disables the insured person as defined in the policy.

12. Disability payments from an insurance policy cannot be the subject of a QDRO.

CHAPTER 9

MARRIAGE AND DIVORCE

§ 9.1   Introduction

Most jurisdictions now accept a spouse's interest in a pension plan as marital property for equitable distribution in divorce. The value of the pension is determined and used as an immediate offset to other marital property. When the pension plan is a defined contribution plan with individual employee accounts (e.g., 401(k) plan or thrift and savings plan), the value of the plan is equal to the value in the employee's account.

§ 9.2   Questions for a New Client

During the initial interview with the client or soon thereafter, counsel to a party in a divorce should ask pertinent questions concerning pensions—whether the client or the client's spouse is a participant in a pension plan, whether both are participants in benefit plans established by their respective employers. Such questions and requests for information should elicit responses and materials that provide counsel with insight on how to proceed and determine the extent of discovery. The following list of questions, although not applicable in all divorce cases, serves as a guide.

1.   What are the full names, addresses, Social Security numbers, and dates of birth of client and client's spouse?

2. Does client or client's spouse have a former spouse living? If so, does the former spouse have any claim on the pension—by settlement agreement, divorce decree, QDRO, or any other means?

3. Is there a prenuptial or postnuptial agreement? If so, does it mention or imply any consideration of pension interests?

4. Prior to the marriage, did client and client's spouse live together in an arrangement that could be considered a common-law marriage? If so, on what date did such arrangement begin?

5. What is the formal, official date of client's marriage?

6. What is the date of client's marital separation? Alternatively, what are the possible dates to be considered as the cutoff date for acquisition of marital property?

7. Does client or spouse have a mental or physical handicap?

The next set of questions applies to the employment of either the client or client's spouse:

8. What is the employment status of client/spouse (e.g., active, on leave of absence or layoff, on temporary or permanent disability, retired, terminated with deferred vested rights to a future pension)?

9. What is client's/spouse's job title, position, class, department, division, location? Is the job considered salaried, paid by the hour, management, or other?

10. What is the employer's official name, address, and telephone number? Is the employer a subsidiary, branch, or division of a parent company?

11. Does the employer have a personnel, human resources, benefits, or compensation department?

12. What is the date of hire? Was there a temporary or probationary period of service?

13. Have there been any breaks in service (e.g., layoff, leave of absence, termination and rehire)?

14. Is client/spouse covered by a collective bargaining agreement? If so, what is the full name of the union and its local? Is client/spouse an officer or holder of any union position? Is client/spouse covered by benefit plans of both the local and the national union?

15. What is client's/spouse's current annual rate of pay? Does client/spouse receive overtime pay, or bonuses, or commissions? What was the Form W-2 pay in the prior calendar year?

16. In what benefit plans does client/spouse participate?

17. What is (are) the formal name(s) of the plan(s)?

18. What kinds of plans are they (e.g., defined benefit, defined contribution, profit sharing, thrift, savings, 401(k), SEP, TIAA-CREF, or other)?

19. Does the covered employee contribute to the plan? If not, were there employee contributions in the past?

20. Is the covered employee's contribution made with pretax or post-tax dollars, or both?

21. Does the covered employee have the following items? (If not, they should be obtained from the employer.)

- Summary plan description
- Summary annual report
- Summary of material modifications
- Routine annual benefit/account statement
- Beneficiary form on file

22. Does the plan provide life insurance? (If so, obtain details.)

23. Has the covered employee purchased service, or does the option to do so exist but is not yet exercised?

24. If applicable, has the covered employee obtained a copy of notice of plan amendment and/or termination?

25. What information, if any, concerning the plan(s) has (have) been published in company newsletters or as announcements, memos, letters, or notices?

26. Is client/spouse an employee of a government organization? If so, what type of employment (e.g., civilian, uniformed, law enforcement)?

27. Is client/spouse currently, or was client/spouse formerly, in military service? (If either spouse was or is in military service, ask whether in active duty or in the reserves and in which branch of service. If enlisted, ask for rate or rank and date of enlistment; if officer, ask for rate or rank and date of induction.)

The following questions concern client's/spouse's past employment, if any:

28. Is client/spouse a terminated, deferred vested participant with rights to a future benefit? (If so, obtain details.)

29. Is client/spouse retired, in pay status? Was a lump-sum distribution received? (If so, when and how much?) Is a monthly annuity pension being received? (If so, ask the gross and net amount, form or type of annuity, option, starting date, and beneficiary if any.)

30. Has there been a withdrawal of employee contributions?

31. Has there been a loan from the plan?

32. Has there been a hardship or any other type of withdrawal of funds from the plan?

The following questions and requests may be addressed to the client/spouse or sent directly to the employer(s):

33. What is the employer's tax identification number?

34. What is (are) the formal name(s) of the plan(s)?

35. What is (are) the identification number(s) of the plan(s)?

36. What is (are) the effective date(s) of the plan(s)?

37. What is (are) the most recent amendment(s) to the plan(s)?

38. Are any plan amendments pending?

39. Is (are) the plan(s) in the process of terminating?

40. Who is the plan administrator of each plan?

41. Who is the designated agent for service of legal process for each plan?

42. What are the QDRO procedures for the plan(s)?

43. What is the employer's fiscal year?

44. What is the plan year of each plan?

45. Is the plan subject to ERISA? To the PBGC?

46. Are annual benefit/account statements furnished to participants?

47. Please provide a copy of the following:

    • Summary plan description
    • Summary of material modifications
    • Most recent summary annual report

48. Please provide the following information from your records for this employee (client or spouse):

    • Date of birth
    • Date of hire
    • Union or non-union
    • Current employment status
    • Job title and position
    • Normal retirement age
    • Normal form of benefit payment

        —For a defined benefit plan: Accrued pension benefit for most recent service to date, excluding any future pay or service, payable at normal retirement age.

        —For a defined contribution plan: Most recent available account balance.

        —Have there been loans, withdrawals, or payments?

   The last question is for the client:

49. Would you prefer a current offset of the present value of the pension, if other marital property is sufficient to arrange it, or would you rather wait until normal retirement age to receive pension payments by court order?

§ 9.2 QUESTIONS FOR A NEW CLIENT

The following questionnaire may be sent to client's employer to elicit information about the plan.

PENSION BENEFIT QUESTIONNAIRE

Employer's Name: _____

Employee's Name: _____

1. Date of birth: _____   2. Date of hire: _____
3. Date participation   4. Normal retirement
   commenced: _____   date: _____
5. Date fully vested: _____
6. Accumulated employee contributions, if any:
   a. Separation date _____ $ _____
   b. Complaint filing date _____ $ _____
   c. Current date _____ $ _____
7. Rate or Basis of employee contributions, if any:
   _____

8. Name of pension program: _____

9. Rate or basis of employer contributions: _____

10. General nature of pension program:
    a. Defined benefit: _____
    b. Defined contribution: _____
    Other (explain): _____

11. Normal form of retirement benefit:
    _____

12. Monthly pension benefit at retirement accrued as of:
    a. Separation date: _____ $ _____
    b. Complaint filing: _____ $ _____
    c. Current date: _____ $ _____

                    By: _____

Date: _____   Title: _____

§ 9.3 Necessary Documentation

The documentation concerning a pension plan can be voluminous and complex. Over the years, a plan accumulates amendments, reprints of plan summaries, and annual governmental filings to the Internal Revenue Service, the Department of Labor and, if applicable, the Pension Benefit Guaranty Corporation. When a plan is an asset in a divorce case, counsel must decide what items to request, how important each item is, and the time it may take to obtain the items. Casting a wide net may not be the best approach if it takes too long to gather all of the requested materials or if the requested items, when received, require a great deal of time to review. In any case, much of the information is irrelevant to determining the value of a pension for property distribution in divorce cases.

One item of information that is essential is the fundamental nature of the plan. Is the plan sponsor, the entity that maintains and administers the plan, a governmental organization or a private concern (business, partnership, or union)?

A governmental plan may have been established by federal law, state statute, county or municipal ordinance, or by contract between the governmental unit and its employees or the union representing them. Because ascertaining what the plan's governing documents are can be difficult, counsel may wish to bypass formal plan documentation and request instead a copy of the most recent actuarial valuation report for the plan. Such a report, if available, is likely to contain a summary of the plan's major provisions. This suggestion applies more to pension plans for municipal, county, and state employees than it does to plans for employees of the federal government. Summaries and reviews of the details of federal plans are available from commercial publishers. For discussion of plans for postal workers, see §§ 5.7–5.10.

As for private plans, major corporations generally have sophisticated plan booklets that summarize the plan and can furnish benefit information for an individual upon request. When the employer is a small business, however, counsel should make sure the plan details provided are current.

Every private defined benefit pension plan must have an actuarial valuation report. The report advises the employer concerning the amounts and timing of contributions and the plan assets and liabilities. The report may list the plan participants with their accrued and projected pension benefits as well as their individual present values as calculated by the plan's actuary.

The actuary retained by counsel to determine the present value of a pension in a divorce matter should have the following documents:

1. A letter from the employer (or union) setting forth the employee's accrued pension benefit for service as of a particular date, payable at normal retirement age.
2. The employee's benefit statement, containing sufficient information for identification and verification of the amount in question.
3. The summary plan description (SPD).

4. The summary of material modifications (SMM), if applicable, which is provided without charge. The SPD may be reprinted to include plan amendments in an SMM.

5. The legal plan document, if time permits and if the case so warrants by its size or complexity. The plan document may be substantial, and the employer may charge a reasonable amount for the expense of duplicating it. Copies of any and all plan amendments—including any pending plan amendments—should be requested at the same time.

To probe deeper into the plan, counsel may request the following items:

6. The IRS approval letter for the plan and for its amendments. If the letter is more than five years old, inquiries should be made as to plan amendments not yet submitted for approval or pending administrative processing.

7. The summary annual report (SAR). The SAR does not provide pension information on an individual employee basis and is not particularly useful in a divorce matter unless the plan is small and one of the spouses controls the company.

8. Copies of IRS Form 5500s and other forms in the 5500 series filed by the plan. (See § 7.8 for a discussion of required filings.)

§ 9.4 Marital Agreements

Marital agreements concerning community property, marital assets, and other issues are divided by a bright line into two time frames: prenuptial and postnuptial. Spousal rights bestowed by federal law in an ERISA plan cannot be abrogated prior to marriage, because the parties have no standing as spouses before that time. Prenuptial agreements may cover pension benefits. What cannot be taken away are spousal rights to survivorship benefits and the spouse's right to consent or withhold consent to the employee's choice of benefit payout options.

For example, a valid agreement cannot be made before or after marriage denying the spouse any share of the employee's pension as marital property determined by actuarial valuation for immediate offset or by a qualified domestic relations order (QDRO). However, the spousal survivorship interest is not affected by an agreement made before the employee married. The employee-spouse may, under certain conditions and following strict details, waive the nonemployee-spouse's right to influence the choice of benefit options and survivorship provisions. An ERISA plan does not have to, and most likely would not, follow the provisions of a divorce decree or settlement unless a proper QDRO is issued and all of the requisite spousal consents are obtained.

Following are the texts of two sample property settlement agreements for situations in which one spouse is a participant in a combination union plan. An actual agreement would be signed and notarized.

SAMPLE PROPERTY SETTLEMENT AGREEMENT 1

Husband is a participant in the Carpenters Pension and Annuity Fund, which consists of two parts: a defined benefit plan and a defined contribution individual account plan.

Wife is awarded 50 percent of Husband's interest in each part of the Pension and Annuity Fund as of December 31, 19XX, or the nearest administratively practicable date.

Wife is awarded a proportionate share in each part of the Pension and Annuity Fund with respect to each of the following items as may be available:

- Early retirement
- Pre-retirement death or survivor benefits
- Post-retirement death or survivor benefits
- Disability benefits
- Withdrawals
- Lump-sum payments
- Cost-of-living pension benefit increases
- Benefit incentives or subsidies
- Investment direction

1. Husband will cooperate with the letter and intent of this Agreement and will properly and timely complete any required forms to accomplish same.
2. Wife does not waive her rights to survivorship benefits.

SAMPLE PROPERTY SETTLEMENT AGREEMENT 2

Wife is a salaried employee of the XYZ Corporation with 100 percent vesting as an active participant in the XYZ Salaried Employees Retirement Plan (the Plan), which is a defined benefit plan subject to the federal pension laws of the Employee Retirement Income Security Act of 1974 (ERISA) and the Retirement Equity Act of 1984 (REA).

Husband is awarded 50 percent of the community property portion of Wife's benefits in the Plan, using the marital time rule.

The intent of this settlement agreement is to implement this award in an equitable manner, taking into account the presently unknown factors of Wife's total creditable pension service, options, elections, and benefit commencement age, consonant with the 50 percent portion and the time rule.

1. The parties have agreed and stipulated that the current actuarial present value of the community interest of Wife's benefits in the Plan following application of the time rule is $ _____.

2. The award to Husband of 50 percent of Plan benefits with a current actuarial present value of $ _____ is $_____ in current actuarial present value terms.

3. The actuarial conversion of a current present value of $ _____ into a lifetime monthly pension annuity payable to Husband is $ _____ for benefit commencement when Husband reaches age 65. That is, a monthly pension benefit of $ _____ payable from the plan to Husband beginning at his age 65 and continuing for the rest of his life has a current actuarial present value of $ _____.

4. The award to Husband shall be adjusted as may be needed if benefits commence before or after age 65, to maintain his current actuarial present value as close to $ _____ as is reasonably possible.

5. Husband is awarded his 50 percent share in all aspects of the Plan as they interrelate with respect to each of the available actuarially equivalent options under the Plan, including one or more of the following items as may be available based on the award:

- Early retirement
- Pre-retirement death or survivor benefits
- Post-retirement death or survivor benefits
- Cost-of-living increases, and/or
- Benefit improvements.

6. Husband does not waive survivorship.

§ 9.5   Sample Interrogatory

To elicit pension information early in the divorce proceedings, counsel for the nonemployee-spouse may serve on the employee-spouse the following interrogatory concerning retirement and deferred income plans.

1. Are you now in one of the following categories with respect to a pension, retirement, thrift, savings, profit-sharing, Keogh, or other deferred compensation plan or system?

- Employee
- Member
- Participant
- Alternate payee or otherwise covered

2. Were you formerly in any of the categories named in Question 1? If so, which one?

3. What is the name of each plan that you are or were in?

4. What is your current status in each plan?

- Active
- Terminated with deferred vested rights
- Retired in receipt of a pension

5. On what date did your participation in the plan(s) commence? Name the plan(s).

6. When did benefit credits start to accrue for you? Name the plan(s).

7. Did you have any breaks in service in plan coverage? If so, name the plan(s) and state the dates.

8. What is your vesting status in each plan?

9. When did you or when will you attain full vesting?

10. What is the name of each plan and its nature?

- Defined benefit plan
- Defined contribution plan
- Profit sharing plan
- Thrift plan
- Savings plan
- 401(k) plan
- Simplified employee pension plan
- Deferred compensation plan
- Other (specify)

11. Have you made employee contributions or has your salary been directly reduced for contributions?

12. Are your employee contributions voluntary or mandatory?

13. Are your employee contributions pretax or after-tax?

14. Is the rate or amount of your employee contributions fixed or up to you?

15. If the rate or amount of your employee contributions may vary as you choose, what is the history of your employee contributions?

16. Do you have any investment selections in the plan?

17. What investment selections are available?

18. What investment selections have you made?

19. What is the total of your employee contributions as of the following dates?

- Date of marital separation
- Date of filing of the divorce action
- Date of your completion of this interrogatory

20. What is the total of your employee contributions with interest as of the following dates?

- Date of marital separation

- Date of filing of the divorce action
- Date of your completion of this interrogatory

21. What is the rate or amount of employer contributions?

22. What is the normal form of retirement benefit?

23. What optional forms of retirement benefits are available?

24. What is the amount of the monthly pension benefit that you had accrued under the plan as of the following dates?

- Date of marital separation
- Date of filing of the divorce action
- Date of your completion of this interrogatory

25. What is your account balance in the plan as of the following dates?

- Date of marital separation
- Date of filing of the divorce action
- Date of your completion of this interrogatory

26. What is the minimum benefit provided by the plan?

27. What is the maximum benefit provided by the plan?

28. Are your benefits under the plan linked to or related to benefits or accounts in any other plan?

29. Does the plan that you are in provide for cost-of-living increases in the benefits that you may receive?

30. Does the plan that you are in provide for early retirement incentives or enhancements in the benefits that you may receive?

31. Are you covered by Social Security?

32. Is the plan that you are in covered by ERISA?

33. Is the plan that you are in covered by the federal law of pensions concerning unions and multiemployer plans?

34. Is the plan that you are in a plan of a governmental unit at the local, county, state, or federal level?

35. Is the plan that you are in a plan of a nonprofit organization?

36. Do you have retirement credits for military service, active or reserves? (If so, give details.)

37. If you are in the category of deferred terminated vested, what is the earliest date that your pension may be paid and the amount?

38. Do you have a former spouse with any claim on your pension, retirement, or other deferred compensation?

39. Is a domestic relations order, or its equivalent, in effect concerning your retirement or other benefits?

40. Is there a prenuptial or postnuptial agreement in effect concerning your retirement or other benefits?

41. Are you covered by a collective bargaining agreement?

42. Is there insurance on your life in the plan?

43. If there is life insurance, what is the face amount, the premium, and dividend structure, and who is the named beneficiary?

44. Have you purchased creditable service for the plan?

45. Are you eligible to purchase creditable service?

46. Do you have any outstanding loans from the plan? (If so, give details.)

47. Have you made any withdrawals or received any refunds or other payments from the plan(s)? (If so, give details.)

48. Do you regularly receive annual benefit or account statements?

49. Provide copies of each of the following items as may be appropriate:

   • Plan document and amendments, plus any pending amendments
   • Plan booklet (SPD)
   • IRS forms with schedules and attachments
   • PBGC forms with schedules and attachments
   • Individual benefit or account statements

50. What was your last day worked?

51. What was the last day for which you received pay?

52. What was the date of your retirement?

53. What was the date of your first pension check?

54. Did you receive a lump sum or other cash distribution?

55. Did you receive a refund of tour employee contributions?

56. Was your retirement considered normal, early, or late?

57. What optional forms of pension are you receiving?

58. Who is the named beneficiary of your post-retirement death benefits?

59. Is your pension amount scheduled to change at a certain age or date, or in accordance with changes in the cost of living? (If so, give details.)

§ 9.6   Bifurcation

If the financial aspects of a property settlement, including the pension, are to be determined after the divorce is granted, the nonemployee-spouse, if he or she has a former spouse, must maintain the appropriate beneficiary forms to protect the former spouse in case the employee-spouse dies before the pension value is settled. If a QDRO is pending, the former spouse must be protected until the divorce decree is finally and formally qualified.

CHAPTER 10

DEATH AND SURVIVOR BENEFITS

§ 10.1   Introduction

Death benefits may be available in pension plans in two time frames: before and after retirement. Depending on the time frame, the name or description of the death benefits may change. For example, a benefit payable to a beneficiary when a plan participant dies before retirement is usually called a *death benefit* or *pre-retirement death benefit*. When a participant dies after retirement, the benefit is generally known as a *survivor benefit* or *post-retirement survivorship benefit*. These designations are not exclusive and may be used interchangeably—that is, a pre-retirement benefit may be called a survivor benefit and a post-retirement survivor benefit may be called a death benefit.

Upon divorce, part or all of a participant's pre-retirement and post-retirement death benefits in a plan subject to the Employee Retirement Income Security Act of 1974 (ERISA) may be secured for the former spouse by a qualified domestic relations order (QDRO) served on the plan.

§ 10.2   Pre-Retirement and Post-Retirement Death Benefits

In pension plans subject to ERISA, the benefits payable upon a participant's death have specific names. If the participant dies while in active service, the plan pays the participant's spouse a pre-retirement death benefit called a *qualified pre-retirement survivor annuity* (QPSA). In defined benefit pension plans subject to ERISA, the pre-retirement death benefit may take the form of either a lump-sum distribution or monthly annuity payments. After a participant's death, some plans allow the beneficiary to elect the form of payment. A defined contribution plan is more likely to make a lump-sum distribution of the balance of the deceased spouse's account to the surviving spouse.

Upon the death of a retired plan participant, the primary mandated form of death benefit available to his or her surviving spouse is called the *qualified joint-and-survivor annuity* (QJSA). The QJSA is not the only form of post-retirement death benefit available, however. ERISA plans permit a participant who is retiring as well as the participant's spouse to apply in writing to waive the QJSA or replace it with another form of death benefit. If not properly waived or replaced, the QJSA must go into effect at the retirement of a married participant.

Pension plans not subject to ERISA are not required to provide death benefits when employees die either before or after retirement, although plans that require or allow employee contributions often provide a minimum death benefit when an employee dies before retirement. An employee's pre-retirement death benefit is the sum of his or her contributions, sometimes plus interest added by the plan. When death occurs after retirement, the sum of the retired employee's contributions may serve as a decreasing term death benefit that diminishes with each monthly pension payment.

Pension plans for civilian employees of the federal government provide death benefits automatically when a covered employee dies before retirement. At retirement, a covered employee may elect a post-retirement survivor annuity. Military pension plans do not provide a specific pre-retirement death benefit. However, retiring military personnel may elect, for a fee, a post-retirement survivor annuity under a survivor benefit plan.

§ 10.3   Death Benefits and Divorce

The death benefits available in an ERISA plan may be preserved for a former spouse through a legal agreement in which the participant formally agrees to name the former spouse as a beneficiary. The disadvantage of this method is that if the participant later changes the beneficiary designation, the former spouse may not be informed of the change and the plan will not enforce the agreement made years ago.

The preferred method of preserving death benefits for a former spouse is by a QDRO served on the plan, which can secure for the former spouse part or all of either the participant's pre-retirement benefits or post-retirement death benefits, or both. Note that a participant's former spouse may not receive a form of pension under which a subsequent spouse becomes a beneficiary of a joint-and-survivor (J&S) annuity.

Example: Harry, a participant in an ERISA defined benefit pension plan, is divorcing his wife, Sally. The divorce attorney draws up a QDRO awarding Sally a portion of Harry's pension as well as a portion of Harry's pre-retirement death benefit and requiring that Sally be named the beneficiary of Harry's J&S annuity when Harry retires. The QDRO may award Sally a separate, independent pension, almost as though she had been the employee. At her retirement, Sally may elect from several options. Federal law precludes one option—namely, if Sally remarries, she will not be allowed to elect a J&S annuity naming her new husband as beneficiary.

§ 10.4   QDRO Survivor Benefits

Whatever portion of the death benefit that is not awarded to a former spouse by a QDRO remains available for the participant to bequeath to some other beneficiary. Of course, if the total death benefit is awarded to a former spouse by QDRO, then there is nothing to leave to another beneficiary.

If a participant has begun to receive pension benefits under a specific option, the plan usually will not allow a change to the selected option following the participant's divorce. In drafting a QDRO, therefore, counsel for the spouse should recognize and incorporate this contingency. A QDRO also should be drafted to avoid double-dipping. *Double-dipping* can occur if the former spouse (or alternate payee) is awarded a separate, independent lifetime pension that continues even though, upon the death of the retired employee, the former spouse is a beneficiary of the death benefit.

A post-retirement death benefit that is to be awarded to a former spouse by QDRO should take one of two forms. The former spouse should receive either a separate, lifetime pension that continues after the death of the retiree or a pension that ends with the death of the retiree and is replaced by a death benefit. If a separate, independent lifetime pension is not available by QDRO under a particular plan, the QDRO should specify that the alternate payee is a beneficiary of the post-retirement death benefit.

In all divorce cases involving a pension plan, the nonemployee-spouse should make sure that he or she continues to be named the employee-spouse's beneficiary until such time as the court order is formally approved as a QDRO. Taking this precaution would avoid a situation in which the employee-spouse is still active, the parties are legally divorced without a QDRO in place, and the employee-spouse dies after changing the beneficiary designation. In the absence of a formally approved QDRO, the nonemployee-spouse would be left with no benefits at all.

A non-ERISA plan may or may not permit the award of death or survivor benefits by a court order in divorce. For example, a pension plan for state or municipal government employees may allow survivor benefits after retirement to go only to a spouse beneficiary, not a former spouse.

With respect to death benefits, the easiest type of plan to deal with is an ERISA individual account defined contribution plan. Before retirement, the death benefit is usually the balance in the employee's account. At retirement, assuming the employee receives a lump sum, nothing is left to provide a post-retirement death benefit. When a QDRO is served on a defined contribution plan, the plan sets up a separate account for the alternate payee. Thereafter, the separate account shares in investment gains (and losses), but no contributions are credited to it. The employee's death has no effect on the plan benefits of the alternate payee. The death of the alternate payee releases that separate account to be paid to the alternate payee's beneficiaries.

If the parties to the divorce live their normal lifespans, the issue is of little importance. The only concern a former spouse—say, a former wife—may have is that, if she dies prematurely, the pension amount awarded to her as part of the divorce settlement is lost. She may not bequeath her portion to anyone else or to her estate. If her former husband—the plan participant—predeceases her, she will receive a survivorship benefit if the divorce settlement so states.

Pennsylvania is one of the few states that allow a *state* pension awarded to a former spouse to be paid to the former spouse's estate after the former spouse's death. In general, pension systems, both public and private, do not permit this practice, although the federal system may permit it if properly instructed.

Continuation of a former spouse's annuity in the federal pension system is possible if the court order directs that the annuity be continued after the former spouse dies. If such continuation is provided, payments may be made as specified in the order—either to the court, the children of the parties, or the estate of the former spouse (but only if the former spouse predeceases the federal employee). In such an event, benefits from the federal system are payable only during the lifetime of the retired federal employee.

If the court order so specifies, when the former spouse survives the retired federal employee, the former spouse becomes the beneficiary of the federal employee's post-retirement death benefit, and the benefits continue until the death of the former spouse following the death of the retired federal employee ends all benefits.

Following are six hypothetical cases in which a QDRO may be used to award death benefits in an ERISA defined benefit pension plan (assuming in each case the husband is the participant).

Example 1: Divorce occurs before retirement and Husband dies before retirement. If so stated in the QDRO, former Wife receives payment of Husband's pre-retirement death benefit as a QPSA in lieu of her otherwise awarded pension benefit. If the entire death benefit is not designated to former Wife, Husband has some benefits left to be paid to other beneficiaries, if any, such as Husband's new wife.

Example 2: Divorce occurs before retirement and former Wife dies before her benefits under a QDRO commence. As a rule, former Wife's interest would be extinguished. In special situations, however, it may be possible for benefits to be paid to her estate or for the QDRO to name a contingent alternate payee.

Example 3: Divorce occurs before Husband retires. Husband retires and dies first. Counsel must determine whether Wife has her own separate, independent pension. If former Wife has a separate, independent pension, her benefits are not affected by Husband's death. If her pension is a portion of his, however, her pension stops at his death. In this case, the QDRO should contain a provision that names her as the beneficiary of Husband's post-retirement death benefit, or QJSA.

Example 4: Divorce occurs before Husband's retirement. Husband retires and former Wife dies first. If the QDRO established former Wife's own separate, independent pension, she may have elected a post-retirement death benefit (if the plan so allowed) payable to her beneficiary. If the QDRO named former Wife as beneficiary of a J&S annuity that Husband elected to receive at retirement, former Wife's death ends her interest in any further benefits. Husband's pension remains reduced (because the reduction provided for the J&S coverage) unless the plan provides a ''pop-up'' feature that restores his benefits as if there had been no J&S annuity. If the QDRO did not establish former Wife as beneficiary or create a separate, independent pension for her, then full benefits are restored to Husband.

Example 5: Husband's retirement occurs before the divorce. After the divorce, Husband dies first. Husband's election at retirement determines whether former Wife will receive any benefits because of his death. Most plans do not allow a change in retirement option selection after the participant retires, regardless of a change in marital status.

Example 6: Husband's retirement occurs before the divorce. After the divorce, former Wife dies first. In the circumstances, former Wife's death extinguishes her interest; however, the QDRO may have named a contingent alternate payee.

§ 10.5 Life Expectancy

Life expectancy is not a consideration in the valuation of pension plans, but the Internal Revenue Service (IRS) uses life expectancy tables to make certain estate tax computations and to determine minimum required payouts from pension plans for persons over age 70. No actuary, however, would use life expectancy as such in determining rates, factors, values, or premiums for life insurance policies, pension plans, or annuities.

All pension plans, insurance policies, and annuity contracts are based on mortality tables and probability functions, not on the average number of years of a person's expected lifetime. The proper way to value a pension is to use a mortality probability table, such as the 1983 Group Annuity Mortality Table used in the General Agreement on Tariffs and Trade (GATT), to calculate the probability of mortality in each and every year from the present to the end of the table (approximately age 105). That way, death at any time (even tomorrow) is allowed as a factor. The standard pension mathematics used by the IRS, the Department of Labor, the Pension Benefit Guaranty Corporation, and in the GATT is based on probability of mortality, not life expectancy.

When life expectancy tables are used, it is important to choose the correct table from the large selection of such tables that are published and available. It would be incorrect, for example, to use a table based on the life expectancy of the general population of the United States, as opposed to a table that includes only the active population, because mortality is higher among the larger group than it is for workers.

If a pension evaluator should use life expectancy tables in making a valuation, he or she should be asked the date on which the employee is expected to die. That question exposes the problem in using life expectancy as a computational tool.

§ 10.6   Recognition of Reduced Life Expectancy

In valuing a defined benefit pension plan for a divorce, a fundamental assumption is that the plan participant is in normal good health. Usually, this is a safe assumption: if the employee is actively at work, it is presumed that he or she is part of the group to which normal mortality patterns apply. Standard pension mortality and annuity tables are based on the lives of active working persons, not the general population as a whole.

Occasionally, however, the issue of pension valuation arises when a plan participant has some medical or health condition that may affect his or her longevity. In the present state of medical science, it is not unusual to find active employees who have undergone coronary bypasses, organ transplants, and other procedures.

Generally, if an individual is actively engaged in an occupation and is a participant in a pension plan, that individual is covered by the standard mortality tables, regardless of health or medical status. The problematical cases are those involving a participant who has retired and is drawing a pension or who has terminated service with a vested right to a deferred pension. In these cases, sometimes a closer look is needed to decide which mortality table to use.

Three versions of standard pension mortality tables are available. Table A is designed for use with healthy individuals, both active employees and retired or terminated participants in reasonable health. Table B is used for participants who—whether active, terminated, or retired—have health conditions that would be classified as disabilities, but who are not eligible to receive disability benefits under Social Security. Mortality rates in Table B are greater than those in Table A by about 10 percent, so the value of the pension for an employee whose mortality is calculated using Table B is worth about 10 percent less than the pension amounts would be in Table A.

Table C is used for a person who is eligible for or is receiving a Social Security disability pension. Table C's mortality rates for persons age 65 exceed those in

Table A by about 25 percent, so the value of a pension for a person whose mortality is calculated using Table C is about 25 percent less than that for a healthy person at age 65.

An actuary who is not a physician or a life insurance underwriter is not qualified to make the determination whether to use Table B or Table C. Actuaries normally use Table A, unless counsel provides sufficient documentation to warrant the use of a table with heavier mortality rates.

§ 10.7   Life Insurance

Defined benefit pension plans with few participants may be partially funded by life insurance or may allow the purchase of life insurance policies by the trust fund. If the plan is funded, its documents should be reviewed to determine whether the plan itself is the beneficiary of any life insurance or whether the employee has named a beneficiary directly.

In a defined contribution plan involving life insurance, the proceeds upon death before retirement may be paid into the account of the deceased employee and thence to a beneficiary; if a beneficiary was named previously on the policy, the proceeds of life insurance will be paid by the insurance company to the named beneficiary.

There are two general kinds of insurance: (1) part or all of the plan assets may be invested in insurance products or contracts; and (2) individual life insurance policies on employees may be in the pension plan. Generally, individual life insurance policies are found only in small plans covering fewer than 100 participants. If the plan provides individual life insurance, it would be prudent to investigate the source of premiums and the use of cash values and dividends, if any. This may or may not be another value for the participant, depending on the plan structure.

When there is insurance in an ERISA plan, Schedule A must be filed as an attachment to the IRS form in the 5500 series that the plan is required to file annually.

§ 10.8   Options and Actuarial Equivalents

An ERISA defined benefit pension plan generally contains a set of standard retirement options. Usually, there are joint and survivor (J&S) options with a choice of percentages—e.g., 100 percent, 75 percent, 66⅔ percent, or 50 percent. The higher the percentage for the survivor, the more the employee pays for the option. Some plans subsidize the various J&S options, so that the actuarial cost to the retiree is reduced or eliminated.

Other options in a defined benefit pension plan at retirement include "10-year certain and life," which is also known as "life with 10 years guaranteed" or "10-year certain and continuous." With this option, if the retiree dies before receiving 120 monthly pension payments, the remaining balance is paid to the retiree's beneficiary or beneficiaries. Note that any type of J&S annuity may designate only one beneficiary, and that beneficiary may not be changed in the normal course of events. Other forms of optional post-retirement death benefits may allow any number of beneficiaries and contingent beneficiaries.

Some plans provide for a combination of post-retirement death benefits that may encompass both a J&S provision and a guaranteed payment for a certain number of years. Such an arrangement must be reviewed with care to determine whose death at what time affects which benefit after retirement.

At retirement, a participant may choose among different forms of pension payments, all of which have equivalent actuarial value. A married participant in an ERISA plan has limited pension choices at retirement. The retiree must either elect to receive a lump-sum payment or a 50 percent J&S annuity, which pays a fixed amount monthly until death. Upon the retiree's death, the plan would pay 50 percent of the monthly pension benefits that the retiree had been receiving to the retiree's spouse, unless both the retiree and the spouse had signed a waiver, properly witnessed. The waiver allows the retiree to receive a lifetime pension, ending at death, leaving nothing to any survivor.

If the named beneficiary predeceases the retiree, the retiree continues to receive the fixed monthly amounts that began at retirement. Most plans do not allow the retiree to name a new beneficiary upon the death of the named beneficiary.

Example: Harry reaches age 65 under a pension plan formula that provides him with a monthly pension of $1,000 for the rest of his life. That is the plan's normal pension form, a lifetime pension. The pension is computed based on Harry's pay and years of service. If this pension is converted into a 50 percent J&S pension, the dollar amount paid each month will be reduced to maintain the plan in actuarial balance. Because it costs the plan more to pay a pension over the span of two lives than it would over one life, the monthly amount is reduced to keep costs the same. Harry would receive a monthly pension of $850 instead of $1,000. He gives up or "loses" $150 a month to provide for a form of insurance for his wife, Sally. When Harry dies after retirement, his wife will receive one-half of Harry's reduced pension, or $425 (0.50 × $850). Sally will receive $425 a month for the rest of her life. But if Harry retires and Sally dies before he does, Harry will continue to receive the reduced amount of $850 for as long as he lives. He cannot name a new beneficiary after Sally dies.

The J&S option is a mortality risk that a husband and wife should consider carefully before deciding about death benefits.

Using a form of deferred distribution to award a portion of the employee's pension to a spouse, it is possible to include some form of death benefit if the details are worked out correctly. A former spouse may be named as the beneficiary under a J&S option. In this way, the nonemployee-spouse receives a portion of the employee-spouse's pension payments while the employee-spouse is alive, and a guarantee of continued payments after the employee-spouse dies.

CHAPTER 11

DEPRIVATION OF BENEFITS

§ 11.1   Introduction

The possibility of loss of benefits always exists. An employee's benefits are exposed to various types and amounts of loss, usually not contemplated or understood by the employee. The underlying benefit plan might be terminated or amended by the employer; the employee's service could be counted in such a way as to provide less than the expected benefit; breaks in service may interrupt the accrual of benefit credits; and death could deprive the employee's beneficiaries or estate of any benefit at all, or provide a reduced benefit.

In community property matters especially, counsel and the employee-spouse should be aware of the downside potential in benefit matters. The treatment of benefits as community property makes the benefits vulnerable to attachment in a divorce action. In plans that allow loans and hardship withdrawals, the actions of the employee could diminish the value of benefits, as could poor investment choices by the employee in plans that allow some investment control in an individual account.

Early retirement of an employee can reduce the benefits, and deferred retirement may delay benefit payments to a former spouse under a court order. These contingencies should be considered by counsel in reviewing marital assets and advising a client in a pending divorce action. Thorough discovery and discussion are warranted so that all parties are fully informed of the potential for reduced benefit amounts.

In a defined benefit pension plan, the benefit is structured to be paid at retirement as a monthly annuity. When, as part of a divorce settlement, the employee's spouse is awarded a portion of the employee's pension benefit, he or she may expect it to grow with interest until the employee-spouse's retirement. This is not the case. The pension benefit is based on the pension plan formula. No interest is credited to increase the benefit or to reflect the waiting period until it becomes payable. Interest applies only to benefits in individual accounts in defined contribution plans, such as 401(k) plans, not to those in defined benefit pension plans.

If an actuary is performing a valuation to determine the present value of a pension benefit to be used as an immediate offset to other marital property, interest is a vital component in the calculation. Discounted interest is an inherent component of the current worth of any payment due in the future. The actual pension benefit itself, as it is earned, has nothing to do with interest. From one point of view, the lack of interest growth on a current pension award could be considered a benefit loss. This should be explained and understood before negotiations are finalized.

§ 11.2   Alienation and Attachment

Before the passage of the Retirement Equity Act of 1984 (REA), benefits in ERISA plans were exempt from any kind of alienation or attachment. Federal law protected an employee's benefits once they had vested under the terms of the plan. Even if an action occurred that would be considered against public policy, such as fraud or defalcation, a participant in an ERISA plan could not lose vested benefits. Vested benefits under federal law are deemed "nonforfeitable."

The REA introduced the qualified domestic relations order (QDRO), an order issued by a court of competent jurisdiction that deprives an employee of vested benefits. The QDRO can take a portion or all of the employee's accrued benefits and give them to a former spouse or other dependent. The QDRO can be drastic enough (from the employee's perspective) to take 100 percent of the employee's total benefits at retirement, even though such retirement may occur long after the divorce.

This breach in ERISA's protective wall was followed by other legislation and various court rulings that weaken the vesting and nonforfeitability concept. At present, an Internal Revenue Service (IRS) lien can be applied to pension benefits; bankruptcy in limited cases can affect benefits; and fraud or other criminal activity can result in the loss of benefits.

§ 11.3   Vesting and Forfeitures

Every ERISA plan has a vesting schedule, the most prevalent being the "five-year cliff." Upon the completion of five years of vesting service, the employee is 100 percent vested. If employment ends short of five years, there is no benefit. The vesting applies to benefits accrued up to that time as well as to all future benefits. The employee does not have to achieve separate five-year periods for each increment of benefits—with one exception. Defined contribution plans that have individual accounts are permitted to have phased vesting, with each year's contributions accounted for separately and subject to its own ratcheted vesting schedule. This procedure is not very common, as it is difficult both to track and to explain to plan participants, but it is one point to research in a marital property case.

Regardless of a plan's vesting schedule, when an employee qualifies for normal retirement, automatic 100 percent vesting is obtained. However, this is not automatic at a plan's *early* retirement age. It is possible for an employee to become eligible for early retirement but not to be fully vested. In that case, if the employee elects early retirement, he or she receives whatever portion of the benefit vested by then. This scenario, although possible, is unlikely, because most plans have vesting schedules under which the employee would have reached full vesting long before attaining eligibility for early retirement.

If an employee leaves service without full vesting, the portion that is not vested is forfeited. In a defined benefit pension plan, forfeitures are a financial gain to the plan, in that a contemplated benefit does not have to be paid. In a defined contribution plan, however, depending on the type of the plan and its terms and provisions, forfeitures may be used to increase the accounts of the remaining participants. Counsel is advised to see if a reallocation of forfeitures is available to increase a spouse's account balance in a defined contribution plan.

§ 11.4   Waivers

Ordinarily, a participant does not have the right to waive benefits in an ERISA plan. The theory is that this is for the employee's own protection, so that she cannot be forced or persuaded to give up benefits under pressure by the employer or anyone else. In a small plan, an owner-employee may waive some or all of her pension benefits with permission of the IRS. If a divorce action involves an owner of a small business, the possibility of such a waiver should be investigated. It is not unheard of for an owner to give up her own benefits in an acrimonious divorce case, just to deprive a spouse of getting his fair share.

Defined benefit pension plans in ERISA, as well as certain categories of defined contribution plans, must provide a standard form of benefit payout for married employees. In the absence of a waiver, benefits must be paid in the form of a qualified joint-and-survivor annuity (QJSA) with the spouse as the beneficiary of the employee's post-retirement death benefit. The spouse may waive the death benefit, allowing the employee to elect any other option under the plan. A spouse may do this for a number of reasons, but the principal reason is that electing to receive the death benefit causes the plan to reduce the basic lifetime benefit so as to keep the plan in actuarial balance. The waiver, therefore, means a larger pension while the retiree is alive, but no survivor benefit after the retiree dies.

In a divorce, a QDRO may be drafted to require the employee to elect survivor benefits with the divorced spouse as beneficiary. The court order cannot require a spouse to waive his or her rights under ERISA but, in most cases, at the time of retirement the parties will no longer be married, so there will be no ERISA spousal rights per se. Only a QDRO can continue the rights that a spouse had during the marriage.

If divorce occurs after retirement, and if the spousal waiver had left no survivor benefits, it may be advisable for the spouse's counsel to investigate whether the waiver was properly executed in all respects. If every step of ERISA's technical requirements has not been met, there may be grounds to attack the waiver as improper and thereby restore survivorship benefits to the spouse.

§ 11.5   Reduction in Benefits

ERISA precludes reductions in benefits, with some exceptions. A plan partici- pant's vested benefit could be reduced if the plan terminates with insufficient assets to meet its benefit payments. If the plan is covered by the Pension Benefit Guaranty Corporation, a portion of the vested benefits is guaranteed by the federal government.

A plan may be amended by the employer, or by joint employer and union agreement in collective bargaining, to reduce future rates of benefit accruals. The vested benefits accrued to date are not affected, but the benefit formula or employer funding obligation is changed to provide smaller benefits for future service. In divorce, with a QDRO and a contemplated benefit at retirement, the actual benefit received may not be what was expected at the time of the divorce.

§ 11.6   Breaks in Service

Few employees work for the same employer full-time for their entire career without any lapses, leaves of absences, layoffs, maternity leaves, or other breaks in service. ERISA plans contain complicated rules for the counting and crediting of service for plan vesting and for benefit accrual. When dividing pension benefits in divorce, it is not enough to look at the employee's date of hire, date of marriage, and date of divorce to measure length of service. The plan should be queried on the employee's credited service periods, for vesting and for benefit credits, as well as on the units of measurement used in counting time periods—for example, full or fractional years, months, or other service measurements peculiar to the plan.

For breaks in service, some plans allow credit to be restored by proper application—for example, if the break was due to military service. A plan may permit restoration of service by the payment of past-due employee contributions (with or without interest). If there is a repayment of contributions, it may be on a phased time schedule. If, at the time of divorce, there is an ongoing repayment structure to recapture past service, the issue of whether and how to count the repaid contributions as marital property should be explored. This possibility may be considered in a QDRO.

§ 11.7   Data Correction

Occasionally, an employee's records contain incorrect data. Perhaps the date of birth, or date of hire, or record of time worked is wrong. Correction of data errors may create or denigrate eligibility for benefits or for retirement status. If errors are discovered at the time of retirement, long after the divorce, the expected spousal benefits may differ from the basis on which the divorce was settled. It is advisable, therefore, to verify employment data and plan records at the time of the divorce.

§ 11.8   Inflation

Inflation is a touchy subject. In the valuation of a defined benefit pension, the actuary must decide whether to include a factor for inflation in the calculations. The general trend is not to adjust for inflation unless there is a significant reason to do so. Governmental pension plans, including plans for military personnel, increase pension benefits to reflect inflation by use of a cost-of-living adjustment (COLA). Private plans generally cannot afford to maintain a standard COLA for their pensioners, but may award ad hoc pension increases from time to time.

A QDRO on a defined benefit pension plan should take into account the approximate dollar payout at some future date and an estimate on its purchasing power. For example, awarding 50 percent of the current accrued pension earned at the date of divorce by a 40-year-old employee, payable to the former spouse 25 years in the future, may not provide much when it comes due. An immediate offset of the actuarial present value may be preferable, depending on the facts and circumstances of the case and the type of pension plan.

§ 11.9   Bankruptcy

The bankruptcy of an employer with an ERISA plan usually should not be cause for alarm concerning the protection of benefits. The plan funds are held in a separate trust, insulated from the employer's assets, and in a defined benefit pension plan, insured by the PBGC. In a small plan, however, the "firewall" between employer and plan may be breached if it can be demonstrated that the plan benefited only the owner. Benefits awarded by a QDRO are safe from any bankruptcy action, but if there is a QDRO in place, the bankruptcy court should be notified whether benefit payments have begun or are due to be paid.

§ 11.10   Taxes and Penalties

Benefits paid from plans are taxable, under certain conditions and in certain time frames. If a participant receives a lump-sum distribution or a series of monthly annuity pension payments, personal, ordinary income tax is applied on the amounts in the calendar year in which the monies are received. If a participant receives a plan payment and turns it over to a former spouse as part of a divorce settlement, the payment is taxable to the participant because that is the person to whom the plan paid the money. Payments from a plan, as ordered by a QDRO, receive special tax treatment. If an employee's or retiree's benefits are paid in full or in part to a former spouse under a QDRO, the tax applies to the spouse receiving the payments. If, under the QDRO, payments are made to a dependent child, the tax applies to the plan participant as if the participant had received the payment.

If the payment is in the form of a lump-sum distribution, it may be rolled over to the person's individual retirement account (IRA) within 60 days of its receipt to maintain its tax shelter. However, the payment is subject to mandatory 20 percent federal income tax withholding before it gets to the IRA. A procedure exists for avoiding the withholding: direct transfer of a lump-sum distribution from the plan to the IRA, without the money going through the hands of the participant or the spouse.

A plan participant under the age of $59\frac{1}{2}$ who receives a lump-sum distribution—not with respect to death or disability and not in an annuity form—is subject to a 10 percent excise tax. The 10 percent penalty does not apply when the payment is made under a QDRO, regardless of the ages of the participant and the spouse. This special exception to the penalty is an important tax-planning tool and can be significant in settlement negotiations.

CHAPTER 12

TIME VALUE OF MONEY

§ 12.1   Money Now and Then

From the aphorism "a bird in the hand is worth two in the bush" to the concept that a dollar today is worth more than a dollar tomorrow, we build the entire structure of the time value of money and the theory of interest. One might ask, "If I absolutely must have one dollar one year from now to repay a loan, how much do I need today to be sure of it?" One answer would be to put the dollar in a shoebox and store it under the bed. But we are looking for a financial method, and we would like to be prudent.

Taking interest into account, we can deposit an amount less than a dollar today in the anticipation that it will grow with interest to become the dollar we want a year from now. Some inherent assumptions must be made here, assumptions not always obvious.

First, we must assume that we will be alive in one year to meet that obligation and that the party to whom payment is due will still be here. Second, we must assume that the unit of currency will not change and that the contractual obligation will remain the same. We ignore administrative expenses and shipping and handling charges. We are concerned only with the time value of money in an otherwise perfect world.

It is an axiom that the present value of a sum due in the future bears an inverse relationship to the interest rate. The lower the interest rate, the greater the sum needed now to meet the future payment. The higher the rate at which interest can be earned, the smaller the amount needed now. At the front end, the greater expected yield means that we need less on hand to satisfy the promised payment.

In determining the present value of a pension benefit to be paid at some future date, therefore, the actuary's choice of an interest rate assumption is vital to the outcome. The interest rate assumption must be reasonable and appropriate, one that can withstand scrutiny and be successfully presented in settlement negotiations, and can be explained to the finder of fact if the case goes to trial.

§ 12.2 Interest

There are two fundamental ways of accounting for interest: *simple* interest and *compound* interest. Simple interest may be illustrated as follows: Start with capital of $100, and an interest rate of 5 percent per year. Each year the capital amount earns $5 ($0.05 \times $100). After one year the total is $105. After 10 years, the total is $150.

Compound interest adds interest to both the capital and the previous accumulations of interest. Start with $100 and a 5 percent interest rate. After one year the total is $105, just as in simple interest. In the second year, however, interest is earned on both the base $100 and the $5 of interest earned in the first year. At the end of the second year, the investment equals $110.25 ($100 + $5 + $0.25 + $5). After ten years, at 5 percent compound interest, we have $162.89, a dramatic difference compared to the simple interest 10-year total of $150.

Compound interest means *x* percent per year, compounded annually. Of course, interest may be paid or received more than once a year and its compounding period may be monthly, quarterly or semiannually.

§ 12.3 Discount and Projection

When we want to know the present worth of a given future financial obligation, we *discount* the amount due with interest. Then, if that interest assumption is met in practice, the present worth grows to be the obligation amount at the time it is due. The future obligation may be for a lump sum, an annuity, or a combination of both. If, however, we want to know what we can expect to receive from a given amount on hand at present, we *project* it with interest. If the interest assumption is met, the anticipated amount will be there at the end of the given time period. The discounting of a future payment may be called "reducing to present value," but if this term is used, be careful not to misinterpret the word "reducing." A mathematical computation is made, in which, by assumption, an equivalence is maintained over time. Nothing is actually reduced, in the sense that nothing is lost.

§ 12.4 The Effect of Interest Rates on Present Value

The present value of a pension represents the worth in today's money of a future stream of payments. A major component in the mathematical determination of the present value is the interest rate. The interest rate is sometimes called a discount rate, but in the technical language of compound interest, the discount rate is something different from the interest rate that is used to obtain a present value. It may be said properly, however, that the interest rate is used to discount a future amount to its current value.

Interest rates prevail over two separate and distinct time periods in a pension valuation. The first period encompasses the years before the employee reaches retirement age, the pre-retirement phase. The second period starts at retirement and is known as the post-retirement phase. The interest rate that prevails after retirement is the "immediate" or "primary" rate. The pre-retirement interest rate may or may not be the same as the post-retirement interest rate.

In valuing pensions for divorce, interest is computed per annum and compounded annually. It is the annual yield or annual percentage rate, not merely the nominal rate. When a bank or broker advertises an interest rate, it may state both the nominal rate and the effective annual rate. The effective annual rate is used in pension valuations.

The magnitude of the interest rate and the present value of a pension or any future obligation are always in an inverse relationship. When the interest rate is high, the present value is low. When the interest rate is low, the present value is high. When interest rates are relatively low, the present value of a pension is higher than it would be when interest rates are high. The General Agreement on Tariffs and Trade (GATT), as amended, sets forth a rate that has become a reliable national standard for the computation of present values of pensions in divorce cases. It removes doubt, speculation, and eliminates arguments over what interest rate to use.

§ 12.5   Sources of Interest Rates

Because the interest rate assumption is so significant to the value of an asset—in particular, a pension in a divorce case—it is important to know how and why it is selected by the evaluator. The sources of interest rates are the PBGC, the GATT, the prime rate, the plan's interest rate, and a "best judgment" rate.

PBGC. The PGBC publishes various sets of interest rates each month. The sets differ for various governmental purposes, but the one with any bearing would be the interest rates for a terminating single-employer pension plan. This category includes two subsets, one for lump-sum payments and one for annuities. The monthly information may be obtained by subscription or via the Internet. The PBGC annuity interest rate, the generally recognized standard for use in computing the present value of a pension as property in marital dissolution, has been replaced by the GATT interest rate.

GATT. The Pension Reform Act imbedded in the GATT established a benchmark interest rate for pension plans as the smoothed average of 30-year U.S. Treasury Bonds for a given month. The plan determines the reference month in relation to the time of the calculation. It may be the first month of the plan's fiscal year, the first month of a calendar year (January), or a month that precedes the current month by a fixed interval. The GATT interest rates are generally perceived as being the most reasonable and appropriate for measuring the worth of a pension as marital property.

Prime Rate.   Many financial uses are put to the prime rate as published in *The Wall Street Journal*, but it is a somewhat artificial rate promulgated by major U.S. banks and is not usually adequate for pension purposes.

Plan Rate.   It would seem that the interest rate used by the plan itself would be the financial tool to use in valuing benefits, but that turns out not to be the case. In fact, a defined benefit pension plan under ERISA is subject to a bewildering array of different interest rates for different liability and tax reporting purposes. Further, the actuary for the plan uses a number of financial and demographic assumptions, each of which is intended to be reasonable and in harmony with the others, to provide a comprehensive package pertinent to that particular plan. Selecting out from the group of variables, just the interest rate, would be misleading.

Best Judgment Rate.   Because of the many interest rates, the actuary or pension evaluator in a divorce case may attempt to use some interest rate based on his or her best judgment. This approach is difficult to justify and certainly open to attack by one spouse or the other. Why is interest rate x better in the evaluator's judgment than interest rate y?

Pension practitioners nationwide have come to accept the GATT rate as the principle for valuation of pension assets in marital dissolution. In all discussions of interest rates in pension plans, the most important factor after the interest rate is mortality. The value of a pension benefit payable in the future, or the value of a continuing stream of monthly payments to a retiree, is determined by discounting for interest for the time value of money and for mortality to reflect that the pension benefit stops for the named individual when that person dies. Whether or not a survivor benefit exists, the primary benefit being valued is for a specific individual who has an uncertain lifespan.

CHAPTER 13

VALUATION OF A DEFINED BENEFIT PENSION PLAN

§ 13.1   Information Needed for Pension Valuation

For the valuation of a pension in a divorce case, the actuary or evaluator needs the following information concerning the divorcing couple:

A. Basic data
    Names of the parties
    Dates of birth
    Social Security numbers (optional)
    Date of marriage
    Date of marital separation
    Date of filing of divorce complaint
    Date of divorce (actual or potential)
B. Employment service data
    Name of each spouse's employer and division or department
    Position, job title, general duties
    Hire date; plan entry date
    Dates of other employment
    Dates of military service, if any
    Current employment status (active, terminated, retired)
    Current or last pay rate classification

Copy of recent paycheck stub, retirement statement, or other document accompanying payment of benefit

General health status of each spouse

Any special or unusual matters concerning employment or pension coverage

§ 13.2 Determining Present Value

What is the "present" in present value? In most jurisdictions the present is the date on which the marital property settlement is signed. For pension purposes, the present means the employee-spouse's current age and the prevailing market interest rates.

Proposed Rule on Employee Benefit Plans [6 C.F.R. Part 31, § 3121(v) (1986)] contains the following definition:

> Present Value Defined. "Present value" of a pension benefit in a defined pension plan means the value as of a specified date of an amount or series of amounts due thereafter, where each amount is multiplied by the probability that the conditions on which payment of the amount is contingent will be satisfied, and is discounted according to an assumed rate of interest to reflect the time value of money. The present value must be determined as of the date the value is required to be taken into account using actuarial assumptions and methods that are reasonable as of that date. For this purpose, a discount for pre-retirement mortality is permitted. In addition, the present value cannot be discounted for the risk that payments will not be made (or will be reduced) because of the unfunded status of the plan, the risk associated with any deemed or actual investment of amounts deferred under the plan, the risk that the employer, the trustee, or another party will be unwilling to pay, the possibility of a future change in the law, or similar risks or contingencies.

§ 13.3 Valuation Date

In valuing a pension for immediate offset as marital property in equitable distribution, the date of the valuation must be established. What do we want to know? What the pension was worth on the date of marital separation or on the date the divorce complaint was filed? What the pension is worth at the time the case is settled or at trial?

Consider the analogy of the family dwelling. Assuming the couple jointly own the house in which they have lived during the marriage and that they agree on a real estate appraiser, when should the house be valued to reflect its fair market value as an asset of the marriage? The same answer applies to pensions as to houses: the *real-time value* is the only reliable measure of the worth of property.

A house stands still, but a pension moves in time. Whether it is a defined benefit pension plan with a complex benefit formula or a simple defined contribution plan with individual accounts, the participant accrues pension benefits—usually with each year of service.

The dates for the determination of the benefit and the valuation of the benefit differ. A pension valued at a specified date in the past has a present value that is different from its present value in real time. The pension's past value is not relevant for the divorcing couple's property settlement.

Example: David, who participates in his employer's defined benefit pension plan, separates from Judy and files a divorce complaint in 1993. Six years later, in 1999, the divorce case is settled. In 1993, David's accrued pension benefit was $800 per month, payable for life starting at age 65. In 1999, after six additional years of service and several pay increases, David's accrued pension benefit is $1,200 a month. The issue arises as to which amount—$800 or $1,200—is to be considered marital property. State statute or case law determines whether the couple's marital property is the present value in real time (i.e., 1999) of the 1993 pension amount ($800 per month) or the present value in 1999 of the current 1999 pension ($1,200 per month).

§ 13.4   Coverture Fraction and the Time Rule

To allocate or segregate the amount of pension attributable to the marriage, actuaries use a method known as the *time rule*. The time rule apportions the value of the pension over the time of the marriage divided by the total time the pension was earned for working service. This rule is implemented by use of a *coverture fraction*.

The coverture fraction *numerator* equals the length of time from the later of (a) the date of plan entry or (b) the date of the marriage to the marital property acquisition cutoff date for the jurisdiction, date of marital separation, filing date of the divorce complaint, or date of the trial. The coverture fraction *denominator* equals the length of time from the date of plan entry to the cutoff date for the jurisdiction.

Following are two examples of coverture fractions based on data provided in the preceding example (see **§ 13.3**):

Example 1:
 Plan entry date: August 1, 1979
 Date of marriage: October 1, 1983
 Complaint filing date (or jurisdictional cutoff date): November 1, 1993
 Current valuation date: August 1, 1999

The couple's date of marriage is later than Husband's plan entry date. The time from date of marriage (October 1, 1983) to cutoff date for the jurisdiction in which the couple resides (November 1, 1993) is 10 years and 1 month. The coverture fraction numerator is therefore 10.08333 years. The period from Husband's plan entry date (August 1, 1979) to the cutoff date (November 1, 1993) is 14 years and 3 months. The denominator is therefore 14.25 years.

In this example, the coverture fraction is 10.08333 ÷ 14.25, which equals 0.7076, or just over 70 percent. Whatever the pension's current present value is, based on the accrued pension as of November 1, 1993, the portion considered marital property is arrived at by multiplying the pension value by the coverture fraction, 0.7076.

Therefore, if the present value (in 1999) of Husband's 1993 pension is $50,000, the marital portion of the present value subject to equitable distribution is $35,380 ($50,000 × 0.7076).

Example 2:
    Plan entry date: August 1, 1979
    Date of marriage: October 1, 1983
    Complaint filing date (or jurisdictional cutoff date): August 1, 1999
    Valuation date: August 1, 1999

The coverture fraction numerator in this example is 15.83333. The denominator, representing the time from plan entry date (August 1, 1979) to the jurisdictional cutoff for acquisition of marital property (August 1, 1999), is 20 years. The fraction is therefore 15.83333 ÷ 20, which equals 0.7917. Whatever the pension's current present value is, based on the employee-spouse's current accrued pension as of August 1, 1999, the portion considered marital property is reached by multiplying the amount by 0.7917.

Therefore, if the present value (in 1999) of the 1999 pension is $80,000, the marital portion of the present value subject to equitable distribution is $63,336.

The use of a coverture fraction and the time rule has two aspects as shown in the preceding examples. It is essential to determine first which benefit is being valued—the past or current one—and then to use the appropriate fraction.

The ending time point of the coverture fraction denominator should be exactly the same time point as the date of determination of the accrued pension benefit. That is, if the denominator ends at November 1, 1993, that is the date on which pension benefit is fixed. If the 1999 benefit is used, then the denominator of the coverture fraction must end as of that date in 1999.

In a jurisdiction where the employee's past pension benefit is the one valued, measured as of the date of marital separation or the filing date of the divorce complaint, a question may arise if the pension plan's condition has changed in the interim. Pension plans are amended to remain in compliance with changes in federal laws and with regulations and rulings of the IRS and the Department of Labor.

Plans are also amended by agreement under a union contract, or by the employer to increase benefits or change any particular plan terms and conditions. If a 1993 benefit is valued in 1999 and the plan was amended in 1996 to increase past or future benefits, or both, an argument may be put forward that such change should be included in the marital property component. The divorcing couple may be expected to differ.

It may be argued that changes in future benefits should be ignored under the theory that they would be post-divorce increases. If the case is being settled by deferred distribution instead of immediate offset of present value, the court order should clearly establish the pension amounts being awarded to the nonemployee-spouse and whether future increases in benefits will be included.

§ 13.5   Computation Dates in Valuation

Several dates are of interest in pension valuations. As noted previously, the basic dates required are date of birth, hire date, plan entry date, date of marital separation, filing date of divorce complaint, and actual (or potential) date of divorce (see § 13.1). Table 13–1 lists additional issues to be considered and assumptions to be made concerning dates.

Table 13–1

Issues and Assumptions Concerning Valuation Dates

Assumed Date When Pension Accruals End (Termination of Employment)	Assumed Date When Pension Payments Commence (Annuity Starting Date)

A. Cutoff date:
    1. Date of marital separation
    2. Filing date of complaint
    3. Date of divorce
	Earliest possible retirement age, with reduction

B. Valuation date: Date current work is being done, using current age and interest rates	Various alternative early retirement ages Early retirement age without reduction
C. Retirement date: One or more of the dates shown in column 2	Various alternative normal retirement ages

§ 13.6   Contributions

All contributions to a pension fund after the cutoff date for measuring marital property are the separate property of the employee-spouse, not available for equitable distribution in marital dissolution. The value of the pension at the cutoff date may be credited with passive increases, but not contributions, to the date of trial or other settlement of the property issues in the divorce case. (Depending on the jurisdiction, the cutoff date may be the date of marital separation, the date of filing of the divorce complaint, or the date of the divorce.)

In a routine defined benefit pension plan, employer contributions are made to the general pension fund for all employees covered by the plan, not earmarked for individuals. The continuation or absence of any contributions in this type of plan has no bearing on an employee's pension benefits. For marital property purposes, the proper value is determined in a two-step process, reflecting two time frames. First, the amount of pension benefit that the employee has accrued based on pay and service is determined up to the cutoff date. Second, the value of the pension is determined currently by actuarial factors using the employee's current age and current interest rates. The result is the current present value of the pension benefit at the cutoff date, without respect to contributions.

§ 13.7   Pension in Pay Status

The *right* to receive a future pension by reason of employment during a marriage is marital property subject to equitable distribution by one of two methods: immediate offset or deferred distribution. Some questions have arisen regarding the treatment of a pension when the marital dissolution occurs after the employee-spouse retires and is drawing an actual pension—that is, the pension is in pay status.

One approach was to treat the pension as any other income and to count it, if it was counted at all, in the financial structure of the parties in determining alimony. Using this approach, the present value of the potential future stream of pension payments would be ignored. The opposing argument is that, once the pension has entered pay status, many of the previous contingencies are gone and the pension may be valued on a pure actuarial basis. For example, no assumptions are needed as to the length of time the employee-spouse will continue in employment, nor is any estimate of a future pension needed, because the pension exists in actuality.

The Pennsylvania Superior Court has addressed part of this issue in *Miller v. Miller* [577 A.2d 205 (Pa. Super. Ct. 1990)]. The *Miller* opinion, written by Judge Popovich, indicates that a vested, matured pension that is currently being paid may be distributed on an actuarially based current value. To an actuary, there is redundancy in this phrase because a pension in pay status is by definition matured and vested. If it were not vested upon retirement there would be no pension to pay, and if it were not matured it would not be payable. Nevertheless, the concept is clear that an actual pension is subject to valuation and distribution just as is a deferred future pension.

Miller does not address double-dipping—the practice whereby the pension is addressed twice in the divorce settlement, once in immediate offset of the pension's present value and later as a source of income, as a component in the determination of alimony.

The ruling further clarified the construction and use of the marital coverture fraction to measure the portion of the pension's value that is attributable to the marriage and thus subject to equitable distribution. The parties in *Miller* had been married for 17 years during which the husband retired after 31 years of employment. He had 25 years of service credit before his marriage and 11 years in retirement, receiving a pension before the marital separation occurred. During the couple's six years of marriage, before his retirement, the husband was an active employee participating in the pension plan.

The plan counted the employee's total service from his date of hire in 1942 to the date he retired in 1973, and determined the marital plan period extended from the employee's date of marriage in 1967 to the date he retired in 1973. The court found the correct coverture fraction to be the 6 years of married plan service divided by 31 years of total plan service, or 0.1935.

The husband in *Miller* argued that the value of the pension should be computed as of the date he retired. The appellate court dismissed this argument, agreeing with the lower court that the current value as of the date of the hearing is determinative. Further, there were cost-of-living increases in the pension benefit after retirement and these were correctly included in the valuation process. The court in *Miller* cited the ruling in another case: Where a plan has vested and value increases aside from the contribution of the parties, beyond the date of separation, the increase is marital property. [*Morschauser v. Morschauser,* 516 A.2d 10 (Pa. Super. Ct. 1986).]

Family practice lawyers may derive from these decisions some guidance on the valuation of pensions in divorce, the valuation date, and the coverture fraction. The extension of these concepts to pensions in pay status is a welcome expansion of knowledge in this complex field.

§ 13.8   Sample Pension Plan Valuation

The valuation of a typical ERISA defined benefit pension plan as marital property in divorce is illustrated for a 50-year-old husband whose retirement age is 65.

PENSION VALUATION REPORT

VALUATION DATE March 30, 1999

Name: John Smith	Plan: XYZ Corporation Pension Plan
Birth Date: 02/25/49	Benefit Age: 65
Entry Date: 11/01/73	Benefit Date: 03/01/2014
Marriage Date: 09/10/89	Employee Status: Active
Cutoff Date: 04/01/97	Sex: Male

VALUATION OF A DEFINED BENEFIT PENSION PLAN

1. Age at nearest birthday to valuation date   50
2. Monthly pension accrued for service as of valuation date (from benefit statement received from plan and reviewed by the below signed actuary for reasonableness) $3,340
3. Deferred annuity rate per $1.00 annual pension   3.7688
4. Present value (12 × $3,340 × 3.7688) $151,054
5. Plan service while married from 9/10/89 to 4/01/97   7.58333 years
6. Plan service at valuation date from 11/01/73 to 3/30/99   25.41667 years
7. Coverture fraction (7.58333 years ÷ 25.41667 years)   0.29836
8. Marital present value ($151,054 × .29836) $45,068

The marital portion is contingent on the jurisdictional cutoff date for community property, in the County of _____, State of _____.

Pension form: Life annuity

Calculations in accordance with generally accepted actuarial standards as codified in the GATT, with 5.89% interest rate and mortality table GAM-83.

Prepared by: _____   Date: _____
                  Actuary

CHAPTER 14

VALUATION OF A DEFINED CONTRIBUTION PLAN

§ 14.1   Introduction

The Employee Retirement Income Security Act of 1974 (ERISA), the federal law of pensions, created some unintended confusion in nomenclature. ERISA distinguishes between two types of plans, pension plans and welfare plans, with the term "pension plans" encompassing both defined benefit plans and defined contribution plans. In pension terminology, on the other hand, a pension plan *is* a defined benefit pension plan, whereas a defined contribution plan has various designations, depending on its type and contribution basis.

A defined contribution plan has a structure quite distinct from that of a defined benefit pension plan. The plan maintains an individual account, sometimes more than one account, for each participant. Employer contributions are allocated among participants' accounts, as are investment gains and losses. Some defined contribution plans allow participants to make investment choices for their own account, although the choices are generally limited to certain categories of investments, or subfunds. When a defined contribution plan is part of the marital property involved in a divorce settlement, it is important to learn whether the spouse is permitted to make investment selections for the segregated account portion awarded by the order.

The valuation of a defined contribution plan as marital property does not always need the services of an actuary. The evaluator should have knowledge of the workings of the plan, along with some financial acumen, to report a reasonable and appropriate result.

The defined contribution plan reports the account status to each participant individually at least once a year and often quarterly. Usually, the report shows the account's opening balance followed by the contributions allocated to the account, the share of investment gains or losses, and the balance at the end of the period. The vesting schedule in defined contribution plans is often more generous than it is in defined benefit pension plans. For example, in a typical 401(k) plan—a combination profit-sharing and pre-tax salary reduction employee contribution arrangement—a participant is vested fully and immediately in the account balance.

A popular form of defined contribution plan is the thrift or savings plan constructed in accordance with IRC Section 401(k). The most advantageous feature of this type of plan for the employee is that the employee contribution comes from his or her pay on a pre-tax basis. The employee's contribution is not subject to personal income tax when it is made, but it is taxable when withdrawn or otherwise paid as a benefit distribution. Thrift and savings plans may or may not accept contributions from the employer and they are subject to valuation for immediate offset or for an award of all or part of the account by court order in deferred distribution.

§ 14.2 Complications

Individual account plans might appear to be among the easiest type of plan to evaluate as marital property in a divorce, but there are numerous factors that complicate the evaluator's job. The principal difficulty is not being able to determine the employee's account balance as of a given date. Some plans value accounts on a specific schedule (e.g., annually, semiannually, quarterly, or monthly); other plans are so fully computerized that account balance information is available at any time. Even when a daily balance figure is known, however, there are complications. A defined contribution plan may be a simple plan with an individual account for each participant and investments managed by the trustees of the plan fund. In the most basic type of plan, contributions are made only by the employer, only once a year. Simple plans do exist, but the vast majority of defined contribution plans now allow contributions by both employees and employer at various times throughout the year—as well as after year-end although the contribution is attributable to the prior year. Many defined contribution plans have provisions for loans, hardship withdrawals, employee investment selections, and purchase of life insurance.

In a divorce situation, counsel for each of the parties should become thoroughly acquainted with the plan provisions and know which provisions have been or could be exercised by the employee-spouse. If a qualified domestic relations order (QDRO) is involved, inquiry should be made regarding features that are available to the nonemployee-spouse that could be included in the QDRO.

§ 14.3 Valuation Features

Unlike in a defined benefit plan, the employee's retirement age plays little part in the valuation of a defined contribution account. Once the employee is vested (and vesting is usually fast; typically, 100 percent after five years of service), he or she may leave the job at any time and receive a full benefit cash-out. There are no special provisions for early retirement and no actuarial adjustments for the age at which the cash-out is paid. A lump-sum cash-out is the most common form of benefit payment, although plans offer the option of conversion to a monthly lifetime annuity form for the employee, with or without survivor's benefits.

Some features of a defined contribution plan that can be exercised—and so have a bearing on the value of the account—are loans, hardship withdrawals, and purchase of life insurance. The number and variety of the employee's investment choices and subaccounts should be reviewed. If the plan offers the employee the opportunity to make pre-tax contributions, as in a 401(k) plan, and if the employee has done so, those contributions have a different economic value than money the employee contributed after taxes.

§ 14.4   Sample Valuations

Set forth in this section are four sample valuations of defined contribution plans as marital property. The samples illustrate some of the complexities encountered when valuing a defined contribution account to ascertain the worth of a pension as a marital asset. All the samples use the same basic data but apply different methods.

In the first example, employee's entry into the plan occurred *after* the parties were married, so the employee-spouse's account is 100 percent marital property. Note that the valuation date is not necessarily the date the report is prepared.

PENSION VALUATION REPORT 1

Valuation Date   12/15/98

NAME: Kate Kane
EMPLOYER: ABC Corporation
TYPE OF PLAN: Defined Contribution Plan

Birth Date:	10/28/65	Benefit Age:	Any
Entry Date:	12/03/88	Benefit Date:	At any age
Marriage Date:	11/03/84	Status:	Active
Cutoff date:	12/31/97	Sex:	Female

1.	Age at nearest birthday to valuation date	33
2.	Individual account balance at cutoff date (provided by the plan)	$16,722
3.	Length of plan service while married	9.0833 years
4.	Length of plan service to cutoff date	9.0833 years
5.	Coverture fraction (item 3 divided by item 4)	1.0000

VALUATION OF A DEFINED CONTRIBUTION PLAN

6. Marital present value at cutoff date (item 2 × item 5) $16,722
7. Imputed net investment gains on marital property value from
   cutoff date to present (one year at 6 percent) $ 1,003
8. Marital present value (item 6 + item 7) $17,725

Marital portion contingent on jurisdictional cutoff date and assumed net investment gain of 6 percent per annum, compounded annually.

Pension form: Lump sum.

Calculations in accordance with generally accepted actuarial standards for a defined contribution pension plan.

Prepared by: _____   Date: _____
                    Actuary

The second sample is somewhat more complicated than the first. The employee-spouse entered the plan *before* the parties were married, so a coverture fraction is used to determine the portion of the account that qualifies as marital property under the time rule.

PENSION VALUATION REPORT 2

Valuation Date   12/15/98

NAME: Kate Kane
EMPLOYER: ABC Corporation
TYPE OF PLAN: Defined Contribution Plan

Birth Date:	10/28/65	Benefit Age: Any
Entry Date:	01/01/80	Benefit Date: At any age
Marriage Date:	11/03/84	Status: Active
Cutoff Date:	12/31/97	Sex: Female

1. Age at nearest birthday to valuation date   33
2. Individual account balance at cutoff date
   (provided by the plan) $30,500
3. Length of plan service while married   13.1666 years
4. Length of plan service to cutoff date   18.0000 years
5. Coverture fraction (item 3 divided by item 4)   .7315
6. Marital value at cutoff date (item 2 × item 5) $22,311
7. Imputed net investment gains on marital value from
   cutoff date to present (one year at 6 percent) $ 1,339
8. Marital present value (item 6 + item 7) $23,650

Marital portion contingent on jurisdictional cutoff date and assumed net investment gain of 6 percent per annum, compounded annually.

Pension form: Lump sum.

§ 14.4   SAMPLE VALUATIONS

Calculations in accordance with generally accepted actuarial standards for a defined contribution pension plan.

Prepared by: _____   Date: _____
                          Actuary

The third sample valuation is a variation on the second. The employee-spouse entered the plan *before* her marriage, but the coverture fraction is applied at a different step in the computations to determine the marital property portion of the account, under a variation of the time rule.

PENSION VALUATION REPORT 3

Valuation Date   12/15/98

NAME: Kate Kane
EMPLOYER: ABC Corporation
TYPE OF PLAN: Defined Contribution Plan

Birth Date:	10/28/65	Benefit Age: Any	
Entry Date:	01/01/80	Benefit Date: At any age	
Marriage Date:	11/03/84	Status: Active	
Cutoff Date:	12/31/97	Sex: Female	

1.	Age at nearest birthday to valuation date	33
2.	Individual account balance at valuation date (provided by the plan)	$36,675
3.	Length of plan service while married	13.1666 years
4.	Length of plan service to valuation date	19.0000 years
5.	Coverture fraction (item 3 divided by item 4)	.6930
6.	Marital present value (item 2 × item 5)	$25,416

Marital portion contingent on length of marriage and assumed net investment gain of 6 percent per annum, compounded annually.

Pension form: Lump sum.

Calculations in accordance with generally accepted actuarial standards for a defined contribution pension plan.

Prepared by: _____   Date: _____
                          Actuary

In the fourth sample valuation, subtraction instead of a coverture fraction is used to compute the marital property portion of the employee-spouse's defined contribution account. Subtraction may yield a greater or a lesser result than the one obtained by the time rule methods. In subtraction, of course, the vital difference is in the starting point—the account balance at the date of marriage. Often, this starting figure is not readily available if the couple has had a long marriage.

PENSION VALUATION REPORT 4

Valuation Date   12/15/98

NAME: Kate Kane
EMPLOYER: ABC Corporation
TYPE OF PLAN: Defined Contribution Plan

Birth Date:	10/28/65	Benefit Age:	Any
Entry Date:	01/01/80	Benefit Date:	At any age
Marriage Date:	11/03/84	Status:	Active
Cutoff Date:	12/31/97	Sex:	Female

1. Age at nearest birthday to valuation date — 33
2. Individual account balance at cutoff date (provided by the plan) — $30,500
3. Account balance at date of marriage (provided in correspondence from the plan) — $ 3,850
4. Cumulative account change over time, by subtraction (item 2 minus item 3) — $26,650
5. Imputed net investment gains on marital value from cutoff date to present (one year at 6 percent) — $ 1,599
6. Marital present value (item 4 + item 5) — $28,249

Marital portion contingent on jurisdictional cutoff date, allocated by subtraction and assumed net investment gain of 6 percent per annum, compounded annually.

Pension form: Lump sum

Calculated in accordance with generally accepted actuarial standards for a defined contribution pension plan.

Prepared by: _____   Date: _____
                       Actuary

FUNDING

§ 15.1   Introduction

Pension plans covered by ERISA are required to be funded, with the assets held by trustees. A plan's trustees may be the owners and officers of the company sponsoring the plan, or a bank, or a trust company. When the participants in a plan have investment choices, the investments are maintained within the trust fund. Table 15–1 summarizes the general characteristics of typical investment vehicles.

There is, of course, a variety of other types of investments; the list is intended only to give an idea of the characteristics that participants would be interested in for a particular investment. For any type of investment not listed in Table 15–1, the following characteristics should be researched:

1. Payment of interest and dividends;
2. Gain or loss at sale or maturity;
3. Potential for unrealized appreciation.

Another characteristic of investment vehicles not listed above due to its volatility is marketability, or liquidity. An asset may have a market value, but if there is no purchaser the asset would have insufficient marketability. Alternatively, an asset may have a market value but be insufficiently fungible—its nature is such that it is not readily convertible to cash.

Table 15–1

General Investment Characteristics

Type of Investment Vehicle	Pays Interest or Dividends (cash or stock)	Realizes Gain/Loss on Sale or at Maturity	Potential for Unrealized Appreciation
Cash equivalents (money market, savings account, etc.)	Yes	No	No
Government issues (but not zero coupon bonds)	Yes	Yes	Yes
Corporate bonds (but not zero coupon bonds)	Yes	Yes	Yes
Common and/or preferred stock	Varies	Yes	Yes
Commingled trust funds	Yes	Yes	Yes
Mutual funds	Yes	Yes	Yes
Employer stock	Varies	Yes	Yes
Zero coupon bonds	No	Yes	Yes
Guaranteed investment contracts (insured)	Yes	Yes	No
Individual life insurance policies	Varies	No	No
Universal life insurance policies	Yes	Yes	Yes
Collectibles	No	Yes	Yes

§ 15.2 Typical Funding of a Pension Plan

Investment income varies within each plan, depending on the type and nature of the investments and the level of conservative or aggressive investment philosophy of the trustees. A pension fund may invest in items that do not generate any current yield, such as artwork. The fund's investment is made in anticipation of favorable market appreciation, with the trustees willing to forgo current income.

If the pension plan invests in life insurance products, income may be obtained from cash surrender values of terminated policies as well as from death benefit payments when the insurance is structured with the plan as the beneficiary. An employer may set up a plan with all administrative expenses to be paid by the employer as tax-deductible business costs. That approach leaves more funds in the plan to pay benefits. Alternatively, a plan may be designed so that some or all of the appropriate expenses for administration and investment are paid out of plan funds. An employer cannot make up plan investment losses, however, except in the form of employer contributions within the allowable limits.

Benefit payments are made by the fund, not by the employer, and are paid in accordance with the terms and conditions of the plan and the recipient's elections. If there has been an erroneous employer contribution, perhaps because of faulty data or a computational error, the plan may make a refund to the employer.

The corpus of the pension fund therefore consists essentially of income from contributions and investment results, minus the outgo of administrative and investment expenses and benefit and other payments.

Table 15–2 lists a comprehensive set of income and outgo items that could occur in a large defined benefit pension plan. A smaller plan would not have as many financial components as those shown. There may be no employer contributions in a given year if the plan is fully funded, as actuarially determined (see § 15.3). In a defined benefit pension plan there may be no employee contributions at all, or employee contributions may be permitted only on a limited and voluntary basis. When there are employee contributions, a separate bookkeeping account is maintained for each employee.

Table 15–2

Sample Income and Outgo Items for a Defined Benefit Pension Plan

A. INCOME ITEMS
  Contributions
    From the employer, as actuarially determined
    From the employer in advance of need
    From the employer, to match employees' contributions
    From employees in matching program
    From employees (mandatory)
    From employees (voluntary)
  Investment Income
    Interest on bonds
    Interest on money market funds, bank accounts
    Interest on commercial paper
    Other interest
    Dividends on stocks: cash dividends and stock-in-kind
    Realized gains on sales of investments
    Unrealized gains in market value of investments
    Appreciation on other assets, realized and unrealized
  Other Income
    Employee repayments of loans
    Forfeitures of nonvested benefits
    Repayments of erroneous benefit distributions
    Payments received for reproducing plan copies upon request
    Proceeds received by the plan for life insurance

(continued)

Table 15–2 (*continued*)

B. OUTGO ITEMS
    Administrative Expenses
        Fees paid to trustees, legal counsel, actuary, consultants
        Fees paid to investment advisors, fund managers
        Administrative, clerical, office expenses
        Bank service charges
        Trustees' bonding premiums
        PBGC premiums, IRS filing fees
    Investment Expenses
        Commissions on purchases and sales of investments
        Realized losses on sales of investments
        Unrealized losses on market values
        Depreciation on other assets, realized and unrealized
        Investment administrative, clerical, office expenses
        Defaults in employee loan repayments
    Benefits and Other Payments
        Retirements, normal and early
        Disability benefits
        Death and survivor benefits
        QDRO-ordered benefit payments
        Loans to employees
        Hardship withdrawals
        Refunds of employee contributions
        Refunds of excess employer contributions

§ 15.3   Contributions

All defined benefit pension plans are supported by contributions, some solely by the employer, some solely by the employee, and some by both. The assets of the pension plan are maintained in a tax-sheltered fund that grows with contributions and investment gains and from which benefits—and sometimes expenses—are paid.

    The total amount of an employee's contributions to the pension fund is not the value of the pension. It is an error to look at an annual pension statement to find the total of the employee's contributions and to represent that as the value of the pension benefit. Contributions made by the employer are made for the entire group of plan participants as recommended by the plan's actuary.

§ 15.4   —Individual Contributions

Employer contributions are not earmarked for particular individuals, nor paid into individual accounts. These contributions may be represented as a percentage of covered payroll. For example, if a pension plan includes 100 active participants (not counting retirees) with a total annual payroll of $3,250,000, the employer's contribution to the plan for the year may be $200,000, or 6.15 percent of covered payroll. However, this does not mean that the employer contributes exactly 6.15 percent of each employee's pay to the pension plan that year. The employer's contributions are computed by the plan's actuary based on the number of plan participants, the participants' ages and salaries, the terms and conditions of the plan, the actuarial cost method, and the actuarial assumptions for the group. The amount of the employer's contribution cannot be allocated to specific individuals with any accuracy or relevance. To illustrate, the employer may announce that a contribution has been made to fund the pension plan in an amount equal to more than 6 percent of each employee's pay. In financing the plan, however, the fund may require as much as 25 percent of pay for an older, highly paid employee and as little as 2 percent of pay for a younger, low-paid employee.

§ 15.5   —Employee and Employer Contributions

It is useless to ask the employer for the amount of employer contributions to a defined benefit pension plan in total, or the amount contributed for any one plan participant. Even if the information is available, it cannot help to determine the value of the pension for marital property purposes, nor for eventual deferred distribution under a qualified domestic relations order (QDRO). It is helpful, however, to ask for the person's employee contributions, if any, to see if it is one of the rare cases where the sum of contributions exceeds the computed pension value.

Not every pension plan has employee contributions. When employee contributions are allowed by the plan, they may be mandatory or voluntary. Some plans pay interest on the employee contributions. There are plans that credit interest but pay it only under certain circumstances. At retirement, the amount of the individual's employee contributions serves as a guarantee of minimum benefit payments, especially in the event the individual dies shortly after retirement.

§ 15.6   —No Contributions

It is possible that, in one or more years, no contributions were made to a defined benefit pension plan, either by the employer or by the employee. This may occur in a plan that has no employee contributions at all or in a year when the plan is overfunded. If the plan's assets equal or exceed the total of its actuarial liabilities for pensions, then no employer contribution is made. Alternatively, the plan may have a technical credit balance that precludes an employer contribution for that year.

Whether or not any contributions were made, a pension benefit for each participant exists under the terms of the plan. The pension benefit has a present value, and the benefit may be awarded by a QDRO, regardless of any contributions.

Whenever a defined benefit pension plan is involved in a divorce case, look to the benefits and their values before considering contributions. Contributions play a subsidiary role and may be of some minor interest, but are not determinative of the value of a spouse's property as an asset subject to division.

§ 15.7   Annuity Contracts

One way to provide promised benefits from any type of plan is for the plan administrator or the trustees to purchase an annuity contract from an insurance company. The plan may hold the contract as an asset, or the contract may be distributed to the recipient. When benefits come due, the insurance company makes payments in accordance with the provisions of the annuity contract. Note that the annuity contract is not the plan itself, and the provisions of the contract may be expected to deal with payment procedures, not with plan terms and conditions.

A common trust agreement concerning the assets of a plan of any kind will authorize the plan trustees to purchase an annuity contract. If the cost of the contract is large, the trustees may prefer to pay the benefits periodically out of the trust fund as they come due, instead of sending one large payment to an insurance company when the participant retires (or dies).

Some plans are structured to purchase annuities, regardless of the amount (unless it is very small, in which case a cash lump sum would be paid to the recipient). For example, a prototype plan may be sponsored and established by an insurance company for a number of employers. The sponsoring insurance company would sell annuity contracts to the plans. A large insurance company should be able to accommodate almost any form of annuity payout called for by the plan or elected by the retiree.

Serving a QDRO on an annuity contract often requires extra investigation and discovery. If the contract is owned by the plan, the QDRO will be addressed to the plan as usual. If the contract has been distributed to the individual, the QDRO should be served on the insurance company, under the theory that it is a continuation of the mechanism of a qualified plan.

Annuity contracts are also used to settle cases of personal injury and wrongful death, and as a means of providing a structured settlement.

Care must be taken by the responsible parties in selecting the insurance company from which the annuity is to be purchased. The paying party should be named as the ultimate guarantor to be responsible for payments due if the insurance company should fail.

In 1991 Executive Life, an insurance company, ran into financial difficulties, causing contracted payments to be reduced and eventually stopped. A party had been promised contractual payments as a result of winning a lawsuit in Colorado, but the payments stopped when the insurance company failed. The plaintiff sued the defendant in the original case, maintaining that the defendant had the obligation to provide the payments if the annuity contract defaulted, which it did.

In *Roemmich v. Lutheran Hospitals*, 934 P.2d 873 (Colo. App. Ct. 1996), a local Colorado court ruled against the plaintiff, as did the Colorado Court of Appeals. The court interpreted the settlement between the original plaintiff and the defendant as contract that required the defendant to purchase an annuity from an insurance company in a certain amount with certain payment conditions. The defendant did so. By complying with its contractual obligation under the settlement, the defendant had no other duty. The fact that the insurance company later failed to meet its contracted payments under the annuity contract hurt the plaintiff, but was without recourse to the defendant.

A dissenting opinion held that the deal required the original defendant to purchase an annuity contract to make the agreed payments. In other words, it was a two-part obligation: first, to purchase an annuity contract and, second, to ensure the contract made the payments. When the insurance company that issued the annuity contract failed to make the payments, the defendant, Lutheran Hospitals, was shown to have failed to meet its agreement.

Whenever an insurance annuity contract is involved in any matter, the issuing company must be selected with care, and the parties must consider and decide whether there should be an underlying responsibility for payments in the event of a contract default by the insurance company.

CHAPTER 16

SOCIAL SECURITY

§ 16.1   Introduction

The normal Social Security benefit for a covered individual is computed by a complex formula using pay history, past inflation adjustments, and years and months worked in employment covered by Social Security. After the monthly Social Security benefit begins, it is increased annually in accordance with the cost of living, subject to change by federal law from time to time.

The individual's pay history is measured to age 65, or later if the individual continues in coverage past age 62. The service period used to compute the individual's normal Social Security benefit is measured from a starting point—the time coverage begins—to age 62. Then five years are subtracted from the total.

The starting point is the later of the year 1950 or one year after the year in which the individual attains age 21.

Example: Susan, born in 1957, will attain age 62 in 2019. If Susan entered the work force and came under Social Security coverage in 1978 at age 21, her starting point is 1979 (one year after attaining age 21). At age 62, Susan's covered service would total 40 years $(62-22)$. After subtraction of five years from the total number of years covered, the measured time is 35 years $(40-5)$.

Any person covered by Social Security who has fewer than 35 years of covered service receives a Social Security benefit smaller than the benefit that would be received if the person's covered service attained the 35-year mark.

Example: Bob, born in 1957, entered the work force and came under Social Security coverage in 1987, at age 30. Time coverage for Bob began in 1979, one

139

year after he reached age 21. At age 62 in 2019, Bob's covered service would total 32 years (62 − 30), three years short of the normal 35 years. In this example, the Social Security benefit is smaller than what it would be after 35 years by the ratio of 32 to 35, or 0.914. Thus, the Social Security benefit payable to Bob would be about 8.5 percent less than the benefit payable after 35 years.

§ 16.2   Social Security Retirement Age

Full Social Security monthly annuity benefits are payable when the covered individual attains Social Security Retirement Age (SSRA). The SSRA varies by year of birth and is defined as the attainment of a specific number of years and months of age. The date of attainment of SSRA has been tabulated by the Social Security Administration (see Table 16–1). For the purpose of determining a person's SSRA, the date of birth is assumed to be January 2 of the year of birth. If the date of birth falls on the first day of a month, the prior month is used.

Table 16–1

Social Security Retirement Age

Year of Birth	SSRA Year/Month	Date of SSRA Attainment
1937 or earlier	65/0	N/A
1938	65/2	Mar. 1, 2003
1939	65/4	May 1, 2004
1940	65/6	July 1, 2005
1941	65/8	Sept. 1, 2006
1942	65/10	Nov. 1, 2007
1943–1954	66/0	Jan. 1, 2009–2020
1955	66/2	Mar. 1, 2021
1956	66/4	May 1, 2022
1957	66/6	July 1, 2023
1958	66/8	Sept. 1, 2024
1959	66/10	Nov. 1, 2025
1960 and after	67/0	Jan. 1, 2027

§ 16.3   Early Social Security Retirement

Reduced Social Security monthly annuity benefits are available between age 62 and the person's SSRA. Table 6–2 shows the Social Security Administration's reduction percentages for benefit commencement at age 62. The reduction factor is $\frac{5}{9}$ of one percent per month for the first 36 months that benefit commencement occurs before the person's Social Security retirement age, and $\frac{5}{12}$ of one percent for each additional month before the person's SSRA.

Table 16-2

Social Security Retirement Benefit at Age 62

Year of Birth	SSRA Year/Month	Percentage of Full Benefit
1937 or earlier	65/0	80.0 %
1938	65/2	79.2
1939	65/4	78.3
1940	65/6	77.5
1941	65/8	76.7
1942	65/10	75.8
1943–1954	66/0	75.0
1955	66/2	74.2
1956	66/4	73.3
1957	66/6	72.5
1958	66/8	71.7
1959	66/10	70.8
1960 and after	67/0	70.0

§ 16.4   Social Security as a Surrogate

Are pension benefits for persons not covered by Social Security a substitute for Social Security benefits? This is a controversial issue. Several courts at both state and federal levels have ruled that Social Security benefits are not marital property and cannot be considered for any reason at all in equitable distribution. However, the issue continues to be raised and may yet be decided differently.

Would federal pensions be smaller if federal employees were covered by Social Security? The general answer is yes. The reasoning is based on the fact that there are two federal retirement programs, the Civil Service Retirement System (CSRS), whose members are not covered by Social Security, and the Federal Employees Retirement System (FERS), whose members are so covered. CSRS members have larger pensions than do FERS members; however, FERS members also have a thrift plan. Therefore, it might be argued that a CSRS member's pension in some measure compensates for the lack of Social Security benefits. On the other hand, although CSRS requires contributions from its members, the members do not pay Social Security taxes. In private employment, of course, both the employer and the employee pay Social Security taxes.

Social Security benefits are not affected by any sums received in divorce settlements unless and until the individual's separate total income in any year exceeds that allowed by Social Security regulations, depending on age. It is presumed that application for Social Security benefits is not made before age 62, at which time income is measured. Social Security benefits may be decreased or reduced to zero if other income is too high. Consequently, the amount of a benefit is open to assumption.

How does an actuary adjust the valuation of a CSRS pension to compensate for the lack of Social Security in that case? The procedure is as follows:

1. Determine an estimated Social Security benefit at age 65, as if the person were always covered by Social Security, using as much pay history as is available.
2. Compute the portion of the estimated Social Security benefit that is attributable to the time period of marital pension service.
3. Calculate the present value of the pension benefit as usual (actuarially).
4. Subtract the Social Security present value from the otherwise calculated present value of the marital portion of the non-Social Security pension.

The result is a net pension benefit value, after reduction for a hypothetical Social Security benefit.

§ 16.5   Spousal Social Security Benefits

The divorced spouse of a retired (or disabled) Social Security covered worker is entitled under certain conditions to receive a monthly Social Security annuity benefit. The marriage must have lasted at least ten years. If so, and if the covered employee-spouse had sufficient Social Security coverage, the divorced spouse is guaranteed a benefit as early as age 62, upon proper application. The divorced spouse's benefit does not diminish the employee's Social Security benefit.

Social Security spousal rights cannot be awarded in a divorce settlement or bargained or adjudicated away, as stipulated by the Social Security Act. Counsel or the court may take notice of future Social Security spousal benefit, but in most cases it will not enter into calculations or the distribution of marital assets.

§ 16.6   Social Security in the Pension Formula

The benefit formula in a defined benefit pension plan is permitted under ERISA and by IRS regulations to take into account some of the employee's Social Security coverage. This practice is largely obsolete, but some plans still contain a reference to Social Security in the pension benefit formula.

Prior efforts had been made to recognize that part of a person's retirement package would include Social Security benefits, and that such benefits were based on employee and employer taxes on pay up to a maximum wage base each calendar year. A pension benefit formula could be split into two parts, with different percentages applying to compensation above and below the wage base. This approach, called "Social Security integration," is now strictly limited by federal law. IRS regulations regard it as "permitted disparity."

§ 16.6 SOCIAL SECURITY IN THE PENSION FORMULA

Another form of this approach, currently permitted, is a benefit formula that offsets a portion (usually less than 50 percent) of an estimated Social Security monthly benefit. It does not affect the employee's actual Social Security benefit, but uses it as part of the plan benefit calculation. Upon retirement, the employee is entitled to have this portion of the plan benefit formula recomputed, based on the actual Social Security benefit, as opposed to the estimated figure used by the plan during all of the years of participation. When a plan contains this offset feature, it adds a layer of complexity to benefit estimates.

CHAPTER 17

PENSION COURT ORDERS

§ 17.1   Introduction

Prior to the enactment of the Retirement Equity Act of 1984 (REA), the Employee Retirement Income Security Act of 1974 (ERISA) prohibited the attachment of pension benefits in a divorce action. The REA provided a mechanism for the attachment of all or a part of a spouse's ERISA pension benefits as part of a divorce decree or settlement. That mechanism is a court order known as a *qualified domestic relations order* (QDRO). Other types of court orders, known by different names and acronyms, are used to attach a spouse's non-ERISA plan benefits.

This chapter reviews the basic facts about pension court orders that counsel may use for quick reference or to answer a client's questions.

§ 17.2   DROs and QDROs

When one party in a divorce is covered by a pension or profit sharing plan, a court order is the standard tool for awarding plan benefits to the other party. Typically, counsel for the nonemployee-spouse prepares a draft order—which becomes a domestic relations order (DRO) when it is signed by a court of competent jurisdiction under the REA—and forwards it to the employee-spouse's plan administrator for determination that it complies with federal law and the terms of the plan.

The plan administrator may review and revise a draft order as many times as needed to meet the plan's requirements. The plan administrator may decline to comment on an unsigned draft order or may give low priority to its review, but will give priority consideration to a DRO. If changes are made to a DRO, the document must be resubmitted to the court for signature.

Federal law requires that a plan administrator determine whether a DRO is qualified within a ''reasonable'' time. If the DRO is submitted when the pension benefit is in pay status or is about to be paid, the plan must make the determination within 18 months and must suspend benefit payments until the matter is settled. Upon receipt of a draft order that is not signed by a court, a plan may freeze payments, but it is not required to do so. If a plan administrator is unwilling or unable to rule on a DRO within a reasonable time, counsel for the nonemployee-spouse may petition the court for relief. Such petition may result in findings of contempt against the employee-spouse, the employer, or the plan administrator. In addition, counsel may give consideration to enjoining the employer and/or the plan administrator as parties to the case.

Upon approval by the plan administrator, the DRO becomes a QDRO. The plan administrator sets forth the finding in a memo or letter, or on a form (there is no prescribed format), addressed to the plan trustee. The acknowledgment of the plan administrator that a DRO is qualified is an action separate and distinct from the issuance of a court order. In routine cases, a QDRO is issued following a property settlement in equitable distribution agreed to by the parties to the divorce.

A plan trustee must follow the plan administrator's instructions with respect to the payment of benefits pursuant to a QDRO. For example, if a QDRO calls for annuity payments to the *alternate payee* (technical designation of the nonemployee-spouse named in the QDRO), the plan administrator so instructs the plan trustee, who must start making the annuity payments. If the alternate payee named in the QDRO cannot be located, the plan must hold a reserve until such time as the alternate payee is located or a valid claim is made. The plan is not allowed to charge a direct fee for administering the QDRO. However, there may be an indirect cost to the alternate payee by way of an actuarial adjustment to recognize age, sex, and the form of benefit.

In theory, a QDRO could order that benefits awarded to the alternate payee cease upon that person's remarriage or cohabitation with a third party. A plan may well reject such a provision, however, as being outside the range of plan terms or because such provision is difficult to enforce.

If the plan administrator determines a DRO is not qualified, the court of competence has the power to bypass the plan administrator and declare the DRO qualified. In the case of a direct court order, the plan trustee would follow the court's instructions. A court, in theory, could consider the facts and circumstances and overrule the plan administrator, but that would be an extremely rare occurrence.

§ 17.3 Types of Plans Subject to Pension Court Orders

Every ERISA pension plan is subject to a QDRO, even when there is no mention of QDROs in the plan materials. The major types of ERISA plans are:

- Defined benefit pension plans
- Defined contribution plans (e.g., profit sharing, thrift, and savings plans; 401(k) plans of businesses, professional partnerships, and sole proprietors; money purchase plans; target plans; Keogh plans; employee stock ownership plans (ESOPs); TIAA-CREF plans); and
- Special plans (e.g., deferred compensation plans, tax-sheltered annuities, 403(b) plans, and retirement plans of 501(c)(3) organizations).

Certain non-ERISA plans, such as plans covering military personnel and civilian employees of the federal government, will comply with pension court orders similar in effect to the QDRO. Other non-ERISA plans, such as nonqualified deferred compensation plans and individual retirement accounts (IRAs), may or may not accept pension court orders, depending on their structure, management, and purpose. Because IRAs are not covered by either ERISA or the REA, their inclusion as marital property for equitable distribution in divorce technically does not require a QDRO. Nevertheless, many IRA fiduciaries request a court order before they will release funds to an account owner's former spouse as part of a divorce settlement.

Three types of pension plans for civilian employees of the federal government accept and comply with a court order similar in effect to a QDRO in a divorce proceeding. They are:

1. The Civil Service Retirement System (CSRS), a generous defined benefit pension that covers federal workers whose employment started before January 1, 1983.
2. The Federal Employees Retirement System (FERS), a defined benefit pension benefit plan that covers federal workers whose employment started on or after January 1, 1983.
3. The Thrift Savings Plan (TSP), a defined contribution plan with individual accounts for federal workers who are covered by FERS.

A pension court order served on a CSRS or FERS member is called a "court order acceptable for processing" (COAP). Members of FERS who participate voluntarily in the federal government's TSP may be served with a pension court order called a "retirement benefits court order" (RBCO). Upon approval of a RBCO, the TSP will pay the distribution immediately to the alternate payee, who may elect to have it transferred to his or her IRA.

Other non-ERISA plans include retirement plans for active or reserve military personnel, National Guard and Coast Guard members, civilian employees of federal, state, county, and local governments, as well as certain deferred compensation plans for select groups of executives (i.e., top-hat plans) and special pension plans for partners of law firms or other professionals.

§ 17.4   Information for Preparing a Pension Court Order

In preparing a pension court order in a divorce matter, counsel needs to know the employee-spouse's participant category—that is, whether the employee-spouse is

- Actively working and earning pension credits during current service, with full, partial, or no vesting at present;
- Terminated, with vested rights to a deferred benefit;
- Currently non-active (whether laid off, on leave of absence, or on temporary disability leave) but is expected to return to work; or
- Retired, having received a lump-sum cash-out, or currently receiving periodic pension payments.

In addition, counsel needs information about the employee-spouse's plan, such as the type of plan, whether the plan is subject to ERISA, and the identity of the plan sponsor, plan administrator, and any actuarial or administrative consulting firm that provides services to the plan.

To obtain the necessary information for drafting the draft order, counsel may request from the plan sponsor a copy of the summary plan description, the participant's benefits or account statements, and the formal plan document.

§ 17.5   Considerations in Drafting a QDRO

There are a number of items that merit consideration in process of drafting a QDRO. The standard considerations are discussed below.

Remarriage.   In theory, a QDRO can provide that benefits awarded to a former spouse cease upon that person's remarriage or cohabitation with a third party. The plan administrator, however, may well reject such a provision as being outside the range of plan terms or because such provision is difficult to enforce. The terms of an antenuptial agreement, if one exists, generally have no effect on the QDRO, because it was signed before the parties became spouses.

Taxes.   With certain exceptions, distributions of plan benefits are taxable to the recipient. If the employee-spouse made after-tax contributions to the plan that constitute a favorable tax basis, the QDRO may allocate the favorable tax basis as part of the pension award.

It is important to note that the 10 percent federal excise penalty tax on routine lump-sum distributions from a pension plan to a recipient under age $59\frac{1}{2}$ does not apply to distributions made to a former spouse pursuant to a QDRO, whether or not the distributions are transferred or rolled over into an IRA and regardless of the age of either party.

A lump-sum distribution is subject, however, to 20 percent withholding for personal federal income tax. Withholding applies even if the payment is rolled over into an IRA within 60 days of receipt. The 20 percent withholding does not apply only if the payments to a former spouse pursuant to a QDRO are transferred directly from the plan into an IRA without passing through the hands of the former spouse. For this reason, the pension court should refer to the payment as a "transfer" rather than a "rollover."

When payments pursuant to a QDRO are placed in a former spouse's IRA, they become subject thereafter to the tax rules governing IRAs. If payments under a QDRO are made to the employee's dependent child rather than the former spouse, the employee is taxed on the amounts paid.

A QDRO may allocate contributions or investments between the employee and the employee's former spouse, but it cannot change tax law. Nor should a QDRO attempt to direct a plan to use a specific tax form or comply with a specific reporting requirement. Given the changing nature of tax laws and IRS reporting forms, a plan is within its rights to ignore any such directions.

Loans.   If the participant spouse had a loan from the plan before the divorce, the loan is not considered a taxable distribution unless the participant fails to repay it.

A QDRO cannot order a participant to take a loan, but it may grant loan privileges to the alternate payee if the participant's plan will allow it. A QDRO cannot order a participant to request a hardship withdrawal, but it may make such withdrawal available to the alternate payee. If the plan allows a hardship withdrawal, and if it is clearly specified that the withdrawal is the result of a QDRO, the early payment penalty would not apply.

A defined contribution plan may allow an actively working participant to elect to receive a lump-sum cash payment as a hardship withdrawal. Such a distribution is fully taxable and, if the participant is under age $59\frac{1}{2}$, is subject also to the early payment penalty. The distribution cannot be rolled over into an IRA, because it is intended to alleviate an immediate and pressing financial need. A QDRO cannot require a participant to apply for a hardship withdrawal or order a plan to make a hardship payment.

Liens.   In Letter Ruling 9234014 (May 21, 1992), the Internal Revenue Service (IRS) stated that, under Internal Revenue Code Section 414(p) regarding domestic relations orders, an ERISA plan is permitted to accept a lien on a participant's benefits, and that a lien placed on a participant's interest in his or her retirement plan is not a prohibited alienation when made pursuant to a QDRO. According to the ruling, the creation of a security interest in a qualified plan by means of a QDRO constitutes an assignment permitted by Code Section 401(a)(13)(B).

Withdrawals.   The QDRO should preclude any distributions from the plan, such as new loans to the participant or hardship withdrawals that could impair the alternate payee's awarded amount. Generally, a withdrawal of employee contributions results in a smaller pension benefit or even a forfeiture of the entire pension benefit. It may be possible for the QDRO to prohibit the employee-spouse from withdrawing any employee contributions to avoid dissipation of marital assets.

149

Bankruptcy. The impact of personal bankruptcy on a QDRO is uncertain. If the QDRO is validated as an obligation of the plan and is payable from plan assets, it would not be affected by the employee's filing for bankruptcy. However, if the QDRO is found by the bankruptcy court to be a debt of the employee, the bankruptcy court may block the payment of the QDRO proceeds.

Retirement. Upon retirement, a married participant in an ERISA defined benefit pension plan must receive pension benefits in the form of a joint and survivor (J&S) annuity unless both spouses waived the J&S annuity in favor of either a simple life annuity or another optional form available under the plan. Without a properly executed waiver, the requirement for a J&S pension after retirement continues, even if the parties are legally separated or their divorce is pending. Even after the parties are divorced, a QDRO may require the participant to elect J&S benefits at retirement.

If divorce occurs after the participant's retirement, with a J&S pension in pay status, a QDRO may be used to award all or part of the pension to the alternate payee. Of course, if the participant had elected to a lump-sum distribution at retirement, there would be nothing left to be awarded by a QDRO. However, a plan may purchase an annuity contract from an insurance company for or on behalf of a retired employee. If so, counsel should investigate whether that annuity may be the subject of a QDRO.

When counsel is preparing a DRO affecting a retiree, it is extremely important to ascertain the details of the retirement benefits. If the benefits are in the form of a J&S annuity, counsel should find out from the plan whether the form of the annuity can be changed and, if so, what the actuarial consequences will be. (A plan may not be willing to perform the actuarial exercise of converting an existing J&S pension to a straight life pension.) In addition, counsel should find out whether the pension benefit is a fixed amount or whether it is subject to change at a stated age or upon the occurrence of a future event. For example, a participant who retires early may receive pension benefits in the form of a "bridge" or temporary payment until he or she becomes eligible for Social Security. Then as the plan pension gets smaller, the participant's total pension plus Social Security payments will approximate the amount of the temporary pension before Social Security payments began.

Early Retirement. Early retirement should not be confused with a floating or variable normal retirement age (NRA). A plan may pay full pension benefits to a participant upon reaching age 65 with 5 years of service, or age 60 with 10 years of service, or age 55 with 20 years of service. Retirement before age 65 is not necessarily early retirement.

An ERISA plan is not required to make provision for early retirement. If a plan does provide for early retirement, it will state the requisite conditions (e.g., eligibility upon attaining age 55 and completion of 10 years of service). For purposes of a QDRO, whether or not the plan provides for early retirement, the earliest date at which payment of benefits may commence to an alternate payee is the earlier of:

(1) The earliest date under the plan that a benefit is payable to the participant, or
(2) The later of
  (a) The date the participant reaches age 50 or
  (b) The date the participant could start receiving benefits if he had separated from service.

A profit-sharing plan may permit distributions to start at any time after the funds have been in the participant's account for at least two years. This two-year provision may be interpreted as a sufficient condition to fulfill an early payment requirement of a QDRO.

A defined contribution plan usually does not reduce benefits for early retirement if the benefit is payable as a lump sum upon retirement. A defined benefit plan may reduce pension amounts for early retirement in one of two ways: The first method, *actuarial reduction*, results in a smaller dollar amount of monthly benefit. The smaller benefit is mathematically equivalent to the full benefit because it is payable sooner and for a longer time. If the plan provides for an actuarial reduction, it must set forth the mortality table and interest rate to be used or attach a table of early retirement factors.

The second method, *subsidized early retirement*, provides early retirement benefits on a reduced basis, but the reduction is less than the true actuarial equivalent. A plan that provides for subsidized early retirement must set forth the basis of its reduction (e.g., the pension is reduced by one-half of one percent per month, for each month preceding normal retirement age, a reduction of 6 percent per year early). If a plan provides fully subsidized early retirement benefit at certain ages, the reduction in benefits is only nominal. For example, a plan's NRA may be age 65, but reduced benefits may be payable to retirees at age 62, 63, or 64. There may be a different early retirement adjustment for a plan participant who terminated service with a deferred vested pension. If such person were to elect early commencement of benefits, the reduction in benefits may be more than it would be for an actively employed participant of the same age.

When an alternate payee's pension benefits commence early, the early retirement reduction required by a defined benefit plan applies only to the alternate payee's benefits; the participant's benefits are not affected by either the manner or the timing of the alternate payee's benefit payments.

A QDRO may allow the alternate payee to elect, or be required to, receive benefits when the employee-spouse attains eligibility for early retirement, whether or not the employee actually retires. The following plans, however, will not pay benefits to an alternate payee when the participant becomes eligible for early retirement unless the participant actually retires:

- CSRS
- FERS
- Postal workers pension plan
- Military personnel (active duty and reserves) retirement plan
- Railroad workers retirement plan
- Retirement plans for employees of city, state, or other governmental unit

A pension plan of a small business or professional corporation may allow amendment of plan terms for the special purpose of early distribution of benefits to an employee's former spouse pursuant to a QDRO.

A QDRO should give special care to early retirement incentives or enhancements. If early retirement benefits begin to flow simultaneously to the employee and the alternate payee, and if such benefits are increased under a special plan, the QDRO may allow the alternate payee to share in the increase. A QDRO may allow the alternate payee to begin receiving benefits early, before the employee retires. If, later, the plan should announce a special program that increases early out benefits, and the employee does retire, this occurrence would have been anticipated by a provision in the QDRO calling for the alternate payee's early benefit payments to be recomputed to share in the employee's special early retirement increase.

Death Benefits.   If the employee-spouse dies after the divorce is final but before the DRO is formally approved, the alternate payee is potentially exposed to a loss of benefits. For this reason, existing plan beneficiary forms are maintained in force while a DRO is pending. In addition, the employee-spouse can be legally bound by the divorce decree or property settlement agreement not to change his or her beneficiary designation while the DRO is being processed.

The employee-spouse's death could occur before or after retirement. The plan may make a distinction between "survivorship benefits" and "death benefits," depending on when death occurs, but the terms are otherwise synonymous. If death occurs while the employee is actively working (or terminated with a deferred vested benefit), a death benefit is generally paid to the employee's named beneficiary. If death occurs after retirement, there may not be any death benefit unless the plan provides one automatically or the retiree opted to provide one.

All defined benefit pension plans and defined contribution plans subject to ERISA provide for a pre-retirement death benefit, payable to the spouse, if the participant should die while in active service. The standard pre-retirement death benefit in a *defined benefit pension plan* is known as a qualified pre-retirement survivor annuity (QPSA). The amount is determined on the basis of a 50-percent J&S annuity, based on the participant's accrued pension benefit under the plan as of the day before the date of death. The standard pre-retirement death benefit found in most *defined contribution plans* is the entire amount in the participant's account balance, less any outstanding loans.

If divorce occurs after the participant's retirement, when monthly pension benefits are in pay status, a QDRO may award all or part of the retiree's pension and all or part or none of any survivorship or death benefits to the former spouse. However, if the former spouse was awarded the total available death benefit upon divorce and the retiree subsequently remarried, there would be no survivorship benefits for the new spouse. This is a loophole in the federal pension laws, which are supposed to provide protection for spouses.

When a divorce is pending, it is advisable to prepare a pension court order and have it approved early in the proceedings so that the QDRO is ready to implement the day the divorce becomes final. While the pension court order is under review, it is important to make sure that the participant spouse does not change his or her beneficiary designation to impair the alternate payee's potential interest, because if the participant should die before the QDRO is fully and formally approved, the alternate payee would have no claim.

If the alternate payee should die before the QDRO is fully and formally approved, the QDRO would become null and no benefits would be paid to the alternate payee or any potential beneficiaries he or she may have named. If the alternate payee should die after the QDRO is properly in effect, his or her beneficiary or estate would receive the awarded portion of the participant's account. Once the award is fully distributed in accordance with the QDRO, the alternate payee's death has no effect on the plan.

Whether a death benefit is available after the participant has retired from a *defined contribution plan* depends on the form of payout elected at retirement. If the account was paid out in full or rolled over into an IRA, of course there would be no death benefit available from the plan. If the participant had elected payment in the form of an annuity, however, a survivor benefit may be attached to the annuity.

Once the divorce is final, the former spouse has no rights if the participant dies before the QDRO is fully and formally approved. A QDRO may change the amount of the death benefit payable to the former spouse. That amount may be less than the standard pre-retirement death benefit that the plan provides for an employee's spouse; it cannot be more, because a QDRO is not allowed to award a benefit that is not available under the plan.

If the former spouse dies *before* the QDRO is in place, the order is effectively vacated and no benefits will be paid to the former spouse's estate or any beneficiary thereof. If the former spouse dies *after* the QDRO is fully and formally approved but *before* benefits become due and payable from the plan, there is a potential problem. In the simplest case, assuming neither the employee nor the former spouse had yet attained eligibility for early retirement, the QDRO would become null and no benefits would be paid to the former spouse's estate or any beneficiary thereof. In a more complicated case, assuming the QDRO awarded the former spouse a separate, independent, lifetime pension benefit, the award may be considered to survive the death of the former spouse and the benefits would be conveyed to a named beneficiary or to the former spouse's estate. The actuarial problem that arises is that the amount of the pension benefit awarded by the QDRO depends on the type and form of annuity, taking into account the sex and age of the recipient.

If the former spouse dies after QDRO-awarded benefit payments begin, his or her beneficiary or estate would receive benefits from the plan only if an approved form of annuity was elected before pension benefits began. Whether any death benefit is available after the participant has retired from a *defined benefit pension plan* depends on the form of payout elected at retirement. If the participant elected a single-life annuity, there is by definition no post-retirement death or survivor benefit. No death benefit would be available from the plan unless the participant had elected an annuity form of payout with a survivor benefit attached to the annuity.

The possibility of ''double dipping'' may arise with respect to the death benefit after divorce. For example, the divorce court may have awarded the former spouse a portion of the participant's account, and this portion may have been put into a separate account in the plan or paid in cash, or transferred to an IRA for the former spouse. If the QDRO names the former spouse as the beneficiary of the death benefit, the former spouse would receive the death benefit paid from the plan at the participant's death. This would give the former spouse both a lifetime pension and a death benefit.

Plan Amendment or Termination. The possibility that the pension plan may be amended or terminated with cessation or reduction in benefits should be considered in drafting the court order. Reduction in benefits may affect only the employee. Alternatively, both the employee and the former spouse could share proportionately in any adjustments.

All defined contribution plans maintain individual accounts, and sometimes subaccounts, for each participant. A QDRO served on a participant in a defined contribution plan should indicate the accounts involved and award a pro rata share across all accounts equally. If the participant had some right of control over the investment or allocation of his or her accounts, the QDRO should seek the same right for the alternate payee. A defined contribution plan may allow an immediate distribution to an alternate payee by QDRO or it may establish and maintain a separate account for the alternate payee. Counsel should inquire into the plan's policies in this regard before submitting the court order for review.

In preparing a pension court order to be served on a defined benefit pension plan, counsel should inquire whether the participant's account contains any employee contributions. If such contributions were made, the QDRO should specify whether all or part of the employee's contributions are to be included in the award to the alternate payee.

Plan Funding. The funding status of a plan is usually of little or no concern in drafting a QDRO. In plans covered by the Pension Benefit Guaranty Corporation (PBGC), benefits are protected up to certain dollar limits announced each year by the PBGC. If the plan is a pension plan covering only one person, or very few employees, in a business or professional corporation and the plan is overfunded (i.e., there is a surplus of plan assets), the possibility of allocation or distribution of excess benefit amounts should be considered in drafting a QDRO.

§ 17.6   Standardized QDROs—Pros and Cons

As the use of QDROs in the settlement of pension property in divorces becomes more common, many employers are making available a standard QDRO form customized for their pension plans. A divorce attorney's client, whose employer has a standard QDRO form, would be justified in wanting to know why the standard form should not be used, and why a fee should be paid to the attorney or an outside pension consultant to produce a document that is made available for free. The client's request seems even more reasonable when the employer's standard QDRO form is simple and easy to understand.

Using the employer's standard QDRO form offers certain advantages. There is the hope (if not the assurance) that the plan will approve the standard QDRO more quickly than a pension court order drafted specifically for the client. On the employer's standard QDRO form, at the very least the name of the plan will be correct. (Because most corporate employers maintain more than one plan, the plan considered in the divorce settlement should be clearly identified.) Furthermore, an employer does not charge a fee for making its standard QDRO form available to an employee.

The very simplicity of a standardized QDRO form can cause problems and create controversy at a later stage. The form QDRO is designed for the employer's convenience and administrative ease. It may be a comprehensive standard order form, designed to be used on either a defined benefit pension plan or a defined contribution plan. Its flexibility, however, makes it more difficult for counsel and the client to read through all the options and select the best features for the particular case. If the alternate payee is to be awarded payments from more than one plan, a separate pension court order should be prepared for each plan so as to avoid confusion.

The text of a pension court order should not use the terms "plaintiff," "defendant," or "respondent." Rather, all references in the court order to the divorcing couple should be to the "participant" and the "alternate payee"—not husband and wife or plaintiff and respondent—except in the initial identification of the parties. The introduction to a standard court order, therefore, may state: "The parties hereto were formerly husband and wife, having been divorced on [date], 19XX, by this Court."

When the divorce decree is pending, even the wording of the introduction to the court order may be difficult because it is uncertain whether the final decree will be handed down on the day the judge signs the QDRO or possibly delayed until the pension court order is formally approved by the employer, and whether the judge who signs the pension order will be the one who signs the divorce decree.

A standard court order for a defined benefit pension plan might not offer the alternate payee certain choices because the employer may have designed the form to allow the least onerous administrative procedures, omitting to mention potential alternatives and additions that the employer's plan could provide if the court order mentioned them. For example, a standard court order may allow for a percentage of the employee's pension but not for a fixed dollar amount. If it does allow for a fixed dollar amount, does it account for any possible changes to the figure if there should be an early retirement of the employee or if the alternate payee elects early commencement of her awarded benefit?

A pension court order may allow for the computation of an award based on the benefit as of a date certain, such as the date of divorce. But what if the settlement is based on the benefit that will have been earned at retirement, sometime in the future? Conversely, the order may address the benefit at retirement without a provision to deal with the accrued benefit at some other point in time.

A standard order made available by an employer may be satisfactory for dealing with its plan and its various benefits, but may have neglected to consider that in a divorce it is possible that not all of the pension in question is marital property. The use of a coverture fraction, the time rule, or the subtraction method may well not have been considered or even understood by the employer in preparing a standardized draft pension order. If the employee had earned pension benefit credits before the date of marriage, those credits could be excluded by the divorce settlement, but there has to be a way to do so in the QDRO.

The employer's form may not make clear what would happen in any one of the following circumstances:

1. The employee dies while in active employment before becoming eligible for early retirement.

2. The employee dies while in active employment after becoming eligible for early retirement.

3. The alternate payee dies while the employee is in active employment before becoming eligible for early retirement.

4. The alternate payee dies while the employee is in active employment after becoming eligible for early retirement.

5. The alternate payee dies while the employee is in active employment after becoming eligible for early retirement, and after benefits have started to the alternate payee under his or her early retirement payment election.

6. The employee dies after retirement, survived by the alternate payee.

7. The alternate payee dies after the employee has retired, survived by the retired employee.

8. The employee dies after termination of employment but before deferred benefits have started.

9. The alternate payee dies after the employee's termination of employment but before deferred benefits have started.

A potential problem in an employer's standard QDRO form for a defined benefit pension plan concerns the J&S option. Typical plans offer the participant a choice of percentages for survivor benefits, the most common of which are 100 percent, $66\frac{2}{3}$ percent, 50 percent, and 25 percent. If the form provides a blank for the percentage to be filled in, the participant should carefully evaluate the benefit amounts available upon death and the consequences. It should also be ascertained by counsel whether the participant has the right to make an option selection, and whether the divorce settlement imposes any constraints on this right.

A plan is allowed to assess an actuarial charge on a form of pension benefit to maintain the plan in balance. The charge could be, for example, an adjustment to the dollar amount of a monthly pension for converting a straight life annuity to a J&S annuity. A plan can likewise impose reductions to a participant's pension benefit for early retirement. However, administrative costs are not allowed to be passed on to the participant or the alternate payee, nor can they be charged against the benefit amount. If the employer retains legal, accounting, or actuarial services for the review and administration of QDROs, such expenses must be borne by the employer. However, the employer is allowed to charge a reasonable cost for photocopies of plan documents requested by counsel.

An employer that offers a plan containing special provisions, such as employee loans, hardship withdrawals, or investment choices, may make an administration decision that such special features will not be made available to alternate payees by QDRO. In some cases, special features may be available to alternate payees, but are not mentioned in the employer's standard QDRO form because the employer wishes to discourage their use by alternate payees.

Some of the selections available in a boilerplate draft order may be overlapping or contradictory. The form may provide, by choice or inadvertently, for death benefit double-dipping—for example, it may allow the alternate payee to elect a separate, independent, lifetime pension, whether the employee is alive or dead, and elect a J&S annuity in another section of the form. This arrangement would provide a bonus to the subsequent spouse of an alternate payee upon the participant's death after retirement.

The standard form provided by an employer may not address various other contingencies, such as termination of the participant's employment due to disability. Does the employer's plan provide for a separate disability benefit? If so, would the alternate payee receive a portion of that disability benefit in lieu of the regular pension benefit? Could the alternate payee receive a regular pension benefit even if the participant is receiving a disability pension?

In plans that require or allow employee contributions, it is standard to allow a retiring employee to withdraw some or all of his or her accumulated employee contributions with interest. This withdrawal would, in a standard situation, result in a reduced monthly pension benefit. A QDRO should address the issue of whether the alternate payee's benefit would be affected by the combination of events.

Corporate defined benefit pension plans routinely contain a provision for small benefits that allow the plan to offer a retiring employee a lump-sum cash-out, provided the lump-sum amount is less than a certain sum (usually $3,500 to $5,000). If the value of the employee's pension is $3,500 or less, the plan has the option of paying the lump sum instead of the pension, and the employee cannot insist on a pension in monthly form. A QDRO should contain a provision indicating what the alternate payee's share of the lump-sum cash-out, but a standard QDRO form may not contain this provision simply because the provision was not thought of when the standard form was designed.

A defined benefit pension plan may provide for routine benefit increases payable to pensioners after retirement, with increases linked to inflation or a cost of living index. A boilerplate QDRO may not contain any reference to a cost-of-living adjustment (COLA), however, because the employer reserves the right to adjust or cancel such payments. A well-drafted QDRO will allow for the alternate payee to share in COLA benefits if the divorce settlement says so. The plan may not have such a feature in it at the time of the divorce, and it may never in the past have had such a feature. However, if the divorce settlement makes a contingent provision for a future COLA, the alternate payee will not share in it if there ever is one unless so stated in the QDRO.

An employer-provided QDRO form may be filled with references to various sections of the Internal Revenue Code, ERISA, the REA, and as many other regulations as the employer's advisers deem should be included. Such references should be included only when absolutely necessary to support a court order submitted as a DRO to be qualified. As the laws are amended from time to time, and new regulations, private letter rulings, and other advisories are issued, it would be impossible for a QDRO to always contain all the current, relevant references. Besides, the statutory references that a QDRO does contain may be too limiting because time passes and other appropriate references could come to bear on QDROs.

Participants in defined contribution plans, such as 401(k) plans, may have several subaccounts. The employer's standard form may provide for pro rata distribution across all accounts or it may allow various percentages or dollar amounts to be allocated to the alternate payee from specific named subaccounts. The award should be based on the divorce settlement in order for the parties to receive the appropriate tax treatment and share in reasonable investment opportunities.

An employer's standard form may have designated a particular tax treatment that is at variance with the desires of the parties or out of step with current tax law and IRS regulations or procedures. The advantage of drafting a QDRO specifically for a given client is that it can provide counsel to the parties in the divorce with options among the payout forms available under the plan (e.g., partial or full withdrawal of employee contributions with or without interest, lump-sum distributions, straight life or J&S annuities) or among other commonly available forms of payment. The alternate payee should be allowed the option of a full or partial transfer or rollover to an IRA or other qualified plan. If the QDRO is being drafted years before any payments will become due, flexibility should be built in with the opportunity to change optional elections or to defer the selection of an option or payout form until closer to the time of payment.

In the real world of marital dissolution the family practice attorney is well advised to treat an employer's standard form QDRO as merely the starting point. A QDRO best serves all parties by being comprehensive and carefully designed, taking into account all of the complexities and peculiarities of the particular divorce case and the plan in question.

§ 17.7   Checklist for Reviewing a Pension Court Order

The following checklist is designed for the use of employers when they are reviewing pension court orders served on their employees.

_____ 1. Name, address, and Social Security Number of the employee and the employee's spouse or other alternate payee. If the alternate is other than the spouse, the relationship.

_____ 2. Name of plan or sufficiently identified so the plan is clear.

_____ 3. Court identification: State, County, City, name of court, jurisdiction, and case number. Names and addresses of lawyers for each spouse.

_____ 4. Is the draft for review, or is it already a signed DRO?

_____ 5. What is the status of the divorce proceedings? Is the divorce final? Is the order for the purpose of alimony, child support, spousal support, or property settlement?

_____ 6. Is the benefit in question proper for the plan, that is, if it is a defined benefit pension plan does the order call for a dollar amount or percentage of a monthly pension as opposed to a lump sum?

_____ 7. Is the benefit identified as to an amount as of a specific date, such as the date of marital separation, or the date of filing of the divorce complaint, or the date that the order is approved, or some future date such as the date the employee is eligible for normal or early retirement?

_____ 8. Does the order mention early retirement subsidies or enhancements, cost-of-living increases, or future benefit adjustments?

_____ 9. If there is life insurance in the plan is it mentioned in the order?

_____ 10. If it is a defined benefit pension plan, is a pension awarded to the spouse to be payable during the lifetime of your employee, or is it a separate independent pension that is payable for the life of the spouse regardless of the employee's life?

_____ 11. Does the order propose any onerous tax reporting that the plan would not ordinarily do?

___ 12. Does the order mention loans, employee contributions, in-service withdrawals, disability or any other items that do not apply or that would require special calculations?

___ 13. Does the order attempt to have the plan stop benefits if the spouse remarries or cohabits with another? [If so, decline to accept this provision as being nearly impossible to monitor and enforce.]

§ 17.8 Sample Court Orders Involving Pensions

The eight sample court orders presented in this section are intended to give divorce attorneys and their clients an idea of the distinctions and nuances involved in preparing a properly drafted pension court order.

The material set forth below is not intended as legal advice, and counsel to the parties to a marital dissolution should not rely on it for the legal issues that arise under federal or state law. Nor should the language in these samples be reproduced verbatim for an actual case.

§ 17.8   SAMPLE COURT ORDERS INVOLVING PENSIONS

I. STANDARDIZED QDRO—ERISA DEFINED BENEFIT PENSION PLAN

The following standardized QDRO is for John Jones, an active participant in an ERISA defined benefit pension plan and the plaintiff in a divorce action.

DISTRICT COURT

John Jones,	)	
	)	
Plaintiff,	)	
	)	Case No. Dxxxxxx
vs.	)	
	)	
Jane Jones,	)	Dept No. Family
	)	
Defendant.	)	

QUALIFIED DOMESTIC RELATIONS ORDER

Hearing Date: N/A

Hearing Time: N/A

Based on the findings of the Court,

IT IS HEREBY ORDERED, ADJUDGED, AND DECREED:

1. PLAN. The Plan to which this Order applies is <u>The XYZ Corporation Defined Benefit Pension Plan</u> as it now exists or may from time to time be amended, or any successor plan thereto. The rights of Alternate Payee under this Order are protected in the event of plan amendments, a plan merger, or a change in the sponsor of the Plan to the same extent that rights of participants or beneficiaries are protected with respect to benefits accrued as of the date of the event. The rights granted by this Order must be taken into account in the event of the termination of the Plan as if the terms of this Order were part of the Plan. To the extent that this Order grants Alternate Payee part of Participant's benefits, the Plan Administrator, in terminating the Plan, must provide Alternate Payee with the notification, consent, payment, or other rights that it would have provided to Participant with respect to that portion of Participant's benefits.
2. PARTIES. The parties hereto were husband and wife, and a divorce action is in this Court at the above number, and this Court has personal jurisdiction over the parties, the subject matter of this Order and this dissolution of marriage action pursuant to the domestic relations laws of this State. The parties were married on _____ and divorced on _____.

I.

(continued)

3. PARTICIPANT: John Jones

    Date of Birth: _____

    Social Security Number: _____
    hereinafter referred to as "Participant," is or has been employed by the XYZ Corporation and is or has been a participant in the named Plan.

4. PARTICIPANT ADDRESS. The current and last known mailing address of Participant is: _____ .

5. ALTERNATE PAYEE: Jane Smith, formerly Jane Jones,

    Date of birth: _____

    Social Security Number: _____
    hereinafter referred to as "Alternate Payee," is the former spouse of Participant.

6. ALTERNATE PAYEE ADDRESS. The current and last known mailing address of Alternate Payee is: _____ .

7. LAW. Alternate Payee has an interest in Participant's benefits under domestic relations laws of this State. Participant's pension in the Plan is marital property subject to distribution by this Court under State domestic relations law for the jurisdiction in which this Order is issued and under which the above-named Participant and Alternate Payee are covered. This Order creates and recognizes as to the Plan the existence of Alternate Payee's right, subject to the provisions of this Order, and subject to the terms and conditions of the Plan, to a share of benefits otherwise payable to Participant under the Plan, in the amount and form set forth. If there should be a legal cause by which the Participant's benefits under the Plan may be offset by the amount of a judgment or settlement that Participant is required to pay as a result of a crime involving the Plan, nevertheless, the award in this Order to Alternate Payee shall be based on Participant's benefits before any such offset.

8. COMPUTATION OF AWARD TO ALTERNATE PAYEE.
    a. The marital property component of the Plan is determined by a Coverture Fraction multiplied by the accrued pension benefit as of the Determination Date.
    b. The Determination Date is the earliest of Participant's retirement, separation from service, death or other future break in service, or the date Alternate Payee is eligible and elects to receive her benefits from the Plan.
    c. The Coverture Fraction is a mathematical fraction, the value of which is determined as follows:
        (1) The numerator of the fraction is the period of time during which Participant and Alternate Payee were married up to the cutoff date while Participant was in the Plan, which is exactly ( ) years and ( ) months, or a total of ( ) months, or such other amount of time

162

I.

(continued)

as may be on the records of the Plan as Participant's creditable service dating from the date of marriage and ending on the date of divorce.

   (2)   The denominator is the period of time of Participant's total creditable Plan service as of the Determination Date.

   (3)   The Coverture Fraction is the result of the numerator divided by the denominator.

d.   The Percentage awarded to Alternate Payee is Fifty Percent (50 %).

e.   The basic portion of Participant's pension under the Plan awarded by this Order to Alternate Payee is determined as a percentage of the marital property component, resulting from the product of item (1) times (2) times (3), where:

   (1) is the Coverture Fraction;

   (2) is the Percentage awarded by this Order (50 %); and

   (3) is the accrued pension benefit as of the Determination Date.

   Participant's benefit, subject to division by this Order, is, including any plan amendments, based on (1) Participant's pension-creditable pay as defined in the Plan and (2) Participant's pension creditable service as defined in the Plan, as such pay and service existed on the nearest practicable Plan administrative date to the Determination Date, not counting any such pay nor service thereafter.

f.   The basic award shall be increased if applicable by early retirement incentives, if any, and by enhancements and/or cost of living increases, if any, are granted to Participant as a Retiree under the Plan in proportion to the ratio of the portion of the accrued benefit assigned to Alternate Payee to the benefit otherwise payable to Participant under the Plan before any assignment to Alternate Payee.

g.   [OPTIONAL] Participant shall elect at his retirement a 50% Joint and Survivor Annuity with Alternate Payee as the beneficiary, converted by the Plan from the Plan's standard form as necessary.

9.   PAYMENT. Alternate Payee is awarded, as separate property, the portion of Participant's calculated pension benefit as determined and described in accordance with item 8 of this Order, or its actuarial equivalent under the Plan, to become payable to Alternate Payee as soon as administratively feasible on or about the date Participant commences receiving benefits under the Plan, or as soon as may be otherwise legally available under the terms of the Plan at the request of Alternate Payee but not later than the Participant's normal retirement date. Alternate Payee shall provide the Plan Administrator with at least thirty (30) days' written notice of election to commence receiving pension benefits under this Order, or such other time period as the Plan may require, and shall complete such distribution request forms and provide such additional information as may be reasonably requested by the Plan Administrator. Alternate Payee's benefit shall be reduced as may be required by the Plan to reflect early retirement, age and the form or type of such benefit. The award to Alternate Payee shall not exceed the value of Participant's vested

I.

(continued)

interest in the Plan as of the date coinciding with or immediately preceding the date of payment to Alternate Payee. The remaining amount is the separate property of Participant. Alternate Payee shall share proportionately in any benefit incentives, enhancements, and cost of living adjustments based on the accrued pension as of the Determination Date. Payment shall not be made before notice is given to the parties or their legal representatives from the Plan Administrator that this Order constitutes a Qualified Domestic Relations Order.

10. EARLY. If the Plan allows and if Alternate Payee elects early benefit commencement, Alternate Payee's pension shall be actuarially or otherwise reduced as may be required under the Plan.

    a. [OPTIONAL] If benefit payment begins to Alternate Payee under the terms of this Order when or before Participant's benefit begins, and if Participant elects early retirement benefits under the terms of the Plan, and if there is an enhancement or subsidy that increases said early retirement benefits, then the benefit in payment to Alternate Payee shall be recalculated by the Plan Administrator to share in such increased benefit in the same proportion as Alternate Payee's awarded benefit bears to the benefit otherwise payable to Participant under the Plan before any assignment to the Alternate Payee.

11. PRE-RETIREMENT DEATH.

    a. If Participant predeceases Alternate Payee prior to the commencement of benefits either to Alternate Payee or to Participant, Alternate Payee shall be considered the surviving spouse and shall receive the pre-retirement survivor benefit under the Plan in the amount determined in accordance with subparagraphs b and c below, in lieu of the otherwise awarded benefit. Participant retains the right, to the extent permitted by the Plan, to name a beneficiary or beneficiaries for the balance.

    b. Any pre-retirement survivor benefit payable pursuant to this Order under the provisions of the Plan shall be payable to the Alternate Payee as a QPSA (Qualified Pre-retirement Survivor Annuity) benefit only if Alternate Payee has not commenced to receive benefits under any other provision of this Order, limited to the earlier of her election to commence receipt of her benefit or Participant's election to commence receiving his benefit. If such a QPSA occurs, then no benefit under the Plan other than such QPSA shall be payable to the Alternate Payee.

    c. The amount of such survivor benefit shall be determined based on the accrued pension benefit as of the Determination Date under the terms of the Plan as would be awarded to a spouse upon the death of Participant before retirement adjusted to actuarially equal the amount otherwise awarded by this Order as a pension. Any such surviving spouse benefits are in lieu of the benefits otherwise awarded by this Order. In the event Alternate Payee has already commenced receiving benefits under some other provision of this Order at the time of the Participant's death prior to retirement, Alternate Payee shall continue to receive those benefits and shall not receive any benefits under the QPSA.

I.

(continued)

12. FORM. Alternate Payee's benefits are payable during her lifetime, independent of the life of Participant, or the actuarial equivalent thereof under the Plan, in any other form available under the Plan with the consent of the Plan, including a lump-sum distribution, if available, but not a joint and survivor annuity with a subsequent spouse. Any actuarial or other benefit adjustments required under the Plan shall be applied as may be required to Alternate Payee's benefit. Payments from the Plan to Alternate Payee under this Order may be in any optional form or combination of optional forms as permitted by the Plan and elected by Alternate Payee if not otherwise precluded by any other provision of this Order, or by federal law. Alternate Payee does not have the right to elect a joint and survivor pre-retirement survivor annuity with a subsequent spouse as beneficiary.

    a. [OPTIONAL] The awarded pension payments to Alternate Payee are during the life of Participant. Upon the death of Participant, Alternate Payee then receives the awarded pension payments as the beneficiary of Participant's 50% joint and survivor annuity based on the accrued pension as of the Determination Date.

13. TAX. The Plan shall issue individual tax forms as may be required by the Internal Revenue Service, and for local or state taxes as may be appropriate, to each recipient separately for amounts paid by the Plan to each such person. The Alternate Payee assumes sole responsibility for the tax consequences of the distribution to the Alternate Payee.

14. RIGHTS. In no event shall Alternate Payee have greater rights than those that are available to Participant under the Plan. After segregation of the amount required by this Order, Alternate Payee shall have no further claim against Participant's interest in the Plan. If Alternate Payee has an independent benefit under this Order, then in the event of the death of Alternate Payee, on or after the date of benefit commencement, any death benefit available under the Plan based solely on the form of pension which may have been elected by Alternate Payee and limited to the portion of the accrued benefit assigned to Alternate Payee, and not otherwise precluded by this Order shall be payable to the named beneficiary of Alternate Payee. Alternate Payee is not entitled to any benefit not otherwise available under the Plan. Alternate Payee is only entitled to the specific benefits under the Plan as provided for in this Order. All other rights, privileges, and options under the Plan not granted to Alternate Payee are preserved for Participant. None of Participant's elections, options, or features under the Plan are restricted, limited, or otherwise affected by this Order other than a reduction in the pension based solely on the share that the Alternate Payee is entitled to. Upon approval of this Order the Plan shall recognize no connection between Participant and Alternate Payee as former husband and wife with respect to benefits, elections, options, or other features. This Order does not preclude Participant from electing or receiving any options, forms of benefit, or other entitlements under the Plan.

15. REDUCTIONS. If any reductions in Participant's benefits may be required due to maximum benefit limitations, Participant's being convicted of committing a crime involving the plan, a civil judgment (or consent order or decree)

I.

(continued)

entered by a court in an action brought in connection with a violation of fiduciary provisions, or a settlement agreement between a government entity and Participant in connection with a violation of any fiduciary provisions, or any similar judgments, orders, decrees, or settlement agreements, Alternate Payee's benefit shall nevertheless be computed before applying any such reductions to Participant's benefits under the Plan.

16. INFORMATION. Upon written request from Alternate Payee, the Plan shall provide to Alternate Payee the notices and information to which a beneficiary is entitled.

17. CONTRIBUTIONS. If Participant has ever made any employee contributions to the Plan, and if Participant withdraws or obtains a payment consisting of a refund of all or part of accumulated employee contributions, with interest if any is credited, before Alternate Payee's benefits commence, then a proportionate share of the marital property component of such payment shall be paid by the Plan to Alternate Payee.

18. LUMP SUM. In the event Participant withdraws or obtains a lump-sum payment or distribution before Alternate Payee's benefits commence, a proportionate share of the marital property component of such payment shall be paid by the Plan to Alternate Payee.

19. ADDRESS CHANGE. The parties shall promptly notify the Plan Administrator of any change in their addresses from those set forth in this Order.

20. DISABILITY. In the event Participant becomes disabled as may be defined in the Plan and is entitled to begin receiving a disability pension benefit from the Plan in lieu of a regular pension, if any, prior to the commencement of payments under this Order to Alternate Payee, Alternate Payee may begin receiving benefits at the same time as does Participant, unless Alternate Payee has already commenced receiving benefits under some other provision of this Order.

21. SUSPENSION. In the event Participant returns to work after retirement, and if in such event the benefits may be suspended under the Plan, nevertheless Alternate Payee's benefits shall not be suspended.

22. DEATH. [OPTIONAL] In the event Alternate Payee dies before benefits commence under this Order, the benefit allocated to Alternate Payee is restored to Participant as if this Order had not existed. In the event of the death of a party hereto, the Plan shall be entitled to recover any payments issued on the assumption that such person was alive.

    a. [OPTIONAL] In the event Alternate Payee dies before benefits commence under this Order, the benefit allocated to Alternate Payee is payable to the named beneficiary or to the estate of Alternate Payee. In the event of the death of a party hereto, the Plan shall be entitled to recover any payments issued on the assumption that such person was alive.

23. SMALL VALUE. In the event the present value of the pension for Alternate Payee is five thousand dollars ($5,000) or less, or other amount as may be specified in the Plan, the Plan may make a lump-sum distribution of the amount when payable under the terms and conditions of the Plan.

I.

(continued)

24. RESERVE FOR ALTERNATE PAYEE. If Alternate Payee cannot be located or if for administrative or legal reasons the Plan cannot issue the awarded benefit, the Plan shall establish a reserve in the awarded amount for Alternate Payee on the records of the Plan, until such time as the benefit may be appropriately released. In the event of the requirement of the establishment of such a reserve, nevertheless Participant's remaining benefit shall be payable to Participant as and when due under the Plan.

25. ORDER. The benefits awarded to Alternate Payee by this Order shall not be assigned, pledged, or otherwise transferred, voluntarily or involuntarily, before Alternate Payee (or Alternate Payee's designated beneficiary or estate) has received those benefits. During the period in which the issue of whether this Order is a Qualified Domestic Relations Order is being determined (by the Plan administrator, a court of competent jurisdiction, or otherwise), the Plan administrator shall segregate in a separate account in the Plan or in an escrow account the amounts that would have been payable to Alternate Payee (designated beneficiary or estate) during such period. It is the knowledge and information of the Court that neither it nor the Participant and Alternate Payee are aware of any other orders that purport to dispose of the benefits described herein. No provision in this Order shall be construed to require the Plan to (a) make any payment or take any action that is inconsistent with any federal or state law, rule, regulation, or applicable judicial decision; (b) provide any type or form of benefit, or any option, which is not otherwise provided under the Plan and specifically authorized by this Order; (c) provide increased benefits, determined on the basis of actuarial value; or (d) pay benefits to any Alternate Payee which are required to be paid to another Alternate Payee under another order previously determined to be a qualified domestic relations order. Unless ordered by a court of competent jurisdiction, or otherwise addressed herein, this Order shall not be affected by any change in circumstances of either party, including but not limited to remarriage, cohabitation, or support concerning a dependent child. Notwithstanding any other provision of this Order, in the event that Participant, Alternate Payee, or any other party claiming rights under this Order shall make any claim which the Plan shall determine to be inconsistent with the provisions of this Order or with any provision of law, rule, or applicable judicial decision, the Plan may cease making any further payments to any person whose rights under the Plan, in the sole judgment of the Plan, may be affected by such claim pending resolution of such claim or further order of the Court, and the Plan may also take such further action or actions as may be permitted by law with respect to such claim and/or this Order. No provision in this Order shall be construed to require the Plan, the Plan Administrator, or any trustee or other fiduciary with respect to the Plan to take any action that is inconsistent with any provision of the Plan as now in effect or hereafter amended. The division of the Participant's benefits by this Order shall result in a combined benefit for both the Participant and the Alternate Payee that is neither greater nor less than Participant's original benefit.

I.

(continued)

26. NOTIFICATION. If and when either Participant or Alternate Payee apply for any benefit payments or withdrawals from the Plan, the Plan shall notify each of them and their legal representatives.

27. LIMITATION. Any and all benefits and/or modifications of any kind awarded by this Order to Alternate Payee shall be based on the accrued pension benefit as of the Determination Date. The undertakings and obligations of the Plan as set forth in this Order are solely those of the Plan. Neither Participant's employer, nor any subsidiary or affiliated corporations, nor any officer, employee or agent thereof (other than the administrator of the Plan solely in its capacity as administrator) shall be deemed to have made any undertakings or incurred any obligations of this Order.

28. DESIGNATION. The following attorneys are representatives for receipt of copies of notices pertaining to this Order:

    for the Participant: _____

    for Alternate Payee: _____

29. JURISDICTION. It is intended that this Order shall qualify as a Qualified Domestic Relations Order under the Retirement Equity Act of 1984, P.L. 98-397, in accordance with Section 414(p) of the Internal Revenue Code of 1986, as amended, and the appropriately applicable provisions of the Employee Retirement Income Security Act of 1974, as amended, and its provisions shall be administered and interpreted in conformity with such provisions. If any provision of this Order is inapplicable it shall be ignored and it shall not affect the validity of other provisions or of the Order itself. The Court retains jurisdiction to amend this Order as might be necessary to establish or maintain its status.

SUBMITTED BY: _____

APPROVED AS TO FORM AND CONTENT

Dated and Done this _____ day of _____ , _____ .

_____
Judge

II. STANDARDIZED QDRO—ERISA DEFINED CONTRIBUTION PENSION PLAN

The following is a sample standardized QDRO for John Jones, an active participant in an ERISA defined contribution pension plan, and the plaintiff in a divorce action.

DISTRICT COURT

John Jones,	)	
	)	
Plaintiff,	)	
	)	Case No. Dxxxxxx
vs.	)	
	)	
Jane Jones,	)	Dept No. Family
	)	
Defendant.	)	

QUALIFIED DOMESTIC RELATIONS ORDER

Hearing Date: N/A

Hearing Time: N/A

Based on the findings of the Court,

IT IS HEREBY ORDERED, ADJUDGED, AND DECREED:

1. PLAN. The Plan to which this Order applies is The ABC Company Standard Profit Sharing Pension Plan as it now exists or may from time to time be amended, or any successor plan thereto. The rights of Alternate Payee under this Order are protected in the event of plan amendments, a plan merger, or a change in the sponsor of the Plan to the same extent that rights of participants or beneficiaries are protected with respect to benefits accrued as of the date of the event. The rights granted by this Order must be taken into account in the event of the termination of the Plan as if the terms of this Order were part of the Plan. To the extent that this Order grants Alternate Payee part of Participant's benefits, the Plan Administrator, in terminating the Plan, must provide Alternate Payee with the notification, consent, payment, or other rights that it would have provided to Participant with respect to that portion of Participant's benefits.

2. PARTIES. The parties hereto were husband and wife, and a divorce action is in this Court at the above number, and this Court has personal jurisdiction over the parties, the subject matter of this Order and this dissolution of marriage action pursuant to the domestic relations laws of this State. The parties were married on _____ and divorced on _____ .

3. PARTICIPANT: John Jones

   Date of Birth: _____

   Social Security Number: _____

II.

(continued)

hereinafter referred to as "Participant," is or has been employed by the ABC Company and is or has been a participant in the named Plan.

4. PARTICIPANT ADDRESS. The current and last known mailing address of Participant is: _____ .

5. ALTERNATE PAYEE: Jane Smith, formerly Jane Jones

   Date of Birth: _____

   Social Security Number: _____
   hereinafter referred to as "Alternate Payee," is the former spouse of Participant.

6. ALTERNATE PAYEE ADDRESS. The current and last known mailing address of Alternate Payee is: _____ .

7. LAW. Alternate Payee has an interest in Participant's benefits under domestic relations laws of this State. Participant's account in the Plan is marital property subject to distribution by this Court under State domestic relations law for the jurisdiction in which this Order is issued and under which the above-named Participant and Alternate Payee are covered. This Order creates and recognizes as to the Plan the existence of Alternate Payee's right, subject to the provisions of this Order, to a share of benefits otherwise payable to Participant under the Plan, in the amount and form set forth herein.

8. SEGREGATION. As soon as administratively feasible following approval of this Order as qualified a portion of Participant's Account shall be segregated for Alternate Payee, and shall thereafter be credited separately with earnings (interest, dividends, gain or loss, realized and unrealized, etc.) or charged with losses and allowable administration expenses in their respective accounts during the period the earnings or losses accrued. Alternate Payee's benefit shall consist of employee and company contributions and pre- and after-tax funds in proportion to the pre- and after-tax funds in Participant's total account, if any. Alternate Payee's account shall not be increased by any further contributions subsequent to the effective division date. A physical segregation of assets is not required. Any outstanding loans and interest due thereon are considered as if repaid and the Account made whole for purposes of this Order.

9. AWARD. The portion of Participant's Account awarded to Alternate Payee is [OPTIONAL] dollars ($) or percent (%) of the account as near as administratively practicable as possible to the date of [OPTIONAL] / approval of this Order. The portion of the account awarded to Alternate Payee shall not exceed the value of Participant's account at the time of the award.

10. INVESTMENT. In the event that the payment of all or any portion of Alternate Payee's benefits under the Plan is to be delayed, Alternate Payee shall be permitted to direct the investment of Alternate Payee's interest in the Plan. To the extent that Alternate Payee directs investment of interest in the Plan under this item, the income or loss on such interest shall be determined on

II.

(continued)

a segregated basis in the account of Alternate Payee. Until the appropriate forms are executed by Alternate Payee designating investment instructions, Alternate Payee's account shall be invested in proportion to the investments in Participant's account at the time of segregation.

11. TREATMENT OF PARTICIPANT CONTRIBUTIONS. For purposes of federal and state income taxation and reporting to federal and state taxing authorities, the total amount of any voluntary nondeductible participant contributions made to Participant's accounts under the Plan and not yet distributed as of the date of this Order shall be allocated between the interests of the Participant and the Alternate Payee in proportion to each.

12. DEATH OF ALTERNATE PAYEE. In the event that Alternate Payee dies before the entire interest of Alternate Payee in the Plan has been paid, the Trustee shall distribute the remaining interest in the Plan, determined as set forth in this Order, as soon as practicable to Alternate Payee's named beneficiary or estate, or in the event no valid designation of beneficiary exists at the time of Alternate Payee's death, the death benefit shall be payable to her estate.

13. DISTRIBUTION. Alternate Payee's account shall be payable as a distribution to Alternate Payee upon request on the earliest practicable date, not in contradiction of the Plan or law or regulations, of the following, but not before this Order has been found to be a Qualified Domestic Relations Order by the Plan and written request has been made to the Plan as may be required by the Plan on the election forms prescribed by the Plan, if applicable:
    a. as soon as administratively practical after receipt and approval of this Order by the Plan Administrator;
    b. the approval of this Order as a Qualified Domestic Relations Order by the Plan Administrator as if Participant had retired on such date even if Participant has not actually retired or separated from service;
    c. the date on which Participant attains Normal Retirement Age, as if Participant had retired on that date, even if Participant has not actually retired or separated from service;
    d. the date on which Participant actually retires or otherwise separates from service for whatever reason;
    e. the date of Participant's death;
    f. the date Participant reaches age 50;
    g. the date Participant reaches earliest retirement age under the Plan;
    h. the date Participant enters pay status for whatever reason.
    If Participant has already reached the earliest retirement age under the Plan then payment shall be made to Alternate Payee as soon as administratively available following the determination that this Order is qualified and the receipt of a request for payment by Alternate Payee. Payout may be made before Participant terminates employment if not in contradiction of the Plan or law or regulations, but not before this Order is found to be qualified.

14. FORM. The form of said payment is a lump-sum distribution to Alternate Payee. In accord with the Plan's normal administrative procedures, Alternate

II.

(continued)

Payee may request that the distribution be in the form of a full or partial transfer or rollover to an individual retirement account (IRA) or to the administrator, trustee, or custodian of the IRA. Upon notification from the Plan to Alternate Payee of the approval of this Order, Alternate Payee shall inform the Plan of the IRA transfer details if that is to be done.

15. RIGHTS. Alternate Payee shall have the same account investment direction rights with regard to Alternate Payee's portion of the Plan as are available to Participant. In no event shall Alternate Payee have greater rights than those that are available to Participant. Alternate Payee is not entitled to any benefit not provided under the Plan or by this Order. Alternate Payee is only entitled to the specific benefits under the Plan as provided for in this Order. All other rights, privileges, and options under the Plan are preserved for Participant. Each is responsible for individual tax reporting on payments.

16. ADDRESSES. The parties shall notify the Plan Administrator of any change in their addresses from those set forth in this Order.

17. ORDER. The benefits awarded by this Order shall not be assigned, pledged, otherwise transferred, voluntarily or involuntarily, before Alternate Payee (or Alternate Payee's designated beneficiary or estate) has received those benefits. During the period in which the issue of whether this Order is a Qualified Domestic Relations Order is being determined (by the Plan administrator, a court of competent jurisdiction, or otherwise), the Plan administrator shall separately account for the applicable amounts in the Plan that would have been payable to Alternate Payee (designated beneficiary or estate) during such period. It is the knowledge and information of the Court that neither it nor the Participant and Alternate Payee are aware of any other orders that purport to dispose of the benefits described herein. No provision in this Order shall be construed to require the Plan to (a) make any payment or take any action that is inconsistent with any federal or state law, rule, regulation, or applicable judicial decision; (b) provide any type or form of benefit, or any option that is not otherwise provided under the Plan and specifically authorized by this Order; (c) provide increased benefits, determined on the basis of actuarial value; or (d) pay benefits to any Alternate Payee that are required to be paid to another Alternate Payee under another order previously determined to be a qualified domestic relations order. Unless ordered by a court of competent jurisdiction, or otherwise addressed herein, this Order shall not be affected by any change in circumstances of either party, including but not limited to remarriage, cohabitation, or support concerning a dependent child. Notwithstanding any other provision of this Order, in the event that Participant, Alternate Payee, or any other party claiming rights under this Order shall make any claim which the Plan shall determine to be inconsistent with the provisions of this Order or with any provision of law, rule, or applicable judicial decision, the Plan may cease making any further payments to any person whose rights under the Plan, in the sole judgment of the Plan, may

II.

(continued)

be affected by such claim pending resolution of such claim or further order of the Court, and the Plan may also take such further action or actions as may be permitted by law with respect to such claim and/or this Order. No provision in this Order shall be construed to require the Plan, the Plan Administrator, or any trustee or other fiduciary with respect to the Plan to take any action that is inconsistent with any provision of the Plan as now in effect or hereafter amended. The undertakings and obligations of the Plan as set forth in this Order are solely those of the Plan. Neither Participant's employer, nor any subsidiary or affiliated corporations, nor any officer, employee, or agent thereof (other than the administrator of the Plan solely in its capacity as administrator) shall be deemed to have made any undertakings or incurred any obligations as a result of this Order.

18.   NOTIFICATION. The Plan shall notify each of the parties hereto and their legal representatives when either party makes application for any benefit payments or withdrawals from the Plan, but such notice requirement shall lapse after Alternate Payee's account is established.

19.   DESIGNATION. The following attorneys are representatives for receipt of copies of notices pertaining to this Order:

for Participant: _____

for Alternate Payee: _____

20.   REDUCTIONS. If any reductions in Participant's benefits may be required due to maximum benefit limitations, Participant's being convicted of committing a crime involving the plan, a civil judgment (or consent order or decree) entered by a court in an action brought in connection with a violation of fiduciary provisions, or a settlement agreement between a government entity and Participant in connection with a violation of any fiduciary provisions, or any similar judgments, orders, decrees, or settlement agreements, Alternate Payee's benefit shall nevertheless be computed before applying any such reductions to Participant's benefits under the Plan.

21.   RESERVE FOR ALTERNATE PAYEE. If Alternate Payee cannot be located or if for administrative or legal reasons the Plan cannot issue the awarded benefit, the Plan shall establish a reserve in the awarded amount on the records of the Plan, until such time as the benefit may be appropriately released. In the event of the requirement of such a reserve, nevertheless Participant's benefits shall not be affected.

22.   JURISDICTION. It is intended that this Order shall qualify as a Qualified Domestic Relations Order under the Retirement Equity Act of 1984, P.L. 98-397, in accordance with Section 414(p) of the Internal Revenue Code of 1986, as amended, and the appropriately applicable provisions of the Employee Retirement Income Security Act of 1974, as amended, and its provisions shall be administered and interpreted in conformity with such provisions. If any provision of this Order is inapplicable it shall be ignored and it shall not

II.
(continued)

affect the validity of other provisions or of the Order itself. The Court retains jurisdiction to amend this Order as might be necessary to establish or maintain its status.

SUBMITTED BY: _____

APPROVED AS TO FORM AND CONTENT:

Dated and Done this _____ day of _____ , _____ .

_____
Judge

III. COURT ORDER ACCEPTABLE FOR PROCESSING—NON-ERISA DEFINED BENEFIT PENSION PLAN

The following sample court order is for John Jones, a civilian employee of the federal government and an active participant in the Civil Service Retirement System, a non-ERISA defined benefit pension plan. John Jones is the husband and plaintiff in a divorce action. Note that this court order is called a court order acceptable for processing (COAP), not a qualified domestic relations order.

DISTRICT COURT

John Jones,	)
	)
Plaintiff,	)
	) Case No. Dxxxxxx
vs.	)
	)
Jane Jones,	) Dept No. Family
	)
Defendant.	)

COURT ORDER ACCEPTABLE FOR PROCESSING

Hearing Date: N/A

Hearing Time: N/A

Based on the findings of the Court,

IT IS HEREBY ORDERED, ADJUDGED, AND DECREED:

1. PARTIES. The parties hereto were husband and wife, and a divorce action is in this Court at the above number, and this Court has personal jurisdiction over the parties, the subject matter of this Order, and this dissolution of marriage action pursuant to the domestic relations laws of this State. The parties were married on _____ and divorced on _____ .

2. The Employee: John Jones

    Date of Birth: _____

    Social Security Number: _____
    is a participant in the Civil Service Retirement System (CSRS) and, based on employment with the United States Government, will be eligible for retirement benefits under CSRS.

III.

(continued)

3. The current and last known mailing address of Employee is:
    _____ .

4. The Former Spouse: Jane Smith, formerly Jane Jones

    Date of Birth: _____

    Social Security Number: _____
    hereinafter referred to as "Former Spouse," is awarded this distribution of marital property pursuant to State law.

5. The last known mailing address of Former Spouse is:
    _____

6. Employee's gross self-only retirement annuity benefit in the CSRS is marital property subject to distribution by this Court. The United States Office of Personnel Management is directed to pay Former Spouse's share as set forth in this Order directly to Former Spouse.

7. If Employee purchases or has purchased prior military service with a resulting increase in his CSRS employee annuity, the increased retirement benefit is included as marital property in this Order. If Employee annuity is reduced for purposes of Social Security, whether his own or as a spouse, or because of failure to purchase prior military service when available, the decrease in his employee annuity shall be reflected proportionately in the award to Former Spouse under this Order.

8. For purposes of this Order the employee annuity is a self-only gross annuity with survivor benefits. The self-only annuity with survivor benefits pays a smaller amount than does a self-only annuity that does not provide for survivor benefits.

9. The benefits awarded to Former Spouse by this Order shall be based on Employee's creditable service, including unused sick leave, if any, for purposes of the non-disability self-only annuity and the Former Spouse Survivor Annuity.

10. (a) The marital property component of the CSRS is determined by the marital coverture fraction multiplied by the gross self-only employee annuity.
    (b) The marital coverture fraction is a fraction with a value less than one. The numerator is exactly _____ months (   ). The denominator is the number of months of Employee's creditable service, including unused sick leave if any, at the time of his separation from service with the United States Government.
    (c) The portion of the non-disability self-only gross annuity, before reduction for the Former Spouse Survivor Annuity, awarded to Former Spouse is fifty percent (50%) of the marital property component. Former Spouse's share of Employee's employee annuity will be reduced by the amount of costs associated with providing the Former Spouse Survivor Annuity awarded herein.

11. The specified retirement benefit shall be payable to Former Spouse and shall commence when Employee's annuity begins, unless Employee is to receive an annuity based on disability.

III.

(continued)

12. If Employee becomes eligible for disability retirement payments under the CSRS based on employment with the United States Government, then starting when Employee reaches age 62, Former Spouse is entitled to fifty percent (50%) of a fraction of Employee's gross monthly annuity under the CSRS. The monthly annuity means the amount of Employee's monthly annuity computed as though Employee had retired on an immediate, non-disability annuity on the commencing date of Employee's annuity based on disability, and where the fraction has a numerator of exactly _____ months and a denominator that is the number of months of Employee's total service, in which any time attributable to unused sick leave is not included, at the time of his separation from service with the United States Government.

    In computing the amount of the immediate annuity, the United States Office of Personnel Management will deem Employee to have been age 62 at the time Employee retired on disability, and Former Spouse's share of the annuity will be reduced by the amount of costs associated with providing the Former Spouse Survivor Annuity.

13. When a Cost of Living Adjustment (COLA) is applied to Employee's retirement or disability benefits, the same COLA applies to Former Spouse's share.

14. (a)   Under Section 8341(h)(1) of Title 5, U.S. Code, Former Spouse is awarded a Former Spouse Survivor Annuity under the CSRS.

    (b)   The amount of the Former Spouse Survivor Annuity will be equal to fifty percent (50%) of the marital coverture fraction as defined in this Order, using creditable service, including unused sick leave, if any. The benefits under Former Spouse Annuity apply at the date of death of Employee, whether such death occurs while an employee or while a retiree. Former Spouse's share of Employee's employee annuity will be reduced by the amount of costs associated with providing the Former Spouse Survivor Annuity awarded herein. If Employee remarries before or after retirement, he may elect to provide a survivor annuity for a new spouse with respect to amounts not awarded to Former Spouse by this Order.

15. The term of the regular monthly pension payments to Former Spouse is for life during the life of Employee after retirement, ending at the death of Employee.

16. If Former Spouse dies before Employee, then Employee's entire annuity shall be restored after the death of Former Spouse.

17. The CSRS shall issue individual tax forms to each recipient for amounts paid to each such person with employee contributions, if any, shared as a tax basis in proportion to the benefits awarded by this Order.

18. Former Spouse is only entitled to the specific benefits under the CSRS as provided herein.

19. [OPTIONAL] The United States Office of Personnel Management is directed not to pay a refund of employee contributions.

    a. [OPTIONAL] If Employee becomes eligible and applies for a refund of employee contributions, Former Spouse is entitled to fifty percent (50%) of the marital coverture fraction as defined in this Order, using total

III.
(continued)

service excluding unused sick leave, if any. The United States Office of Personnel Management is directed to pay Former Spouse's share directly to Former Spouse.

20. The CSRS shall notify Former Spouse and legal representative when Employee makes application for any benefit payments or withdrawals from the CSRS.

21. The following attorneys are representatives for receipt of copies of notices with respect to this Order:

for Employee: _____ .

for Former Spouse: _____ .

22. It is intended that this Order shall qualify as a Court Order Acceptable for Processing. The Court has considered the requirements and standard terminology provided in Part 838 of Title 5, Code of Federal Regulations. The terminology used in the provisions of this Order that concern benefits under the CSRS are governed by the standard conventions established in that Part. The Court retains jurisdiction to amend this Order as might be necessary to establish or maintain its status.

CONSENTED TO:

_____

Employee

_____

Former Spouse

SUBMITTED BY: _____

APPROVED AS TO FORM AND CONTENT:

Dated and Done this _____ day of _____ , _____ .

_____

Judge

Note: The CSRS has specific types of annuities available, one of which must be specified in a COAP:

1. Self-Only Annuity. An annuity payable to the retiree for life, with no death or survivor benefits, and no deductions or reductions.

2. Gross Annuity. A self-only annuity adjusted for death and survivor benefits, with the costs of same deducted.

3. Net Annuity. Either a self-only annuity or a gross annuity (depending on death and survivor benefits) reduced by one or more of the following:
—Amounts owed by the retiree to the United States
—Health benefit premiums
—Life insurance premiums
—Medicare premiums
—Federal income tax withholdings
—State income tax withholdings
—Costs of death/survivor benefits, if applicable.

All federal pensions start out as a base self-only annuity. Then adjustments are made as elected by the retiring employee or as mandated by a COAP. The actual pension may remain as a true self-only annuity or become a gross annuity providing death and survivor benefits, or it may become a net annuity subject to the deductions listed above.

IV. DOMESTIC RELATIONS ORDER—NON-ERISA MILITARY SERVICE DEFINED BENEFIT PENSION PLAN

The following is a sample standardized QDRO for John Jones, a member of the Armed Forces and an active participant in the Armed Forces Retirement System, a non-ERISA defined benefit pension plan. John Jones is the husband and plaintiff in a divorce action. This court order is not called a QDRO; it is simply a domestic relations order.

DOMESTIC RELATIONS ORDER

Hearing Date: N/A

Hearing Time: N/A

Based on the findings of the Court,

IT IS HEREBY ORDERED, ADJUDGED, AND DECREED:

1. The parties hereto were husband and wife, and a divorce action has been completed in this Court at the above number.
    This Court has jurisdiction over the parties in accordance with the laws of the State of _____ by reason of the residence and domicile of both parties in the territorial jurisdiction of the Court, other than because of military assignment. No party has objected to this Court's jurisdiction. The parties were married on _____ and divorced on _____ .

2. Participant: John Jones

    Date of Birth: _____

    Social Security Number: _____
    hereinafter referred to as "Participant," has served in the United States [*branch of service*] and is a participant in the Armed Forces Retirement System (the Plan), and has performed more than ten (10) years of creditable service in the U.S. [*branch of service*] during the marriage to the below-named Alternate Payee.

3. The current and last known mailing address of Participant is:
    _____ .

4. Alternate Payee: Jane Jones

    Date of Birth: _____

    Social Security Number: _____
    hereinafter referred to as "Alternate Payee," has raised claims for, inter alia, equitable distribution of marital property under State law.

IV.
(continued)

5. The current and last known mailing address of Alternate Payee is:
    _____ .

6. Participant's interest in the Plan is marital property subject to distribution by this Court, including any Special Separation Benefit (SSB) and any Voluntary Separation Incentive (VSI) benefits.

7. The monthly benefit to be allocated to Alternate Payee is [OPTIONAL] _____ dollars ($) or percent (%) of Participant's pension, provided, however, that the award to Alternate Payee shall not exceed fifty percent (50%) of Participant's actual disposable retired or retainer pay.

8. The specified pension benefit shall be payable to Alternate Payee and shall commence as soon as administratively feasible on or about the date Participant actually retires or otherwise enters pension status for whatever reason, subject to any required actuarial adjustments. Alternate Payee shall share in any scheduled and/or ad hoc increases to pensioners in proportion to the pension awarded by this Order. In the event of the diminution of Participant's disposable retired pay by reason of federal employment, if same should occur, any amount payable to Alternate Payee under this Order that would otherwise be reduced shall become payable from Participant's civil service retirement so as not to diminish the payment to Alternate Payee.

9. Alternate Payee, if living, shall be considered the surviving spouse for the purpose of receiving any pre- or post-retirement survivor benefits under the Plan in the event of the death of Participant, in accordance with the Survivor Benefit Plan. Alternate Payee is only entitled to the specific benefits under the Plan as provided for in this Order. All other rights, privileges, and options under the Plan not granted to Alternate Payee are preserved for Participant.

10. The regular monthly pension payments cease at the first to die of either party. Alternate Payee shall be the beneficiary of any post-retirement death benefits if Participant after retirement predeceases Alternate Payee.

    After benefits commence, if Alternate Payee shall predecease Participant, then Participant's pension shall be restored, for future payments only, to the amount it would have been if there were no Alternate Payee. The Plan shall issue individual tax forms to each recipient for amounts paid to each such person.

11. The Plan to which this Order applies is stated in item 2 hereof, or any successor plan thereto.

12. The parties shall promptly notify the Plan Administrator of any change in their addresses from those set forth in this Order.

13. The following attorneys are their representatives for receipt of copies of notices pertaining to this Order:

    for Participant: _____

    for Alternate Payee: _____

14. It is intended that this order shall qualify under the Uniformed Services Former Spouse's Protection Act, P.L. 97-252, 10 U.S.C. Sec. 1408. The Court retains

jurisdiction to amend this Order as might be necessary to establish or maintain its status. Unless ordered by a court of competent jurisdiction, or otherwise addressed herein, this Order shall not be affected by any change in circumstances of either party, including but not limited to remarriage, cohabitation, or support concerning a dependent child. It is hereby certified that this order has not been amended nor suspended.

SUBMITTED BY: _____

APPROVED AS TO FORM AND CONTENT:

Dated and Done this _____ day of _____ , _____ .

_____
Judge

V. RETIREMENT BENEFITS COURT ORDER—NON-ERISA DEFINED CONTRIBUTION PLAN—THRIFT SAVINGS PLAN (TSP)

The following is a sample standardized QDRO for John Jones, a civilian employee of the federal government and an active participant in a non-ERISA defined contribution plan, the federal government's Thrift Savings Plan (TSP). John Jones is the husband, the plan participant, and the plaintiff in a divorce action. This court order is neither a QDRO nor a COAP; it is called a retirement benefits court order (RBCO).

DISTRICT COURT

John Jones,)
)
    Plaintiff,)
) Case No. Dxxxxxx
vs.)
)
Jane Jones,) Dept No. Family
)
    Defendant.)

RETIREMENT BENEFITS COURT ORDER—THRIFT SAVINGS PLAN

Hearing Date: N/A

Hearing Time: N/A

Based on the findings of the Court,

IT IS HEREBY ORDERED, ADJUDGED, AND DECREED:

1. PARTIES. The parties hereto were husband and wife, and a divorce action is in this Court at the above number, and this Court has personal jurisdiction over the parties, the subject matter of this Order and this dissolution of marriage action pursuant to the domestic relations laws of this State. The parties were married on _____ and divorced on _____ .

2. PARTICIPANT: John Jones

Date of Birth: _____

Social Security Number: _____
hereinafter referred to as "Participant," is a participant in the Thrift Savings Plan (the Plan).

3. PARTICIPANT ADDRESS. The current and last known mailing address of Participant is: _____ .

V.

(continued)

4. ALTERNATE PAYEE: Jane Smith, formerly Jane Jones

    Date of Birth: _____

    Social Security Number: _____
    hereinafter referred to as "Alternate Payee," is the former spouse of Participant. Alternate Payee has an interest in Participant's benefits under the domestic relations law of the State of _____ .

5. ALTERNATE PAYEE ADDRESS. The current and last known mailing address of Alternate Payee is: _____ .

6. PLAN. The Plan in this Order is the Thrift Savings Plan or any amended or successor plan thereto.

7. LAW. Participant's account in the Plan is marital property subject to distribution by this Court under State domestic relations law for the jurisdiction in which this Order is issued and under which the above-named Participant and Alternate Payee are covered. This Order creates and recognizes as to the Plan the existence of Alternate Payee's right, subject to the provisions of this Order, to a share of benefits otherwise payable to Participant under the Plan, in the amount and form as set forth herein.

8. ACCOUNTING. As soon as administratively feasible following approval of this Order as qualified, a portion of Participant's Account shall be separately accounted for Alternate Payee, and shall thereafter be credited separately with earnings (interest, dividends, gain or loss, realized and unrealized, etc.) or charged with losses and allowable administration expenses.

9. AWARD. The portion of Participant's Account from the Thrift Savings Plan awarded to Alternate Payee is _____ dollars ($) of the account as near as administratively practicable as possible to the date of receipt and approval of this Order.

10. DEATH OF ALTERNATE PAYEE. In the event that Alternate Payee dies before the entire interest in the Plan has been paid, payment shall be made to Alternate Payee's named beneficiary or estate, or in the event no valid designation of beneficiary exists at the time of Alternate Payee's death, the death benefit shall be payable to the estate.

11. DISTRIBUTION. Alternate Payee's account shall be payable as a distribution as soon as administratively practical after receipt and approval of this Order by the Plan.

12. FORM. The form of payment is a lump-sum distribution to Alternate Payee. In accord with the Plan's normal administrative procedures, Alternate Payee may request that the distribution be in the form of a full or partial transfer or rollover to an individual retirement account (IRA) or to the administrator, trustee, or custodian of the IRA. Upon notification from the Plan to Alternate Payee of the approval of this Order, Alternate Payee shall inform the Plan of the IRA transfer details if that is to be done.

13. RIGHTS. Alternate Payee is not entitled to any benefit not otherwise provided under the Plan or by this Order. Alternate Payee is only entitled to the specific benefits under the Plan as provided for in this Order. All other rights, privi-

V.

(continued)

leges, and options under the Plan are preserved for the Participant. The Plan shall issue individual tax forms to each such recipient for amounts paid to each such person. Each is responsible for individual tax reporting.

14. ADDRESSES. The parties shall promptly notify the Plan Administrator of any change in their addresses from those set forth in this Order.

15. ORDER. It is the knowledge and information of the Court that neither it nor the Participant and Alternate Payee are aware of any other orders that purport to dispose of the benefits described herein. No provision in this Order shall be construed to require the Plan to (a) make any payment or take any action which is inconsistent with any federal or state law, rule, regulation or applicable judicial decision; (b) provide any type or form of benefit, or any option that is not otherwise provided under the Plan and specifically authorized by this Order; (c) provide increased benefits, determined on the basis of actuarial value; or (d) pay benefits to any Alternate Payee that are required to be paid to another Alternate Payee under another order previously determined to be a qualified order. Notwithstanding any other provision of this Order, in the event that Participant, Alternate Payee, or any other party claiming rights under this Order shall make any claim that the Plan shall determine to be inconsistent with the provisions of this Order or with any provision of law, rule or applicable judicial decision, the Plan may cease making any further payments to any person whose rights under the Plan, in the sole judgment of the Plan, may be affected by such claim pending resolution of such claim or further order of the Court, and the Plan may also take such further action or actions as may be permitted by law with respect to such claim and/or this Order. No provision in this Order shall be construed to require the Plan, the Plan Administrator, or any trustee or other fiduciary with respect to the Plan to take any action that is inconsistent with the Plan now in effect or hereafter amended.

16. DESIGNATION. The following attorneys are designated as representatives for receipt of copies of notices pertaining to this Order:

17. JURISDICTION. It is intended that this Order shall qualify as a Retirement Benefits Court Order in accordance with 5 U.S.C. §§ 8435(d)(1), 8435(d)(2), and 8467, and Part 1653, and its provisions shall be administered and interpreted in conformity with such provisions. If any provision of this Order is inapplicable it shall be ignored and it shall not affect the validity of other provisions or of the Order itself. The Court retains jurisdiction to amend this Order as might be necessary to establish or maintain its status.

SUBMITTED BY: _____

APPROVED AS TO FORM AND CONTENT:

Dated and Done this _____ day of _____ , _____ .

_____
        Judge

VI. DOMESTIC RELATIONS ORDER SERVED ON NON-ERISA RAILROAD SERVICE DEFINED BENEFIT PENSION PLAN

The following is a sample of a standardized court order for John Jones, an employee of a transportation firm and a participant in a non-ERISA defined benefit pension plan—the Railroad Retirement System—under the U.S. Railroad Retirement Board (RRB). John Jones is the husband and plaintiff in the divorce action. This court order is not called a QDRO; it is simply a domestic relations order.

DOMESTIC RELATIONS ORDER

Hearing Date: N/A

Hearing Time: N/A

Based on the findings of the Court,

IT IS HEREBY ORDERED, ADJUDGED, AND DECREED:

1. The parties hereto were husband and wife, and a divorce action has been entered in this Court at the above number. The Parties were married on _____ and divorced on _____ .

2. PARTICIPANT: John Jones
    Date of Birth: _____

    Social Security Number: _____
    hereinafter referred to as "Participant," has been employed by The XYZ Railroad Company and is a participant in the Railroad Retirement Board Pension Plan (the Plan).

3. The current and last known mailing address of Participant is:
    _____ .

4. Alternate Payee: Jane Smith, formerly Jane Jones

    Date of Birth: _____

    Social Security Number: _____
    hereinafter referred to as "Alternate Payee," has raised claims for, inter alia, equitable distribution of marital property.

5. The current and last known mailing address of Alternate Payee is:
    _____

6. By court decree, a portion of Participant's interest in the non-Tier I benefits in the Plan is marital property subject to distribution by this Court. Alternate Payee is awarded, and the Railroad Retirement Board is directed to pay, an interest in the portion of Participant's benefits under the Railroad Retirement Act (45 U.S.C. § 231 et seq.), which may be divided as provided by Section 14 of that Act (45 U.S.C. § 231m). Alternate Payee's share shall be computed

VI.

(continued)

by multiplying the divisible portion of Participant's monthly benefit by a Fraction as set forth below, which incorporates the number of years Participant worked for a railroad employer during the period of the marriage.

7. The Fraction referred to in paragraph 6 above shall be determined as follows:

$$\tfrac{1}{2} \times (24 \div TS)$$

where 24 is the number of years of marriage during which participant was covered by the RRB Plan and TS represents Participant's years of total pension-creditable railroad service at termination of railroad service.

8. The specified pension benefit shall be payable to Alternate Payee and shall commence as soon as administratively feasible on or about the date Participant actually retires or otherwise enters pension status for whatever reason.

9. The term of the regular monthly pension payments to Alternate Payee is for life during the life of Participant. Alternate Payee shall share in any scheduled and/or ad hoc increases to pensioners. The Plan shall issue individual tax forms to each such recipient for amounts paid to each such person. Alternate Payee is only entitled to the specific benefits under the Plan as provided for in this Order. All other rights, privileges, and options under the Plan not granted to Alternate Payee are preserved for the Participant.

10. The Plan to which this Order applies is stated in item 2 hereof, or any successor plan thereto.

11. The following attorneys are representatives for receipt of copies of notices:

    for Participant: _____

    for Alternate Payee: _____

12. It is intended that this order shall qualify as a Domestic Relations Order under the Railroad Retirement Act of 1983 concerning the partition of annuities by court decree. This is part of the final distribution of property between the parties; not an award of spousal support. The Court retains jurisdiction to amend this Order as might be necessary to establish or maintain its status.

SUBMITTED BY: _____

APPROVED AS TO FORM AND CONTENT:

Dated and Done this _____ day of _____ , _____ .

_____
                Judge

187

VII. STANDBY/LIEN QDRO—ERISA DEFINED BENEFIT PENSION PLAN

The following is a sample of a specialized QDRO served on a standby basis as a lien against husband's benefits, to be used if, as, and when needed. John Jones is the active participant in an ERISA defined benefit pension plan and the plaintiff in the divorce action.

DISTRICT COURT

John Jones,	)	
	)	
Plaintiff,	)	
	)	Case No. Dxxxxxx
vs.	)	
	)	
Jane Jones,	)	Dept No. Family
	)	
Defendant.	)	

QUALIFIED DOMESTIC RELATIONS ORDER

Hearing Date: N/A

Hearing Time: N/A

Based on the findings of the Court,

IT IS HEREBY ORDERED, ADJUDGED, AND DECREED:

1. PLAN. The Plan to which this Order applies is <u>The PLM Corporation Defined Benefit Pension Plan</u> as it now exists or may from time to time be amended, or any successor plan thereto. The rights of Alternate Payee under this Order are protected in the event of plan amendments, a plan merger, or a change in the sponsor of the Plan to the same extent that rights of participants or beneficiaries are protected with respect to benefits accrued as of the date of the event. The rights granted by this Order must be taken into account in the event of the termination of the Plan as if the terms of this Order were part of the Plan. To the extent that this Order grants Alternate Payee part of Participant's benefits, the Plan Administrator, in terminating the Plan, must provide Alternate Payee with the notification, consent, payment, or other rights that it would have provided to Participant with respect to that portion of Participant's benefits.
2. PARTIES. The parties hereto were husband and wife, and a divorce action is in this Court at the above number, and this Court has personal jurisdiction over the parties, the subject matter of this Order and this dissolution of marriage action pursuant to the domestic relations laws of this State. The parties were married on _____ and divorced on _____ .

VII.
(continued)

3.   PARTICIPANT: John Jones

Date of Birth: _____

Social Security Number: _____
hereinafter referred to as "Participant," is or has been employed by the Company and is or has been a participant in the named Plan.

4.   PARTICIPANT ADDRESS. The current and last known mailing address of Participant is: _____ .

5.   ALTERNATE PAYEE: Jane Smith, formerly Jane Jones

Date of Birth: _____

Social Security Number: _____
hereinafter referred to as "Alternate Payee," is the former spouse of Participant.

6.   ALTERNATE PAYEE ADDRESS. The current and last known mailing address of Alternate Payee is: _____ .

7.   Participant's benefits in the Plan are marital property subject to distribution by this Court as may be required in satisfaction of a lien. No distributions shall be made from the Plan to Participant during the period of time contemplated by the purposes of this Order, nor shall Participant receive from the Plan any loans nor withdrawals during that time.

8.   When required in accordance with item 9 below, Participant's benefits shall be awarded for accounting and record-keeping purposes to Alternate Payee.

9.   The benefits shall become due and payable from the Plan as a distribution to Alternate Payee, at her request (or, if not then living, her heirs or assigns) on the earliest practicable date, not in contradiction of the Plan or law or regulations, and the Plan shall so pay her if and when the first of the following items occurs:

   a.   A default in the scheduled payments from Participant to Alternate Payee for a period of time in excess of thirty (30) days;

   b.   Notice to Alternate Payee from the Plan, Participant, or any other party that the schedule of payments will be altered or delayed;

   c.   The termination of the Plan;

   d.   The filing by the Employer for bankruptcy under any bankruptcy Chapter or the dissolution of the Employer;

   e.   The filing by Participant for bankruptcy under any bankruptcy Chapter. Payout may be made before Participant terminates employment if so required by the terms and conditions of this Order.

10.   The form of said payment is a lump-sum distribution, if available, or otherwise a lifetime pension.

11.   The following attorney is representative for receipt of copies of notices pertaining to this Order: _____ .

189

VII.
(continued)

12. This Order shall become null and void upon satisfaction of the obligation by Participant completing the schedule of payments to Alternate Payee. In such case the lien shall be considered satisfied upon written notification from Alternate Payee to the Plan.

13. It is intended that this Order shall qualify as a Qualified Domestic Relations Order under the Retirement Equity Act of 1984, P.L. 98-397, for the purpose of the creation of a security interest in the Plan as permitted by Internal Revenue Code Section 401(a)(13)(B) as referred to by the Internal Revenue Service in Private Letter Ruling 9234014. The Court retains jurisdiction to amend this Order as might be necessary to establish or maintain its status.

SUBMITTED BY: _____

APPROVED AS TO FORM AND CONTENT:

Dated and Done this _____ day of _____ , _____ .

_____
            Judge

VIII. QDRO FOR CHILD SUPPORT—ERISA DEFINED BENEFIT PENSION PLAN

The following is a specialized QDRO to charge husband's benefits for past due child support. John Jones is the active participant in an ERISA defined benefit pension plan and the husband and the plaintiff in the divorce action.

DISTRICT COURT

John Jones,	)	
	)	
Plaintiff,	)	
	)	Case No. Dxxxxxx
vs.	)	
	)	
Jane Jones,	)	Dept No. Family
	)	
Defendant.	)	

QUALIFIED DOMESTIC RELATIONS ORDER FOR CHILD SUPPORT

Hearing Date: N/A

Hearing Time: N/A

Based on the findings of the Court,

IT IS HEREBY ORDERED, ADJUDGED, AND DECREED:

1. PLAN. The Plan to which this Order applies is The XYZ Corporation Sample Standard Defined Benefit Pension Plan as it now exists or may from time to time be amended, or any successor plan thereto. The rights of Alternate Payee under this Order are protected in the event of plan amendments, a plan merger, or a change in the sponsor of the Plan to the same extent that rights of participants or beneficiaries are protected with respect to benefits accrued as of the date of the event. The rights granted by this Order must be taken into account in the event of the termination of the Plan as if the terms of this Order were part of the Plan. To the extent that this Order grants Alternate Payee part of Participant's benefits, the Plan Administrator, in terminating the Plan, must provide Alternate Payee with the notification, consent, payment, or other rights that it would have provided to Participant with respect to that portion of Participant's benefits.

2. PARTIES. The parties hereto were husband and wife, with a dependent child, and husband is in arrears in the payment of court-ordered child support for the benefit of the dependent child of the parties. This Court has personal jurisdiction over the parties, the subject matter of this Order, and this action pursuant to the domestic relations laws of this State, having found Respondent to be in arrears for legally awarded child support payments due and owed to the Petitioner. The parties were married on _____ and divorced on _____.

VIII.

(continued)

3. PARTICIPANT. John Jones

   Date of Birth: _____

   Social Security Number: _____
   hereinafter referred to as "Participant," is or has been employed by the Company and is or has been a participant in the named Plan.

4. PARTICIPANT ADDRESS. The current and last known mailing address of Participant is: _____ .

5. ALTERNATE PAYEE. Jane Smith, formerly Jane Jones

   Date of Birth: _____

   Social Security Number: _____
   hereinafter referred to as "Alternate Payee," is the former spouse of Participant, and has an interest in Participant's benefits under the domestic relations laws of this State with respect to child support. As the former wife of Participant, Alternate Payee is the custodial parent of the dependent child who is the subject of the child support arrears payments due from Participant.

6. ALTERNATE PAYEE ADDRESS. The current and last known mailing address of Alternate Payee is _____ .

7. LAW. Participant's interest in the Plan is domestic property subject to distribution for the payment of child support by this Court under State law for the jurisdiction in which this Order is issued and under which the above-named Participant and Alternate Payee are covered. This Order creates and recognizes as to the Plan the existence of Alternate Payee's right, subject to the provisions of this Order, and subject to the terms and conditions of the Plan, to a share of benefits otherwise payable to Participant under the Plan, in the amount and form as set forth herein.

8. TAX. The Plan shall issue individual tax forms as may be required by the Internal Revenue Service, and for local or state taxes as may be appropriate, under the tax provisions relating to child support payments made to the parent of the dependent child under a Qualified Domestic Relations Order, which payments are taxable to Participant, and not taxable to Alternate Payee.

9. PAYMENT. Alternate Payee is awarded, as separate property, the portion of Participant's calculated pension benefit as determined and described in accordance with this Order, or its actuarial equivalent under the Plan, to become payable to Alternate Payee as soon as administratively feasible on or about the date Participant commences receiving benefits under the Plan, or as soon as may be otherwise legally available under the terms of the Plan at the request of Alternate Payee but not later than Participant's normal retirement date. Alternate Payee shall provide the Plan Administrator with at least thirty (30) days' written notice of election to commence receiving pension benefits under this Order, or such other time period as the Plan may

VIII.

(continued)

require, and shall complete such distribution request forms and provide such additional information as may be reasonably requested by the Plan Administrator. Alternate Payee's benefit shall be reduced as may be required by the Plan to reflect early retirement, age, and the form or type of such benefit. The award to Alternate Payee shall not exceed the value of Participant's vested interest in the Plan as of the date coinciding with or immediately preceding the date of payment to Alternate Payee. The remaining amount is the separate property of Participant. Payment shall not be made before notice is given to the parties or their legal representatives from the Plan Administrator that this Order constitutes a Qualified Domestic Relations Order.

10.   JURISDICTION. It is intended that this Order shall qualify as a Qualified Domestic Relations Order for the benefit of a dependent child under the Retirement Equity Act of 1984, P.L. 98-397, in accordance with Section 414(p) of the Internal Revenue Code of 1986, as amended, and the appropriately applicable provisions of the Employee Retirement Income Security Act of 1974, as amended, and its provisions shall be administered and interpreted in conformity with such provisions. If any provision of this Order is inapplicable, it shall be ignored and it shall not affect the validity of other provisions or of the Order itself. The Court retains jurisdiction to amend this Order as might be necessary to establish or maintain its status.

SUBMITTED BY: ―――――――――――――――――

APPROVED AS TO FORM AND CONTENT:

Dated and Done this ――――――― day of ―――― , ―――― .

―――――――――――――――――
Judge

APPENDIXES

APPENDIX A

EXAMINATION OF PENSION EXPERT WITNESS

In a typical divorce case, counsel for one of the parties may retain an actuary to testify as an expert witness regarding the other party's pension. Following is the hypothetical transcript of such testimony, provided by an actuary retained by counsel for the nonemployee-spouse.

Q. Counsel for the parties have stipulated to your appearance as an expert witness on the subject of pensions. Are you ready to proceed?

A. Yes.

Q. Are you appearing here a paid expert witness?

A. Yes.

Q. Is your fee in any way dependent or conditioned on the outcome of your valuation?

A. No, it never is. I do the same valuation, and arrive at the same results and conclusions, regardless of which party may have retained my services and regardless of the fee paid.

Q. Have you prepared a valuation report?

A. Yes.

Q. Has anyone, including myself, directed you as to what methods or assumptions to use in your valuations?

A. No. If that had happened, I would have refused.

Q. Did you receive information about this case?

A. Yes, I received a copy of each of the plans, summary plan booklets for each plan, as well as individual benefit and account statements and copies of correspondence.

Q. Were you informed of certain dates when events occurred?

A. Yes, I received basic data, such as dates of birth, date of marriage, date of marital dissolution, and Mr. X's employment date.

Q. Have you discussed this case or any information with Mr. X or asked him any questions?

A. No. Today is the first time I have seen Mr. X.

Q. Have you discussed this case or any information with Mrs. X?

A. Yes, briefly, this morning in your office.

Q. What did you use for Mr. X's employment date?

A. Mr. X's date of hire was April 1, 1969, and his date of plan entry was January 1, 1970.

Q. What is the difference between hire date and plan entry?

A. The plan requires a waiting or eligibility period.

Q. How did the plan's eligibility waiting period affect Mr. X?

A. Mr. X entered each plan on the first day of the plan year, January 1, following his completion of six months at work.

Q. How does that affect his pension, if it does?

A. Mr. X's credited service in this plan starts on his date of plan entry, not his date of hire, so it counts from January 1, 1970.

Q. Is that an unusual feature, peculiar to this plan?

A. No, it is relatively common.

Q. In what case would it be different?

A. Some plans count an employee's service from the date of hire for pension benefit credits.

Q. In your experience, how do plans usually count service?

A. Some plans count in years and months, others in years and fractions of a year.

Q. How do these plans count credited service?

A. Both of the plans in question count credited service in years and completed calendar months.

Q. Doesn't Mr. X's date of hire count for anything?

A. Yes, of course. It establishes the starting point for counting time for his eligibility to enter the plan.

Q. In what kinds of plans does Mr. X participate?

A. Mr. X is a participant in a defined benefit pension plan as well as in a defined contribution plan.

Q. Please define or describe the two plans.

A. In the defined benefit pension plan, Mr. X is earning a pension benefit each year, based on his pay and service. At retirement, the pension benefit will be paid to him as a monthly annuity for the rest of his life.

Q. What about the second plan?

A. In the defined contribution plan, a 401(k) plan, Mr. X is accumulating an account balance through his own contributions as an employee, his employer's contributions, plus investment gains. When he retires, the account balance will be paid to him as a lump-sum distribution or rolled over into an individual retirement account (IRA).

Q. What is Mr. X's account balance in the 401(k) plan?

A. Mr. X's account balance in the 401(k) plan was zero on January 1, 1970. At the date of marriage, the account balance was $10,000.

Q. Please identify each exhibit I hand to you.

A. Exhibit 1 is the formal plan document for the defined benefit pension plan. Exhibit 2 is the formal plan document for the savings plan. Exhibit 3 is the plan booklet for the pension plan, and Exhibit 4 is the plan booklet for the 401(k) plan.

Q. What is the difference between a plan booklet and a formal plan document?

A. The plan booklet is a summary describing the main features of the plan and is written in language designed to be understood by the typical employee. The plan document is the legal written plan in full. It is a formal and technical document, much longer than the summary.

Q. Would the important items in the full plan appear in the booklet distributed to employees?

A. Yes. That is a requirement for the booklet.

Q. What is a summary plan description?

A. That is the technical name of the plan booklet.

Q. What is a summary of material modifications?

A. That is a communication to employees from the employer, telling them that there has been a plan amendment.

Q. Do the plans in question today have formal documents and plan booklets?

A. Yes, and I have already identified them.

Q. What about amendments and modifications?

A. The only ones in the materials that I received are from several years ago and are included in the plans and booklets already.

Q. What is a summary annual report?

A. A summary annual report (SAR) is a general financial report that a qualified plan issues annually to plan participants.

Q. Does the summary annual report give participants details of their benefits or account balances?

A. No. The SAR is the overall report of total plan assets.

Q. What is a "qualified plan"?

A. A plan that has filed with the Internal Revenue Service and received a favorable determination letter in accordance with ERISA is a qualified plan.

Q. What is ERISA?

A. ERISA stands for Employee Retirement Income Security Act of 1974, the basic federal law governing pensions.

Q. Are the plans under discussion today covered by ERISA?

A. Yes, they are.

Q. Are there different ways of referring to the two plans?

A. Yes, the defined benefit pension plan may simply be called the pension plan. The defined contribution plan has several informal names—savings plan, profit-sharing plan, or 401(k) plan.

Q. What is a 401(k) plan?

A. A profit-sharing or savings plan established under Section 401(k) of the Internal Revenue Code that allows pretax employee contributions. Section 401 begins the part of the Code that deals with pensions.

Q. Is such a tax-favored employee contribution feature permitted in defined benefit pension plans?

A. No, this feature is restricted to defined contribution plans.

Q. With respect to these two plans, what does "vesting" mean?

A. Vesting is the employee's rights to his or her benefits. Once vested, an employee's benefits cannot be lost or forfeited, except for certain special exemptions.

Q. What is an example of a special case where a vested benefit could be lost or diminished?

A. One example would be an error in data, such as the plan records having the wrong date of birth or date of hire.

Q. Are there any other examples?

A. An example is a defined benefit pension plan with insufficient assets to pay all vested benefits.

Q. What would happen in a plan termination?

A. If the plan is covered by the Pension Benefit Guaranty Corporation (PBGC), the PBGC will cover most, but not necessarily all, of the covered plan's vested benefits.

Q. Does the PBGC cover the savings plan?

A. No, the PBGC covers only defined benefit pension plans.

Q. Does the PBGC cover all defined benefit pension plans?

A. No, it applies only to plans qualified by the IRS under ERISA, and there are some exceptions to that.

Q. Is this defined benefit pension plan covered by the PBGC?

A. Yes, it is.

Q. Are there any other ways in which a benefit can be reduced or lost in a qualified plan?

A. Yes, a plan could be amended to reduce future benefit accruals or to reduce future contribution levels.

Q. How does an employee acquire vesting?

A. Plans have schedules using years of employment service. Also, vesting is automatic when the employee reaches normal retirement age in a plan, regardless of service.

Q. Is the service for vesting different from the service for benefits or contributions?

A. Yes. Vesting service starts on the first day of full-time employment. Benefit credit service or contributions usually start at the date of plan entry, which could be up to one year later than the first day of full-time employment.

Q. Is there any way a vested benefit could be diminished for a participant in a qualified plan?

A. Yes, in theory there are some ways in which a vested benefit could be diminished for a participant in a qualified plan. For example, a tax lien on an individual may be satisfied by the IRS's attaching some or all of the person's benefits or the person's account balance.

Q. Are you aware of any such actual or potential action by the IRS against either Mr. X or Mrs. X in this case?

A. No, but I would have no way of knowing that unless I had been told. Nothing about a tax action was in the material.

Q. How else could an employee's benefits be lessened?

A. In a divorce action, a qualified domestic relations order (QDRO) can attach all or some of a pension benefit or an account balance as marital property, for distribution to the nonemployee-spouse.

Q. Is Mr. X presently vested in each plan?

A. Yes, he is fully vested at 100 percent in his accrued pension benefit in the defined benefit pension plan, and he is fully vested at 100 percent in his total account balance in the savings plan.

Q. Is Mr. X's account balance guaranteed because it is vested?

A. No. The account balance is subject to investment fluctuations.

Q. Please identify the next exhibit.

A. Exhibit 5 is a copy of Mr. X's individual annual benefit statement, which was issued to him for the defined benefit pension plan.

Q. Do you see any differences in these two items?

A. Yes. The pension plan statement illustrates a monthly pension benefit that he had accrued or earned and a projection of what his benefit might be if he continued to work until age 65.

Q. In the projection benefit shown on the pension plan statement, what is considered?

A. The projected benefit is illustrated on the assumption that Mr. X remains employed and in the pension plan.

Q. Does this projected benefit assume anything else?

A. It assumes Mr. X's pay never changes.

Q. What is shown on Mr. X's saving plan account statement?

A. It shows the account balance as of the statement date and the various internal investments that he selected.

Q. Does the account statement show what Mr. X's account would be at age 65, similar to the pension benefit plan statement?

A. No, it does not.

Q. Would it be helpful to have an account projection?

A. No. That would be a useless projection, because it would depend on future investment results in addition to future contributions, both of which are unknown at present.

Q. Where do contributions come from for the savings plan?

A. The employee's pretax and after-tax contributions and the employer's contributions.

Q. Who controls the investments in a pension plan?

A. In a defined benefit pension plan, there are trustees of the plan who make the investment decisions for the plan in total. There are no individual investments.

Q. Who controls the investments in a savings plan?

A. A defined contribution plan generally has subaccounts for each participant. Employees make contributions to their own accounts and the employer makes contributions to their accounts.

Q. May employees control their own accounts?

A. A defined contribution plan may allow the employees limited investment direction over their individual accounts.

Q. At my request, have you prepared valuations of Mr. X's interests in both of these plans?

A. Yes, using my standard professional actuarial method.

Q. Have you formed an opinion about the marital property values?

A. Yes, I have.

Q. How accurate are your findings?

A. The findings are mathematically correct, and I offer my professional opinion with reasonable certainty. It takes into account mortality and interest rates. It reflects the current price of a deferred pension annuity sold by a typical insurance company on the basis of the facts of this case.

Q. Is that what an employee would pay at retirement to obtain a pension if it were being privately purchased?

A. No, the amount at retirement is only part of it. It must be discounted to today's present value.

Q. Why is it discounted?

A. The "discount," or "bringing to present value," allows for two functions. First, mortality, because the employee may die before reaching retirement age, and, if the employee survives to retire, then at some time after retiring, the employee will die.

Q. How do you allow for the possibility of death before retirement?

A. It is built into the factors by use of a standard mortality table.

Q. What is a standard mortality table?

A. There are several mortality tables available, compiled and published by a national actuarial professional organization.

Q. How do you know which mortality table to use?

A. The General Agreement on Tariffs and Trade (GATT) mandated the use of a specific mortality table for pension work. It is the 1983 Group Annuity Mortality Table, referred to either as GAM 83 or 83 GAM.

Q. Do your calculations allow for a possible termination of employment before retirement age?

A. No, it is not necessary to make this allowance.

Q. Why is it not necessary? Can't it happen?

A. Certainly. Mr. X could terminate employment before becoming eligible for retirement. He could quit, be fired, or lose the job for any number of reasons.

Q. Why, then, does termination of employment not feature in your calculations?

A. Because Mr. X is already 100 percent vested in both plans.

Q. So what would happen to his account and to his benefits?

A. Mr. X is fully entitled to everything presently accrued in each plan in his behalf, whether his employment ends or continues.

Q. If his employment did end prematurely, let us say, would that change your results?

A. No.

Q. Why not?

A. For the defined benefit pension plan, I have computed the actuarial present value of his accrued and vested pension benefit. No future changes in his employment service are relevant. This is the value now of his benefit as it stands.

Q. What about termination of service for the savings plan?

A. Mr. X is fully vested in that plan, too.

Q. What would happen to his account balance upon termination of service?

A. Upon termination of employment, Mr. X would receive his account balance from the plan in a lump sum or he could request that the funds in the account be transferred to an IRA in his name.

Q. In your valuation of the pension, what else, if anything, is included besides mortality?

A. There is an interest discount to reflect the time value of money. A debt or obligation due in the future has a smaller value today than it will have when it must be paid. An interest discount is used in the calculations to arrive at the current figure that will be appropriate when it appreciates with interest to meet the amounts due, to provide the monthly pension annuity benefit at retirement.

Q. What interest rate are you using, and why?

A. The rate used is 6.60 percent per year, compounded annually. This is the prevailing rate announced by the Federal Reserve Board for the smoothed average of 30-year U.S. Treasury bonds.

Q. What do you mean by "the smoothed average"?

A. The yields on Treasury securities are measured daily by the U.S. Treasury and averaged to obtain a figure for the month. The average is also known as the "interpolated" average or "constant maturity." It is a mathematical curve that relates the yield on a security to its time to maturity.

Q. What is your source for these interest rates?

A. The rates are published by the Federal Reserve Board.

Q. In general, how is the present value of a defined benefit affected by one interest rate being higher or lower than some other interest rate?

A. There is a standard relationship between present values and interest rates that is always true in every pension situation. It is an inverse mathematical relationship; the higher the interest rate, the lower the present value.

Q. What if there is a lower interest rate?

A. Then the present value would be higher.

Q. One would think that if the interest rate is higher, the value would be higher. Why is that not so?

A. That is true for the savings plan, but not for the defined benefit pension plan.

Q. How does interest affect the employee's account in a savings plan?

A. There are individual accounts that grow with favorable investment results. If the account items receive more interest, then more money is earned in the account.

Q. Does higher interest mean a higher level of benefits?

A. In a defined contribution plan, yes. In a defined benefit pension plan, no. Pension benefits are determined by plan formula, based on service and salary. The investment earnings of the pension fund have no bearing on pension benefits.

Q. In a defined benefit pension plan, why does a higher interest rate produce a lower value?

A. The value is the amount of money needed today in order to provide a benefit in the future. The more that money can earn through higher interest investments, the less is needed to start with.

Q. Does the Pension Benefit Guaranty Corporation publish interest rates for pension plans?

A. Yes.

Q. Did you use PBGC rates in your valuation?

A. No, the PBGC rates are no longer applicable for this purpose.

Q. Why not?

A. Because they have been replaced by GATT rates.

Q. Have you formed an opinion of value in this case?

A. Yes.

Q. In your professional opinion, what is the actuarial present value of Mr. X's defined benefit pension plan?

A. It is valued at $31,801, but that is not the marital portion.

Q. What is the marital portion?

A. The marital portion is valued at $26,384, which is approximately 83 percent.

Q. Have you arrived at these pension values as of a certain date?

A. Yes, the valuation date is today.

Q. When you were preparing the valuation, how did you know to use today's date as the valuation date?

A. Some months ago, I did a preliminary pension valuation at your request. Last month, you informed me that today was the scheduled date of trial. So I used today's date as the valuation date.

Q. What is the significance of the valuation date?

A. The valuation date is very important for calculation purposes. It determines the person's age nearest birthday.

Q. What does "age nearest birthday" mean?

A. It means the age of the individual on the birthday that is nearest to the calculation date. We find what age occurs within six months either way of today as the valuation date.

Q. How does age affect the pension value?

A. The older the employee and the closer the employee is to retirement age, the larger the value of the pension.

Q. Does that mean that given the same pension benefit for two employees in the same plan, the older of the two would have a greater pension value?

A. That's right. All other things equal, the younger employee's pension would be worth less.

Q. Please identify the next exhibit.

A. It is my report with my findings. There is a forwarding letter, a page of computations, a graph illustrating the marital coverture fraction, supporting materials, and references.

Q. What are the steps in your calculations?

A. I start with a male, age 47, whose normal retirement age is 65.

Q. How do you know retirement age is 65?

A. The normal retirement age in the plan is 65.

Q. Does the pension plan have an early retirement age?

A. Yes, an employee may retire at any time between ages 55 and 64.

Q. Did you account for the possibility of Mr. X's early retirement?

A. Yes. I checked my computations using three different early retirement ages.

Q. With what result?

A. Virtually the same as the basic valuation, because the benefits are reduced by the plan for any early retirement. The combination of the reduced benefit and the actuarial factors at an earlier age results in just about the same value as for the full benefit at normal retirement age of 65.

Q. Will Mr. X retire at age 65?

A. It doesn't matter.

Q. Why doesn't that matter?

A. Mr. X's accrued and vested pension benefit in the plan has been determined by the plan formula using his known pay and service to date. This benefit is payable when he reaches age 65.

Q. What is your next step?

A. I learn from Mr. X's benefit statement that his current monthly pension is $1,000. If he never works another day, he will receive from the plan a lifetime pension of $1,000 a month, starting at age 65.

Q. Then how do you determine its value?

A. Using the standard mortality table and the current interest rate, the factor for a 47-year-old male, with retirement age 65, is 2.6501.

APPENDIX A

Q. Is that 2 or 3 percent interest?

A. Neither, 2.6501 is the factor, not the interest rate. Multiply the factor of 2.6501 by the monthly pension benefit of $1,000, and then multiply the result by 12.

Q. Why do you multiply by 12?

A. The factor is on annual basis, but the benefit is in monthly form. So there must be a multiplication of the monthly benefit by 12 to annualize it or to represent it as a pension benefit payable annually, to be consistent with the way the factor is produced.

Q. What is the result of all of those multiplications?

A. The result is $31,801, or 12 times $1,000 times 2.6501.

Q. How do you allocate or determine the marital portion?

A. By the use of the marital coverture fraction, which is equal to the number of years and months that the parties were married while Mr. X participated in the plan, divided by the number of years and months of Mr. X's total plan participation.

Q. Is the time rule the same as the time value of money?

A. No. The time rule allocates the marital portion as part of the total benefit value, whereas the time value of money is a step in the calculation of the actuarial present value of a pension in a defined benefit pension plan.

Q. What do you mean by the time the parties were married?

A. As part of the time rule allocation, I count the length of time that the parties were married during the time the employee-spouse was earning benefit credits.

Q. What are the steps in that calculation?

A. You start with the later of the date of marriage or the date of plan entry. In this case, Mr. X entered the pension plan on January 1, 1970, and the date of marriage is July 4, 1974, so the starting point for measuring the marital portion is July 4, 1974.

Q. What is the marital coverture fraction?

A. It is .82965, or just under 83 percent.

Q. What is your professional opinion as to the marital present value of Mr. X's interest in the defined benefit pension plan?

A. In my professional opinion, it is $26,384.

Q. With respect to the benefit statement from the defined benefit pension plan, in addition to the accrued and vested pension benefit, are any other pension benefits shown?

A. Yes, it shows an illustration of Mr. X's projected pension benefit at age 65, assuming no increase in pay.

Q. What does the statement show that pension to be?

A. The estimated pension benefit is $2,075 per month, payable at age 65, if Mr. X works until then and retires with no increase in pay.

Q. Is the monthly benefit of some $2,000 in addition to Mr. X's vested and accrued pension benefit of $1,000 a month?

A. No. The current amount of $1,000 is part of the estimated total benefit.

Q. Would it be fair to say that so far he has accumulated about one-half of his total retirement pension?

A. That would be a reasonable approximation in comparing the pension benefits for him in this plan, but it assumes his pay will never change.

Q. Would it be fair to say that the marital portion of the value of his pension currently is about one-half of his ultimate pension?

A. No, it doesn't work that way. The pension amounts as benefits are roughly in proportion to the current benefit as one-half of the total benefit, but the values are skewed in a different relationship.

Q. What is the actuarial present value of the estimated age 65 pension benefit of $2,075 per month?

A. The actuarial present value is $65,987, or 12 times $2,075 times 2.6501.

Q. Is 2.6501 the same factor that you used earlier?

A. Yes, because Mr. X is still a 47-year-old male.

Q. When the pension has been valued and reduced to present value, and the marital portion has been allocated, what next?

A. The parties agree to the value, or the court finds that the value is proper and correct, and then the value is compared and set off against other marital property or assets.

Q. Is there a general name for that procedure?

A. Yes, the procedure is generally known as "immediate offset."

Q. If, for whatever reason, immediate offset of pension values is not appropriate in this case, is there an alternative?

A. Yes, the alternative is deferred distribution.

Q. Explain "deferred distribution."

A. In deferred distribution, both parties wait until the employee-spouse retires. When the employee-spouse's pension becomes payable, the plan pays benefits to the employee-spouse and to the former spouse by use of a special kind of court order.

Q. And what is that special kind of court order called?

A. It is called a domestic relations order (DRO).

Q. What is the difference between a DRO and a QDRO?

A. When a DRO is approved by the court, it becomes a QDRO.

Q. Is a deferred distribution possible in the present case?

A. Yes, if the court so finds.

Q. What federal law allows DROs and QDROs?

A. The basic federal law of pensions is ERISA.

Q. Are there other federal laws that apply?

A. Yes, the Retirement Equity Act of 1984 (REA).

Q. Are Mr. X's plans covered by the REA?

A. Yes.

Q. Must the employee consent to the use of a court order that attaches or assigns his or her pension to a former spouse?

A. No. It is an order of the court in adjudication of the case, as part of the distribution of marital property, and neither party can refuse to honor it.

Q. Must the plan accept this kind of court order?

A. If the plan is covered by ERISA and the REA, as these plans are, the plan administrator must accept the court order for review.

Q. What happens during the review?

A. The plan administrator is responsible for determining whether a court order is qualified under federal laws and regulations. Qualification changes the DRO into a QDRO.

Q. May the DRO or QDRO address the subject of early retirement?

A. Yes. If the plan has an early retirement feature, the court order may (but is not required to) include that feature.

Q. If Mr. X were to elect early retirement after the divorce, how would it affect the pension payments?

A. Mrs. X's share of the benefits would be paid to her at the time Mr. X takes early retirement.

Q. Is the benefit amount the same upon early retirement?

A. The defined benefit pension plan reduces the monthly pension benefit if it is paid before normal retirement age.

Q. Would that affect Mrs. X's share of benefits?

A. Yes, if payments of her monthly pension under the QDRO start before she is at the plan's normal retirement age, her pension payments will be reduced.

Q. May QDROs be used for both the 401(k) plan and the defined benefit pension plan?

A. Yes, but a separate order is needed for each plan.

Q. How would a QDRO work on the 401(k) plan?

A. A common approach is for the court to order the payment of a current distribution from the defined contribution plan to Mrs. X as soon as the DRO is qualified by the plan.

Q. How does income tax apply in a QDRO?

A. No taxes are due until benefits are paid.

Q. When are taxes charged?

A. Each party reports and pays taxes on benefits received, whether in the form of a pension annuity or a lump sum.

Q. Is a rollover to an IRA an option?

A. Yes, for the lump-sum distribution, but not for annuity payments.

Q. Is there current taxation with a rollover to an IRA?

A. Not if it is done correctly.

Q. What is the correct way to effect a rollover to an IRA?

A. The trustees of the pension fund must transmit the money directly to the trustee or custodian of the IRA account or to another qualified plan, bypassing the employee.

Q. Is there a time period in which a rollover must be done?

A. Not if the funds are transferred directly from trustee to trustee.

Q. Is there any time limit at all?

A. The only stipulation is that the rollover must be accomplished in a "reasonable" period.

Q. Isn't there a 60-day time limit?

A. If the individual receives the money that is eligible to be rolled over into an IRA or to a successor plan, he or she must transfer the money within 60 days of receipt. There is no time limit for a trustee transfer.

Q. Is there income tax withholding on a benefit payment?

A. Yes, if a lump-sum distribution is made to an individual.

Q. What if payment is to an individual under a QDRO?

A. If there is a direct trustee transfer, there is no withholding. But if a lump-sum distribution is paid to an individual, whether an employee or the alternate payee under a QDRO, there is a mandatory personal income tax withholding of 20 percent.

Q. Assuming that a proper distribution from a QDRO has been rolled over into an IRA, when are taxes assessed?

A. The regular IRA taxation rules apply. When a distribution is paid out of the IRA, the recipient will have to pay taxes. In other words, when the IRA monies are paid to the retiree, he or she reports that money as income and pays taxes on it.

Q. Does the investment of the plan assets affect their value?

A. In a defined benefit pension plan, the benefit is fixed by plan formula based on pay and service; the value of plan assets is not relevant.

Q. How does the amount of the fund affect an employee's pension benefits?

A. The trust fund does not affect benefits except in rare cases. If the plan is underfunded and if the plan terminates with insufficient assets, it is possible that some benefits of employees may be reduced.

Q. Is there PBGC protection?

A. If the plan is a covered defined benefit pension plan, the PBGC will protect pension benefits up to a limit. The amount guaranteed increases each year with inflation.

Q. What if a defined benefit pension plan is overfunded?

A. If such a plan terminates with surplus assets, the alternatives include reallocating monies to increase pension benefits.

Q. Thank you, no more questions.

Cross-Examination

Q. Have you been retained on behalf of Mrs. X.?

A. Yes, but my report would be the same if Mr. X had retained me.

Q. Did counsel for Mrs. X give you any directions as to what methods or assumptions to use in your computations?

A. No. If she had, I would not have proceeded.

Q. Did counsel for Mrs. X discuss appropriate case law with you on points deemed pertinent to this case?

A. Yes, she did. However, I was already familiar with the cases mentioned.

Q. Did you independently verify the accuracy of the pension data you received?

A. No. I checked it for reasonableness.

Q. If you had used a different interest rate, would your results be different?

A. Yes.

Q. What is the current prime rate?

A. When I last checked in *The Wall Street Journal*, it was at 8.5 percent.

Q. Do you accept *The Wall Street Journal* as authoritative?

A. Generally, yes.

Q. So why didn't you use the rate cited in the authoritative source?

A. The published prime rate has no bearing on pension values.

Q. Do you know how municipal bond interest rates are reported and where that information is found?

A. Yes, generally in The Wall Street Journal, but there are many other sources of financial information that would report the rate.

Q. Is it fair to say that municipal bond interest rates are a reasonable measure of the financial markets?

A. No, I do not agree with that statement. Municipal bonds are just one of many possible financial measures, and municipal bond interest rates are not sanctioned by the IRS or the PBGC for pension purposes.

Q. You have testified that a different valuation date would produce a different valuation result, is that right?

A. Yes.

Q. Did anyone tell you what valuation date to use?

A. No, but I was told that this trial was scheduled for today so I used today's date as the valuation date, as is my standard practice. When I know the scheduled date of a conference, hearing, or trial, I prepare the valuation as of the scheduled date to the extent possible.

Q. Is it correct to say that if you had performed the pension valuation when the parties first separated, the value would have been lower because the individuals were younger?

A. Not necessarily. It would depend also on what the interest rates were at the earlier date.

Q. In your valuation of Mr. X's defined benefit pension plan, what was your assumption for the age at which he would die?

A. That is not part of my calculations.

Q. How can you determine a pension value without an assumed age of death?

A. An estimated age of death is not appropriate for establishing a pension value.

Q. When Mr. X dies, won't his pension stop?

A. Certainly.

Q. But you have not considered it, have you?

A. Yes, I have, as a standard actuarial requirement. It is accounted for in the use of mortality in the actuarial computation of present value. The probability of death exists at each point of future time, and that probability is an important component of the pension value.

Q. Couldn't that be done by reference to a standard life expectancy table?

A. Using a standard life expectancy table would not be correct for several reasons. The standard life tables apply to the general public. In this case, however, we are concerned with active employed individuals. The age at death in a standard life table is an overall average that allows for only one outcome. No insurance company or pension fund uses life expectancy to establish benefits, liabilities, values, or premiums. It would introduce gross inaccuracies.

Q. Are you saying that life expectancy plays no role in pension valuation?

A. Yes, it is not appropriate for a pension valuation. However, there are other uses for the concept of life expectancy. The IRS uses life expectancy in the requirements for minimum distribution amounts at age $70\frac{1}{2}$.

Q. Are you aware that in this state the concept of life expectancy is embodied in a great many court decisions?

A. Yes, but not pension cases.

Q. Why do you think the state courts have used life expectancy?

A. They use it for personal injury and wrongful death cases, but not in pension work.

Q. Thank you. No more questions.

SAMPLE SUMMARY PLAN DESCRIPTION FOR A DEFINED BENEFIT PENSION PLAN

The summary plan description (SPD) presented here is an example of a typical plan booklet for a defined benefit pension plan. The plan is funded by the employer, with benefits based on service and average pay, and it allows voluntary employee contributions. The plan is covered by Employee Retirement Income Security Act of 1974 (ERISA) and by the Pension Benefit Guaranty Corporation (PBGC).

The author's comments and interpretations, which follow the sample SPD, point out the explicit intent and purpose of the various sections of the plan booklet as well as what is left unsaid. For easy cross-referencing, the comments are numbered according to the numbered headings of items in the SPD.

SUMMARY PLAN DESCRIPTION
OF THE CORPORATION COMPANY, INC.
PENSION PLAN

I. IDENTIFICATION

    A. The name of the plan is the Corporation Company, Inc. Pension Plan.

    B. The Corporation, your employer, is the Sponsor of the plan with the address, telephone number, and identification numbers shown below:

        1. Name: Corporation Company, Inc.

        2. Address: 123 Any Street, Anywhere, USA 12345

        3. Telephone number: (555) 555-5555

        4. EIN: 00-0000000

        5. PN: 001

    C. The plan administrator is a Pension Committee (EIN 11-1111111) named by the Corporation, at the address and telephone number shown above.

    D. The Trustees of the Pension Fund are:
        Joe Boss and Charles Chief

    E. The original effective date of the plan was May 1, 1970.

II. ADMINISTRATION

    A. This plan is a defined benefit pension plan administered by a Pension Committee.

    B. The Corporation is designated as agent for service of legal process in its position as Employer and Sponsor at the address shown above. The plan is administered on a plan year basis.

    C. The plan year begins May 1 and ends April 30.

    D. The mailing address is the same as that of the Corporation. Any service of legal process may be made on the Administrator (Pension Committee) or a Trustee.

III. ELIGIBILITY

    A. If you are in an eligible classification and if you work at least 1,000 hours a year, you are eligible to be in the plan after age 21 and with one year of employment with the Corporation.

    B. You enter the plan on the May 1st nearest to your eligibility date.

IV. CONTRIBUTIONS

    A. The Corporation pays the entire cost of the plan. Annual contributions to the plan are determined actuarially upon recommendation of the plan's enrolled actuary.

    B. You may make voluntary contributions to add to your retirement benefits. Your own contributions are not tax-deductible, but any earnings on them are tax-sheltered until withdrawn or paid out as benefits. You are always 100 percent vested in the current value of any voluntary contributions you may choose to make.

V. PLAN COMPENSATION

    A. For purposes of determining your benefits under the plan, the average of your plan compensation is taken for the highest five consecutive years. Generally, this will be the average over the period from ages 57 to 62 but need not be, if some other five-year period provides a higher average.

    B. Your plan compensation is your base pay each plan year, not including any bonus or overtime pay.

VI. PENSION FORMULA

    A. Your pension benefit at retirement is established as a monthly amount by a formula based on your average plan compensation and service.

        1. Determine your highest consecutive five-year average plan compensation, on a monthly pay basis.

        2. Multiply item (1) by .025.

        3. Multiply item (2) by your expected total years of service.

    B. *Example:* Average plan compensation $1,000 a month and 30 years expected total service at retirement.

$$.025 \times \$1,000 \times 30 \text{ years} = \$750 \text{ per month}$$

VII. ACCRUED BENEFIT

    A. Each year of participation in the plan you are "earning" or "accruing" credit toward your retirement pension. Once a year we determine the amount of pension benefit accrued so far for you.

    B. The amount of benefit you have accrued is computed as a fraction of the pension benefit expected to be payable when you retire. First, your retirement benefit at age 62 is calculated based on your current age and pay level. Then it is multiplied by a fraction, the numerator of which is your years of credited service at present and the denominator of which is years of credited service you will have if you work until age 62.

    C. *Example:* Expected pension at age 62 is $750 a month, credited service so far is 10 years, total credited service at age 62 is 30 years.

$$\text{Your accrued benefit is } 10/30 \times \$750 = \$250 \text{ a month}$$

VIII. VESTING

    A. You achieve non-forfeitable rights to your accrued benefit, known as vesting.

    B. The following table shows how your vesting increases with your years of employment with the Corporation.

Years of Employment	Vesting Percentage
Less than 5	0%
5 or more	100%

IX. NORMAL RETIREMENT

    A. Your normal retirement age is 62. Your normal retirement date is the first day of the month following your 62nd birthday (or on your 62nd birthday if that is the first day of a month).

    B. You are 100 percent vested at your normal retirement date.

X. EARLY RETIREMENT
   A. You may elect to retire early, at or after age 55.
   B. The plan reduces your pension if you retire before age 62 with an early retirement benefit. The Administrator will discuss this with you at your request.

XI. DISABILITY
   A. If you suffer a mental or physical incapacity, which is presumed to be total and permanent as certified to the Corporation by competent medical authority satisfactory to the Corporation, you will be eligible to receive your vested benefit.
   B. If this happens, the Administrator will discuss the various forms of payment available.

XII. DEATH BENEFIT
   A. In case of your death while an active participant, your beneficiary will be eligible to receive your vested benefit. The Administrator will discuss the various forms of payment available to your beneficiary as a pre-retirement death benefit.

XIII. POSTPONED RETIREMENT
   A. If you wish to continue working past age 62, you may remain in active employment and continue to be an active participant in the plan. Your pension will start when you actually retire.
   B. This is not, of course, any guarantee of continued employment.

XIV. BENEFIT PAYMENTS
   A. The normal form of pension if you are single is a monthly lifetime pension annuity. This means that if you are scheduled to receive, for example, $1,000 a month, you would receive the $1,000 monthly for as long as you live. Upon your death your pension stops.
   B. The normal form if you are married is a reduced pension paid as a qualified joint-and-survivor annuity with your spouse as beneficiary. This may be waived to be replaced by any form allowed by the plan if you and your spouse sign the proper forms and have your signatures notarized.
   C. You may elect from one of the following optional forms of pension with actuarial reduction if you are single or if the qualified joint and survivor form of annuity has been waived:
      1. A joint and survivor annuity with a percentage of 25 percent, 50 percent, 75 percent, or 100 percent.
      2. A life and period certain annuity with guaranteed payments for five or ten years.

XV. CLAIMS AND REVIEWS
   A. Claims for benefits should be submitted on forms available from the Administrator. If your claim is denied, you will be notified in writing by the Administrator within 30 days with the reason for denial.

    B.   If you wish to appeal, your appeal must be written to the Administrator within 90 days of your receipt of the notice of denial, requesting a review of the denial.

XVI.   AMENDMENT OR TERMINATION

    A.   The Corporation expects to continue the plan indefinitely. However, the Corporation as Sponsor has the right to amend this plan at any time. Such an amendment may not cause any part of the Trust Fund to be used other than for the benefit of the participants or their beneficiaries. Also, such an amendment may not reduce your accrued benefit.

    B.   The Corporation as Sponsor also has the right to terminate this plan at any time.

    C.   If the plan should terminate, your accrued benefit will become 100 percent vested.

XVII.   ASSIGNMENT OF BENEFITS

    A.   You cannot sell, assign, or pledge your benefits under this plan. Your benefits are not subject to attachment or garnishment by creditors prior to your right to receive payment.

    B.   In a divorce action, your benefits may be subject to a court order for division as marital property.

XVIII.   PENSION BENEFIT GUARANTY CORPORATION

    A.   Benefits under this plan are insured by the Pension Benefit Guaranty Corporation (PBGC). Generally, the PBGC guarantees most vested normal retirement age benefits, early retirement benefits, and certain disability and survivor's pensions. However, the PBGC does not guarantee all types of benefits under covered plans, and the amount of benefit protection is subject to certain limitations.

    B.   The PBGC guarantees vested benefits at the level in effect on the date of plan termination. However, if a plan has been in effect less than five years before it terminates, or if benefits have been increased within the five years before plan termination, the whole amount of the plan's vested benefits or the benefit increase may not be guaranteed. In addition, there is a limit on the amount of monthly benefit that the PBGC guarantees.

    C.   For more information on the PBGC insurance protection and its limitations, ask your Administrator or the PBGC. Inquiries to the PBGC should be addressed to the Office of Communications, PBGC, 1200 K Street NW, Washington, D.C. 20005.

XIX.   YOUR RIGHTS UNDER THE LAW

    A.   As a participant in the plan, you are entitled to certain rights and protections under the Employee Retirement Income Security Act of 1974 (ERISA). ERISA provides that all plan participants shall be entitled to:

        1.   Examine without charge, at the Administrator's office, and at other specified locations, all plan documents, including any insurance contracts, and copies of all documents filed by the plan with the U.S. Department of Labor.

2. Obtain copies of all plan documents and other plan information upon written request to the Administrator. The Administrator may make a reasonable charge for the copies.

3. Receive a summary of the plan's annual financial report. The Administrator is required by law to furnish each participant with a copy of this summary financial report.

4. Obtain a statement telling you whether you have a right to receive a pension at normal retirement age (your age at normal retirement date) and if so, what your benefits would be at normal retirement age if you stop working under the plan now. If you do not have a right to a pension, the statement will tell you how many more years you have to work to get a right to a pension. This statement must be requested in writing and is not required to be given more than once a year. The plan must provide the statement free of charge.

B. In addition to creating rights for plan participants, ERISA imposes duties upon the people who are responsible for the operation of the plan.

C. The people who operate your plan, called "fiduciaries" of the plan, have a duty to do so prudently and in the interest of you and other plan participants and beneficiaries. No one, including your employer or any other person, may fire you or otherwise discriminate against you in any way to prevent you from obtaining a plan benefit or exercising your rights under ERISA. If your claim for a plan benefit is denied in whole or in part, you must receive a written explanation of the reason for the denial.

D. You have the right to have the plan review and consider your claim. Under ERISA, there are steps you can take to enforce the above rights. For instance, if you request materials from the plan and do not receive them within 30 days, you may file suit in a federal court. In such a case, the court may require the Administrator to provide the materials and to pay you up to $100 a day until you receive the materials, unless the materials were not sent because of reasons beyond the control of the Administrator.

E. If you have a claim for benefits that is denied or ignored, in whole or in part, you may file suit in a state or federal court. If it should happen that plan fiduciaries misuse the plan's money, or if you are discriminated against for asserting your rights, you may file suit in federal court. The court will decide who should pay court costs and legal fees. If you lose, the court may order you to pay these costs and fees, for example, if it finds your claim is frivolous.

F. If you have any questions about your plan, you should contact the Administrator. If you have any questions about this statement or your rights under ERISA, you should contact the Administrator or the nearest area office of the U.S. Department of Labor.

NOTICE

This Summary Plan Description has been prepared as required by regulations of the Department of Labor under the Employee Retirement Income Security Act of 1974.

It is intended only as a summary of your plan's highlights and not as a detailed legal description. In the event of any inconsistencies between this summary and the actual plan provisions, the plan will be followed. If you wish to read the actual plan, a copy is available for inspection upon request at our main office during regular working hours. We will show it to you and secure answers to any questions you may have. You may obtain a copy of the plan for a small reproduction charge per page. If you want a copy, let us know and we will tell you the cost.

Comments on the Summary Plan Description

I. IDENTIFICATION. This section states the formal name of the plan, which may be different from the name that appears on the cover or title page of the SPD.

The Internal Revenue Service (IRS) assigns every employer an employer identification number (EIN). The EIN identifies the employer and its federal tax returns. A plan will not have its own EIN in most cases, but the trust fund may have one, and the plan administrator should have its own EIN. The plan administrator may be a named individual, a committee, or the corporation itself. The SPD tells us which it is and gives the administrator's identification number.

The plan number (PN) that the employer must assign to each of its plans is unique, not to be reused or reassigned even if the particular plan no longer exists. Plan numbers for pension and profit-sharing plans begin with the numerical sequence "001," whereas welfare plans are numbered starting with "501." The PN is always a three-digit number.

When a plan has been amended many times, its SPD may give only the date of the most recent amendment, not the plan's original effective date. In some cases, to determine the length of an employee's plan service, it may be necessary to know the initial effective date of a plan. Further, it may be advisable to learn whether credited service for benefits was granted for periods of time prior to the plan's effective date. This information may not be found in the SPD description, so further inquiries would have to be made if it appears that prior service could have been involved.

II. ADMINISTRATION. This section states the type of plan, which, in this example, is a defined benefit plan. It also indicates that a committee, rather than an individual or an officer of the corporation, is responsible for the administration of the plan and its day-to-day operations.

The administrative duties are probably performed by one person, even though a committee is named. The SPD does not have to identify any outside pension consulting firm or actuary providing services to the plan. If such information is given, it may be useful.

It is important to distinguish between the concepts of (1) plan services and administration and (2) the plan administrator. Under federal law, only the plan administrator is responsible for plan decisions. Plan administration may be spread among many persons; some employees of the employer and some from outside administrative, actuarial, accounting, and legal firms.

Every plan runs on a 12-month designated plan year. The most common plan years are January 1 to December 31 and July 1 to June 30, but even unusual plan years, such as August 16 to August 15, are acceptable. The trust fund holding the plan assets is run on a fiscal year that, in general, may be expected to coincide with the plan year.

When a plan is first established, the employer may not be certain of getting a corporate income tax deduction for the first year's contribution, so the very first year of the plan will be a short year for technical accounting or tax purposes. The plan year basis is of interest in valuing or distributing pensions in marital dissolution because it provides convenient administrative cutoff dates for benefit information. For example, if the plan year ends on December 31, it may be expected that the plan will have readily available accrued pension benefit figures on December 31.

III. ELIGIBILITY. The eligibility provisions are somewhat interesting but may not be helpful if they do not indicate when benefit credited service starts. In one plan, it may be that even though an employee has to wait a year before entering the plan, that year counts toward benefit and vesting credits once it has been completed. In another plan, benefit service credits may start only when the employee has officially entered the plan. Vesting, however, in most cases, will be counted from the first day of full-time employment.

IV. CONTRIBUTIONS. A plan may require employee contributions or may allow them on a voluntary basis or may combine both. This section of the SPD shows the plan's arrangements. In the sample, the employer must make actuarially required contributions while an employee has the individual option to make voluntary contributions. The SPD does not go into detail on the restraints imposed by the IRS and the PBGC on the minimum and maximum limits of contributions.

Because it is a defined benefit pension plan, the amount and timing of employee contributions has no effect on the benefits provided by the plan. The benefits are established by formula, described later in the SPD. If the plan allows voluntary employee contributions, there will be a separate set of rules and regulations concerning the details of the times and amounts when contributions may be made and the provisions under which they may be withdrawn. In marital dissolution discovery, the details concerning employee contributions should be requested if there is any possibility that the employee has participated in this feature. When there are employee contributions, the contributions are always fully vested regardless of the plan's vesting schedule for pension benefits. The advantage of voluntary contributions to the employee is that they provide the employee with a tax-sheltered investment. The contribution itself is not tax-deductible, but its earnings remain tax-sheltered until paid out or withdrawn.

V. PLAN COMPENSATION. Not all defined benefit plans use pay in the pension benefit formula, but when they do, the basis of pay must be described. The plan may be using one year's pay—the final year before retirement—or an average of pay over three or five years, or any particular number of years could have been selected by the employer when the plan was first designed.

The definition of ''pay'' in the actual formal plan document is usually quite extensive. For purposes of the SPD, generally the overall type of pay will be mentioned. The SPD will probably indicate whether overtime pay or bonus, for example, is counted in the pay used as the basis for benefits.

VI.   PENSION FORMULA.   Here is the heart of the SPD, the description of the pension benefit formula. The formula for determining the pension benefit may run on for several pages or may be encompassed in one sentence, depending on the plan's complexity. There may be minimum amounts and maximum amounts, and there may be alternative formulas for different classes or categories of employee. In the sample SPD, the pension benefit formula is 2.5 percent of five-years' average pay times the number of years of service. An example is given showing how this works. The example assumes that the employee's pay remains level. Occasionally a summary or a benefit statement will illustrate what the possible projected benefit at retirement would be if the employee's salary increases at a certain rate or by a certain amount.

VII.   ACCRUED BENEFIT.   In pension terminology, accrued benefit is the current portion of the ultimate or projected benefit that has been ''earned'' by the employee as of any particular date, based on pay and service to the date in question. A benefit is not fully earned until it is fully vested by the plan's vesting schedule, but it is accrued even if not yet vested. There are other means of obtaining full vesting, such as upon termination of the plan or attainment of normal retirement age.

The most common method of accruing benefits is the fractional method as illustrated in the sample SPD. The fractional method of benefit accrual proceeds as follows:

1.   Estimate the ultimate pension at normal retirement date, using the individual's current pay in the pension benefit formula, assuming that employment continues to normal retirement date. *Example:* $ 750 per month at age 65 with 30 years of service.

2.   Determine the number of years of credited service worked so far by the person, say ten years.

3.   Determine the total number of years of credited service that the person would have at normal retirement date, say 30 years.

4.   Compute the accrual fraction by dividing the number of years so far (10) by the total number of years of service at retirement (30) and multiply that fraction (10/30) by the estimated pension at retirement ($750 per month): $10/30 \times \$750 = \$250$.

The result in the example is $250 per month. This is the employee's current accrued monthly pension benefit. It is payable at normal retirement age, subject to vesting. If the person left employment now, fully vested under the plan's vesting schedule, he or she would be entitled to receive the monthly pension of $250 starting at age 65.

VIII.   VESTING.   Vesting refers to the nonforfeitable portion of a plan participant's benefits. Once vested, the benefit cannot be lost except under extreme circumstances—for example, if the plan were to terminate with insufficient funds to provide all accrued benefits and if the individual's accrued pension benefit exceeds the current maximum amount covered by the PBGC.

The vesting schedule presented in the sample SPD is typical of corporate defined benefit pension plans. It is sometimes called "five-year cliff vesting." Upon meeting the requirement of five years of service, the employee is fully vested in all past and current pension benefits and continues to vest as future benefits accrue. If an employee has between four and five years of service and if vesting is an issue in a matter, it should be investigated further. The plan's formal legal document will have an extensive definition of "service" for vesting purposes. A period of time that is somewhat more than four years, but not exactly five years, may still meet the requirement for five years under the plan's definition of "years of service."

Upon attainment of the plan's normal retirement age, vesting becomes automatic if not otherwise yet attained in the vesting schedule in the plan. Voluntary employee contributions are always fully vested. Contributions made by the employer are not looked at in a defined benefit pension plan to determine an employee's benefits or vesting status.

IX. NORMAL RETIREMENT.   Every pension plan will have one or more normal retirement dates. That is the date at which full vesting occurs automatically and the date at which the employee may voluntarily cease employment and receive a full pension benefit based on the plan's pension benefit formula and pay and service as defined therein. The normal retirement date is the date at which benefit payments would begin to former employees who had terminated service with vested benefits. In the sample SPD, only one normal retirement age is given—age 62.

Normal retirement age and normal retirement date have some different meanings in pension plans. The age may refer to the last birthday attained by the employee, or to the birthday that is nearest—within six months—of a specific date, such as the end of a plan year. The normal retirement date must be defined and specific. A common definition is the first day of the month coincident with or next following the completion of the later of two events: (1) the actual attainment of the 65th birthday (for example) and (2) the completion of five years of credited plan service.

A plan may have a complicated arrangement for normal retirement dates, involving age, service, and/or the attainment of a combination age and service. For example, in a "30 and out" situation, the completion of 30 years of service equals normal retirement date no matter what the age is then. In a "magic number" situation, the attainment of the sum of age plus years of service—equal to, say, 85—results in the normal retirement date. Thus, at age 60 with 25 years of service, the person has reached the 85 number and may retire with full benefits.

X. EARLY RETIREMENT.   Early retirement refers to retirement with pension benefits before normal retirement age. The pension is reduced to reflect its early commencement because, presumably, it will be paid over a longer time period than if the person had retired at the normal retirement age. The plan may have only an age requirement for early retirement, or a combination of age and service. The earlier the retirement occurs, the more the benefit will be reduced.

For example, retiring at age 64 when normal retirement age is 65 might result in a 6 percent decrease in the pension, leaving a 94 percent benefit, while retiring ten years early at age 55 might reduce the pension by 60 percent, leaving a 40 percent benefit. These details may or may not be spelled out in the SPD, but they will appear in full in the formal plan document.

XI. DISABILITY. A plan may, but is not required to, have a disability benefit provision. The specifics will be in the plan document. It would not be unusual for a disability benefit to provide only the same vested benefit an employee would receive for any termination of employment. The only advantage then of calling it a disability benefit may be for favorable federal personal income tax treatment. The plan may, however, have a generous disability benefit that pays an immediate pension to the disabled employee equal to the accrued pension benefit, without reduction for early retirement. A plan may state that the disability pension will be payable to age 65 at which time, if living, the former employee would then start the regular pension based on pay and service at the time the disability occurred. A very generous plan would start the person's pension at age 65 with credit for all of the years on disability as if the time had been worked for purposes of the pension benefit formula.

XII. DEATH BENEFIT. There are two time frames for death benefits in pension plans. In the period before retirement, if the employee died, a pre-retirement death benefit would be paid to a beneficiary as provided for in the plan. After retirement, death would provide benefits only if the employee so elected at the time of retirement or if death benefits were otherwise provided by the plan.

All defined benefit pension plans subject to ERISA must provide a pre-retirement death benefit for married employees with the spouse as beneficiary. Most plans have a pre-retirement death benefit whether or not the employee is married. If there have been voluntary employee contributions, they would constitute at least part of the death benefit. A common pre-retirement death benefit in a defined benefit pension plan would be the amount determined as the actuarial present value of the employee's accrued pension benefit at date of death, based on pay and service as of that date, payable immediately to the beneficiary as a single-sum amount or in the form of a pension annuity. A plan may limit the death benefit to the vested benefit if the accrued benefit at date of death has not yet become fully vested. The plan will have beneficiary forms that every employee should have completed at some time during service.

The choice of the form of payment of the pre-retirement death benefit is usually left up to the beneficiary, but in some cases it may be pre-selected by the employee. A qualified domestic relations order (QDRO) may award all or part of a pre-retirement death benefit to a former spouse. It is important to ensure that there is no conflict between the beneficiary form on file with the plan and any conditions affecting a pre-retirement death benefit that may be set forth in a QDRO.

XIII. POSTPONED RETIREMENT. This section may also be referred to as deferred retirement or late retirement. It deals with the decision an employee makes to continue working after normal retirement age. In a plan with multiple definitions of ''normal retirement age,'' it is not considered postponed retirement until the latest possible of the various retirement ages has been passed in employment. Rarely will a plan start payment of pension benefits at normal retirement age even though the employee continues to work. When the pension is delayed by working beyond retirement age, the benefit will be increased either by actuarial factors or by continued operation of the plan's pension benefit formula. In a generous plan the pension benefit will be increased for working beyond retirement age by both an actuarial adjustment and continued counting of pay and service in the pension benefit formula.

XIV. BENEFIT PAYMENTS. A distinction is made between the normal form and the standard form of pension payments in an ERISA defined benefit pension plan. The terms are not standardized, so different plans may use different benefit terminology. ERISA requires that when a married employee retires from a defined benefit pension plan, the pension benefit must be paid in the form of a qualified joint-and-survivor (J&S) annuity unless properly waived by the employee and by the spouse, witnessed by an authorized plan representative, or notarized.

A qualified J&S annuity is defined as a reduced pension payable to the retiree that, upon the retiree's death, continues in payment of a certain percentage to the pre-designated survivor beneficiary, if then living. In the usual plan, the beneficiary may not be substituted after retirement. The percentages of benefit available in a qualified J&S annuity may range between 50 percent and 100 percent of the retiree's reduced pension benefit. The percentage must be designated at the time of retirement. The amount of reduction applied to the retiree's pension is determined actuarially based on the ages of the retiree and the spouse and on the percentage of the survivor annuity. A survivor annuity of 100 percent requires a greater reduction in the basic pension than does a survivor annuity of 50 percent. If the designated survivor beneficiary dies before the retiree, the retiree's pension nevertheless remains reduced for life except in the special case where the plan has a "pop-up" provision. A pop-up provision restores all or part of the reduction in benefits to the retiree in recognition of the death of the potential beneficiary.

The requirement for a married retiree to have a qualified J&S annuity may be waived within a limited time period immediately prior to retirement. The waiver form must explain the options and the effects of the waiver on potential benefits. It must be signed by the employee and the employee's spouse. The signatures of employee and spouse must be attested to either by a notary public or by an authorized plan representative.

An unmarried employee at retirement is free to elect from among the benefit payment options offered by the plan. A plan may have only one or two benefit payment options, or it may have a large number of elections available that will be explained to the employee shortly before retirement. In most plans, post-retirement death benefits are not free. The election of any of the options that will provide survivor benefits after retirement generally requires an actuarial reduction in the retiree's pension benefit.

A QDRO that is placed on the records before retirement may require the employee to elect a particular option and to irrevocably name the former spouse as a survivor beneficiary for part or all of potential post-retirement death benefits.

If divorce occurs after retirement, it may be difficult or even impossible to change the form of pension benefit payment that the retiree has been receiving or to change an already designated beneficiary.

XV.   CLAIMS AND REVIEWS.   There is usually not much of a problem in corporate defined benefit pension plans under ERISA when an employee retires and requests pension benefit commencement. Occasionally, a problem may arise in a union plan.

The standard provision on claims and reviews that appears in all ERISA plans may be of some importance with respect to QDROs. While QDROs have their own forms and procedures, it is within reason to use the plan in its entirety when constructing or administering a QDRO, and this claims provision may be of use in a troublesome case. It is always a good step to obtain claim forms and any other necessary administrative paperwork from the plan administrator.

XVI.   AMENDMENT OR TERMINATION.   ERISA has strict rules governing how and when plans may be amended or terminated. There are detailed notification requirements to inform employees of such pending actions. A plan termination requires the full vesting of all accrued benefits regardless of where they may stand on the plan's vesting schedule. Benefits that have been earned or accrued under the plan may not be reduced by plan amendment other than under very special circumstances that must be approved in advance by the IRS. But, a plan may be amended to reduce or eliminate future pension benefit accruals. All benefits up to the effective date of the plan amendment would be preserved, but there would be no future benefit increases, or, depending on the terms of the amendment, future benefit increases would be at a lower level than benefits had been set at prior to amendment. The plan's pension benefit formula could be changed for future benefits only.

If a plan terminates with enough assets to pay off all accrued pension benefits and if there is any money left in the plan's trust fund, it may revert to the employer. There are complicated rules and special taxes applied to asset reversions to the employer. Alternatively, the employer may designate an allocation of any surplus assets to be divided among the employees upon termination of the plan.

XVII.   ASSIGNMENT OF BENEFITS.   Prior to the federal law that created the concept of a QDRO, employees were prohibited from assigning or pledging their pension benefits, and the benefits could not be attached or subject to garnishment. With the advent of the QDRO, benefits may now be divided as marital property if the terms and conditions are met as set forth in the federal guidelines and if not in disagreement with the terms and provisions of the plan itself. A QDRO may be used as a form of lien or collateral on a conditional basis and not be in violation of these provisions.

XVIII.   PENSION BENEFIT GUARANTY CORPORATION.   This is a key section in any SPD. This section tells us whether or not the plan is covered by the PBGC. One would expect most defined benefit pension plans subject to ERISA to be covered by the PBGC, but some plans are exempted by federal law, rules, and regulations. For example, a professional corporation with fewer than 25 plan participants is exempt from PBGC coverage.

A pension plan that covers only one person who is the owner of the company is exempt from the PBGC. Plans that are not defined benefit pension plans are not covered by the PBGC. The summary of PBGC provisions in the sample SPD uses the standardized language pre-approved by the IRS and the PBGC. This language will be found in almost all SPDs that are written for plans covered by PBGC. If the plan is not so covered, the SPD will say so. When a plan is not covered by PBGC, it generally states the reason in its SPD.

The amount of monthly pension benefit guaranteed by PBGC is subject to limits concerning whether there has been a recent plan amendment increasing benefits and a stated dollar amount that increases with respect to inflation as measured by a cost of living index. The dollar amount limit is announced each year by the PBGC.

XIX.   YOUR RIGHTS UNDER THE LAW.   This is a required section in all SPDs. However, it may be reworded by the plan if the meaning is communicated as intended by the federal regulations. The formal plan document may run to 50 or 100 pages. There may have been numerous plan amendments over the years that remain as separate items or that have been incorporated in amended and restated documents.

A request for all formal plan documents and amendments could be expensive if the plan imposes even a moderate copying charge. However, the SPD must be provided free of cost.

The plan's annual financial report is a generalized overview of the plan's financial operations by categories. Its technical name is "summary annual report." It has no individualized benefit or asset information for any particular employee.

The reference in the SPD to the right to obtain a benefit statement is important, but its explicit statement is sometimes omitted from the summary plan description. Whether or not it appears in the SPD, the action is still required to be performed upon request. The plan must provide a benefit statement to the employee if requested by the employee in writing. The plan does not have to honor more than one request per year from an employee for benefit information.

The plan does not have to provide benefit statements routinely or automatically to employees. There is no charge for the requested benefit statement. The plan's requirement to furnish such a requested statement pertains to the current timeframe. Upon request, the plan will provide current benefit information. Many plans will honor a request to provide information as to what the person's accrued benefit was at some certain prior date, such as the date of marital separation, but a plan is not required to do so. Further, the plan does not have to furnish this information to a spouse or to counsel for a spouse. A subpoena to obtain it may suffice if the corporate headquarters of the employer is in the same state as that in which the divorce is occurring.

NOTICE. Most SPDs will contain a disclaimer such as the one appearing at the end of the sample SPD. A defined benefit pension plan is complicated, and the formal plan document must cover many points in exhaustive detail. The SPD is intended to provide general guidance to the important features of the plan, but it is not the final arbiter of plan operations or administrative details or procedures.

SAMPLE SUMMARY PLAN DESCRIPTION FOR A DEFINED CONTRIBUTION INDIVIDUAL ACCOUNT PLAN

**SUMMARY PLAN DESCRIPTION
OF THE XYZ COMPANY
MONEY-PURCHASE PENSION PLAN
AS OF MARCH 31, 1998**

Table of Contents

Article I
Purpose and Basic Information

This booklet will introduce you to the most important parts of your Company's money-purchase pension plan (the Plan). It will try to explain how these important parts of the Plan apply to you in most situations. But please remember that this booklet is only a summary of these important provisions; it is not the Plan itself. A summary cannot cover in detail each provision of the Plan and how each provision might work in every situation for everyone. You'll still have to look to the Plan for details.

That is why we urge you to read the whole Plan. Your Plan Administrator will lend you a copy to read free of charge. You can have one to keep by paying a reasonable charge to cover production expenses. We also believe that you should read the Plan again whenever your employment circumstances may be about to change or have changed. You will want to know the effect, if any, that the change will have on your Plan benefits. Also, whenever you have a question about how the Plan's coverage and benefits apply to you, we want you to contact your Plan Administrator.

Several important terms that have special meanings are explained in the "Definitions" section at the end of this summary. You should look at that section as you read this summary to make sure you understand what these important terms mean.

Your rights under the Plan are governed entirely by the terms of the Plan document itself and by the related trust agreement.

Before going into the important parts of the Plan, we have to provide you with the following basic information:

1. Your Company's full Name and Address: _____ .
2. Your Company's Employer Identification Number: _____ .
3. The Plan Administrator's Name, Address, and Business Telephone Number:
   _____ .
4. The Plan Trustee's Name, Title, and Address: _____ .
5. The Plan Number for the Department of Labor: 00 _____ .
6. The Last Day of the Plan Year: _____ .
7. Service of Legal Process: Service of legal process may be made upon the Plan Administrator or the Trustee.

Article II
Overview of the Plan

We call your Plan a money-purchase plan because the Company promises to pay a definite amount each year into the Plan on your behalf. Your benefit upon retirement will be based on these yearly contributions. The Plan costs you nothing; all basic contributions are paid by your Company.

The assets of the Plan are held in a Trust Fund by _____ , which acts as the Trustee for our Plan. An administrative committee serves as the Plan Administrator for the Plan and is responsible for the management and administration of the Plan.

Article III
Participation in the Plan

When Am I Eligible to Participate?

You will be eligible to participate in the Plan after you reach age 21 and have satisfied the Plan's minimum service requirement. You are not eligible to participate if you are covered under a collective bargaining agreement that does not provide for participation in the Plan or if you are a leased employee.

How Do I Satisfy the Plan's Minimum Service Requirement?

You satisfy the Plan's minimum service requirement by completing an eligibility computation period in which you are credited with 1,000 Hours of Service. Your first eligibility computation period will be the 12-consecutive-month period that starts on the first day on which you are credited with at least one Hour of Service.

If you do not complete 1,000 Hours of Service in your first eligibility computation period, we will use Plan Years as your eligibility computation periods, starting with the first Plan Year that begins after you first complete an Hour of Service.

Example 1: Mary is initially hired on February 1, 1990. For her first 12 months of employment Mary is paid for 140 hours a month, including vacations, holidays, and sick days. On January 31, 1991, Mary has completed 1,000 Hours of Service in her first 12 months of employment (her first eligibility computation period). She has satisfied the Plan's minimum service requirement.

Example 2: John is initially hired on February 1, 1990. For his first 12 months of employment John is paid for only 80 hours a month, including vacations, holidays, and sick days. On January 31, 1991, John has not completed 1,000 Hours of Service in his first 12 months of employment. His next eligibility computation period is the first Plan Year that begins after his first Hour of Service. That Plan Year begins on January 1, 1991, and ends on December 31, 1991. If John is credited with 1,000 Hours of Service during that Plan Year, he will satisfy the Plan's minimum service requirement. If John fails to complete 1,000 Hours of Service during the Plan Year, but remains employed, his next eligibility computation period is the Plan Year beginning on January 1, 1992. [This example assumes the plan year is the calendar year.]

When Do I Actually Become a Participant?

Once you are eligible to participate, you actually become a Plan Participant on the Entry Date that occurs on or after the date on which you satisfied the requirements.

Example 3: Assume John, aged 28, is hired on April 1, 1990, and has completed 1,000 Hours of Service on March 31, 1991. John becomes a Participant in the Plan on _____ [insert appropriate Entry Date].

Example 4: Mary is hired on April 5, 1990, and has completed 1,000 Hours of Service on April 4, 1991. She was hired on her eighteenth birthday. If Mary is still employed on her twenty-first birthday (April 5, 1993), she will become a Plan Participant in the Plan on _____ [insert appropriate Entry Date]. This date is the first Plan Entry Date on which Mary satisfies both the age and service requirements of the Plan.

When Does My Participation End?

Your participation in the Plan will end when you retire, or when you terminate your employment with the Company for any other reason, including death. Your participation also will end if you become a leased employee or if your employment becomes covered under the terms of a collective bargaining agreement that does not provide for participation in the Plan.

What if I Leave and Am Rehired?

Special rules cover your eligibility to participate if you leave the Company and are later rehired. Look in Article VII, where we talk about your rights when you are rehired.

Article IV
Plan Benefits

What Benefits Can I Get Under the Plan?

Your benefits are based on the amount of money in your Employer Contribution Account. Once you are a Participant in the Plan, we will open an account in your name called your Employer Contribution Account. When the Company makes a contribution for which you are eligible to the Plan for a Plan Year, your account will be credited with your share of the Company's contribution. Your Employer Contribution Account will also be credited with its share of any income, gains, or losses of the investments in the Trust Fund. Finally, your Employer Contribution Account will also be credited with your share of any forfeitures under the Plan that are allocated to Participants.

When Will I Get These Benefits?

You will be entitled to receive your Employer Contribution Account when you retire, die, become disabled, or otherwise terminate your employment with the Company. See Article XV for details. However, only that part of your Employer Contribution Account in which you have a vested right will be paid to you. Article VI tells you what a vested right is.

Article V
Company Contributions to the Plan

When and How Much Will the Company Contribute?

Each Plan Year, your Company will contribute an amount equal to five percent (5%) of the Compensation of all eligible Participants.

How Do I Get to Share in the Company's Contributions?

You will share in the Company's contribution to the Plan in any Plan Year in which you are a Participant and have also completed 1,000 Hours of Service. If you do not complete 1,000 Hours of Service but the reason is Retirement, Disability, or Death, you still will be eligible to share in the Company's contribution.

How Much Is My Share of the Company's Contribution?

We determine your share of the Company's contribution to the plan each year under our two-step Plan formula as follows:

Step 1: Under the first step, your share of the Company's contribution will be based on your Compensation in excess of the Taxable Wage Base for the Plan Year, which is called "Excess Compensation." Your share will equal the product of the Company's contribution multiplied by a fraction, the numerator of which is your Excess Compensation and the denominator of which is the total Excess Compensation of all Plan Participants for the Plan Year. The amount allocated under this step cannot exceed a specified percentage of your Excess Compensation, based on the portion of the social security tax imposed on your Compensation that consists of old-age, survivors, and disability insurance. For 1991, this percentage is 6.06 percent. If you do not have Excess Compensation during the Plan Year, you will not share in an allocation under Step 1.

Step 2: If any portion of the Company's contribution remains to be allocated after Step 1, your share will be determined by multiplying the remaining contribution by a fraction, the numerator of which is your total Compensation for the Plan Year and the denominator of which is the total Compensation of all Plan Participants for the Plan Year.

Example 5: Joe's Compensation in 1990 is $47,000. His Excess Compensation is $2,000 ($47,000 − $45,000). The total Compensation of all Plan Participants in 1988 is $350,000 and the total Excess Compensation, $55,000. The Company's contribution for 1988 is equal to $20,000. Joe's share is determined as follows:

Step 1:

$$\$20,000 \times \frac{\$2,000 \text{ (Joe's Excess Compensation)}}{\$55,000 \text{ (Total Excess Compensation of all Participants)}} = 727.27$$

However, as indicated above, no more than 6.06 percent of Joe's Excess Compensation may be allocated to his Employer Contribution Account pursuant to Step 1, so his allocation in Step 1 is limited to $121.20.

After allocation to all Plan Participants pursuant to Step 1, $8,200 of the Company's contribution remains to be allocated in Step 2. Joe's share is determined as follows:

Step 2:

$$\$8,200 \times \frac{\$47,000 \text{ (Joe's Total Compensation)}}{\$350,000 \text{ (Total Compensation of all Participants)}} = \$1,101.14$$

Joe's total share of the Company contribution for 1990 is equal to:

$$\$121.20 + \$1,101.14 = \$1,222.34$$

Article VI
Vesting

What Does the Plan Mean by "Vested"?

If you leave the Company for any reason other than Retirement, Disability, or Death, you may not get all of your Employer Contribution Account. You may forfeit some of it—that part to which you don't have a vested right. You become vested in your Employer Contribution Account by receiving credit for Years of Service. When you have enough Years of Service, or if you attain age 65 while employed by the Company, you are fully vested and entitled to all of your Employer Contribution Account, regardless of why you leave the Company.

What Happens to Forfeited Amounts?

When a Plan Participant who leaves the Company is not 100 percent vested in his or her Employer Contribution Account, the part in which he or she is not vested is forfeited. Once these forfeitures become available, they are used to reduce future Company Contributions to the Plan.

APPENDIX C

How Do You Measure My Vesting?

When we compute how much of your Employer Contribution Account is vested and nonforfeitable, we generally give you credit for one Year of Service for each Plan Year in which you complete 1,000 Hours of Service with the Company.

If you leave the Company for any reason after _____ [insert effective date of Plan], and are later rehired, special rules cover whether you get back your Years of Service earned before you left. Look in Article VII, where we talk about your rights when you are rehired.

Example 6: Joe is employed on January 1, 1984, and completes at least 1,000 Hours of Service each year until December 31, 1991. Joe is credited with eight Years of Service.

Example 7: Sue is employed on January 1, 1984, and works until December 31, 1989. She completes the following Hours of Service in each Plan Year:

Plan Year	Hours of Service
1/1/84 to 12/31/84	520
1/1/85 to 12/31/85	1,800
1/1/86 to 12/31/86	1,800
1/1/87 to 12/31/87	700
1/1/88 to 12/31/88	1,800
1/1/89 to 12/31/89	1,000

[Examples 6 and 7 assume the Plan is a calendar-year plan.]

Sue is credited with four Years of Service for vesting purposes because she completed 1,000 Hours of Service in four Plan Years.

What Is Our Vesting Schedule?

Our vesting schedule tells us to what extent, expressed as a percentage, you will be vested in your Employer Contribution Account after each year of Service. It is as follows:

Years of Service	Vested Percentage	Forfeited Percentage
less than 4	0	100
4 but less than 5	40	60
5 but less than 6	45	55
6 but less than 7	50	50
7 but less than 8	60	40
8 but less than 9	70	30
9 but less than 10	80	20
10 but less than 11	90	10
11 or more	100	0

Example 8: Joe, in Example 6, will be 70 percent vested in his Employer Contribution Account.

Example 9: Sue, in Example 7, will be 40 percent vested in her Employer Contribution Account.

If your employment ends because you die, your beneficiary will be fully vested and entitled to the entire amount in your Employer Contribution Account.

Article VII
Reemployment

What Happens When I Am Rehired?

If you leave the Company after _____ [insert effective date of Plan] and are later rehired, special rules tell us when you will be eligible to participate in the Plan again and whether you will get credit for any Years of Service (for vesting) you earned before you left.

When Will I Participate Again?

If you were not a Participant before you left, or you were a Participant, but at the time your employment terminated you did not have any vested interest in your Employer Contribution Account, you will become a Participant in the Plan immediately if you were credited with 1,000 Hours of Service in an eligibility computation period prior to your termination of employment, had attained age 21, and had One-Year Breaks in Service that were fewer than the greater of five years of the aggregate number of your pre-Break Years of Service. (If you were credited with 1,000 Hours of Service in a 12-month period that is other than a Plan Year, you will be credited with two years of Service for purposes of eligibility to participate upon reemployment only.) Otherwise, you must meet the eligibility requirements as if you were a new employee. You will be eligible to become a Participant on the Entry Date that occurs on or after the date you meet the eligibility requirements.

If you were a Participant with a vested interest in your Employer Contribution Account before you left, you will become a Participant again on your date of reemployment.

Will I Get Vesting Credit for My Prior Years of Service?

If you were a Participant with a vested interest in your Employer Contribution Account before you left, your prior Years of Service, attributable to your previous period of employment, will be reinstated on the date of your reemployment.

If you were not a Participant before you left, or were a Participant but did not have any vested interest at the time you left, your prior Years of Service will be reinstated on the date of your reemployment if your One-Year Breaks in Service were less than the greater of five years or the total number of your pre-Break Years of Service.

Can I Get Back My Forfeiture?

If you are not totally vested in your Employer Contribution Account when you leave, any amount in which you are not vested is immediately forfeited. The actual amount that you forfeit is determined by the number of your Years in Service. The Company will restore to your Account the amount you forfeited if you are rehired before you incur five consecutive One-Year Breaks in Service and if (before incurring five consecutive One-Year Breaks in Service or five years after you are reemployed by the Company, whichever is earlier) you repay any amount that was distributed to you from your Employer Contribution Account when you left. If you don't pay back the amount distributed to you before incurring five consecutive One-Year Breaks in Service (for five years after you are reemployed by the Company, if earlier), or if you return after incurring five consecutive One-Year Breaks in Service, your Account will not be restored.

Example 10: Joe terminates employment on April 1, 1987, with three Years of Service. He has no vested interest in his Employer Contribution Account when he terminates. He is reemployed on April 1, 1990. When Joe is reemployed, his three prior Years of Service are reinstated and he is eligible to participate in the Plan immediately because the number of his One-Year Breaks in Service (three) does not exceed the greater of five years or the number of Joe's pre-Break Years of Service (three).

Article VIII
Participant Contributions to the Plan

May I Make Voluntary Contributions?

You are not permitted to make voluntary contributions to the Plan.

Article IX
Adjustments of Accounts and Investments

The Plan's assets themselves are pooled in the Trust Fund. However, we also keep individual Accounts so that we can keep track of how much you or your beneficiary has coming to you. Your Account is adjusted to reflect the following:

a. Withdrawals and Distributions. Any withdrawals you make and any Plan distributions to you are charged to your Account as of the date withdrawn or paid.
b. Trust Income. The Trust Fund's income, gain, or loss is allocated on each Valuation Date to your Account in the proportion that your Account balance bears to the total amount in the Trust Fund immediately after the preceding Valuation Date, reduced by any distributions or withdrawals since the last Valuation Date.
c. Company Contributions. Your Employer Contribution Account gets your share of the Company's contribution to the Plan in any Plan Year in which you are eligible to share in that contribution.
d. Forfeitures. Any forfeitures that have become available during a Plan Year are used to reduce future Company contributions to the Plan.

The value of your Account is determined as of Valuation Dates under the Plan. Valuation Dates will always occur at least once a year—on the last day of the Plan Year—and sometimes more frequently. When you are entitled to a distribution under the Plan, it will be paid to you as of the Valuation Date that coincides with or next follows the date on which you or your beneficiary has a right to receive a distribution. Payments will be paid to you as soon as administratively possible after that Valuation

Date. If your vested Account balance exceeds $3,500 and you do not want to receive the distribution at the first possible date, your Account will continue to be held in the Trust Fund. Your Account will continue to share in earnings, gains, and losses until distributed, but it will not receive further Company contributions or forfeitures. Your Account will not be distributed to you (or your beneficiary) until the Valuation date that coincides with or next follows the date you attain age 65 (or the date of your death, if earlier).

Do I Have Any Investment Control Over My Account?

You may not direct the investment of amounts credited to your Employer Contribution Account. The Trustee will have the responsibility of investing Plan assets.

Article X
Payment of Plan Benefits

This article sets out the events that will trigger your right to get the money in your Account. It also tells you about the exact time and way you or your beneficiary can get that money.

What Happens on My Retirement or Disability?

When you Retire or leave the Company because you are Disabled, you have the right to get the entire amount credited to your Employer Contribution Account (even if you are not then fully vested).

Your Retirement Date is the first day of the month coincident with or next following the day you attain age 65. Of course, if you continue working for the Company after age 65, you are still eligible to participate in the Plan.

Example 10: Gary becomes 65 on March 24, 1990. Gary's Retirement Date is April 1, 1990.

What Happens if I Leave the Company for Any Reason Other Than Death?

If you leave the Company for any reason other than Death or Disability, you will have the right to get the vested percentage of your Employer Contribution Account.

In What Form Will My Benefits Be Paid?

The Plan Administrator is required by law to use the balance in your Account to buy you an annuity from an insurance company unless you elect to the contrary, as explained below. If you are married at the time benefits are to begin, the Plan Administrator is required to use the balance in your Account to buy a special type of annuity, called a Qualified Joint and Survivor Annuity, from an insurance company. An annuity is a series of payments (generally paid every month) that is guaranteed to be paid to you for as long as you live, with all benefit payments stopping upon your Death. A Qualified Joint and Survivor Annuity also is a series of payments that is guaranteed to be paid to you for life. However, upon your Death, a Qualified Joint and Survivor Annuity will provide a series of payments to your Spouse (equal to not less than 50 percent and not more than 100 percent of the amount you were receiving, depending on what you elect) until your Spouse dies.

The amount of the monthly payments that your annuity will provide depends on several factors. First, the amount in your Account at the time the annuity is purchased obviously will affect the amount of monthly benefit. Second, mortality tables, projections of interest earned, and rates the insurance company charges for an annuity all will affect the amount of the benefits. Finally, if the annuity is a Qualified Joint and Survivor Annuity—one that will make payments over two lives, to you until your Death, then to your Spouse until his or her Death in an amount equal to not less than 50 percent and not more than 100 percent of what you were receiving, depending on what you elect—the amount of monthly benefit payable to you will be less than if the annuity payments stopped at your Death.

> Example 11: John Rogers has an Account at the time of his retirement. If he is not married, the Plan Administrator will use his Account to purchase an annuity that will provide him with monthly payments for his life. The actual monthly benefit will depend on the rates the insurance company charges at the time John's benefits are to begin. If he is married, his monthly payments under a Qualified Joint and Survivor Annuity will be less than those he would receive if he were single, since benefits probably will be paid over a longer period of time (that is, at least one-half of the payments will continue to his Spouse after his Death).

The law, however, allows you to choose to receive your benefit in a form other than an annuity. If you are not married, you may make this choice by electing out of an annuity. If you are married, your Spouse must agree in writing (by executing a spousal consent form that a notary public or a representative of the Plan Administrator must witness) to any election that denies your Spouse lifetime benefits upon your Death. Your choices are:

1. A lump-sum payment;
2. Installment payments in substantially equal amounts at least annually over a period not to exceed your life expectancy or the joint and last survivor life expectancies of you and your beneficiary; or
3. A combination of a lump-sum payment and installments.

You will have an opportunity to choose the form of your benefit payments and to designate your beneficiary by completing forms that the Plan Administrator will give to you before your benefits are to begin. Remember, your benefits will automatically be paid in the form of an annuity unless you (and, if you are married, your Spouse) elect otherwise.

The rules discussed in this section assume the value of your Account exceeds $3,500. If the value of your Account is not greater than $3,500, benefits automatically will be paid in a lump sum.

What if I Die Before My Benefits Begin?

If you die before benefits begin, all benefits will be paid to your beneficiary.

If you are not married, all benefits will be paid to your beneficiary in a lump sum or installments, depending on what you elected for your beneficiary.

If you are married, more complicated rules apply. The law requires the Plan Administrator to use your Account to buy an annuity for the life your Spouse. The amount of the monthly benefits provided under the annuity will depend on the amount in your Account at the time of your Death and the rates the insurance company charges for the annuity.

If you are married, and you have reached age 35, there is a procedure that will allow you to choose to have your benefits paid (upon your Death) in a form other than an annuity to your Spouse. The Plan Administrator will give you forms to choose the form of your benefit and to designate your beneficiary. Your Spouse must agree in writing (by executing a spousal consent form that a notary public or a representative of the Plan Administrator must witness) to any election that denies your Spouse lifetime benefits upon your Death.

If you are married but have not reached age 35, the law prohibits you from electing out of an annuity for your Spouse should you die before benefits begin. (There is an exception to this rule if you terminate employment before age 35 and have a vested interest in your Account. In this case, you may elect out of the annuity for your Spouse with respect to the vested portion of your Account that you had earned as of the date you terminated employment.) Even if you do not elect out of an annuity for your Spouse, your Spouse will have the opportunity to choose how benefits will be paid upon your Death if your Spouse does not want the annuity.

The rules discussed in this section regarding the death of a married participant assume the value of your Account exceeds $3,500 at the time of your Death. If the value of your Account is not greater than $3,500, benefits automatically will be paid to your Spouse in a lump sum.

Who Is My Beneficiary?

Subject to the rules regarding spousal consent explained earlier in this section, you can pick any one, or more than one, person you want as your beneficiary, and you can change your mind whenever you wish. You may also list a trustee of a trust you have set up (say, under your will) as your beneficiary. You choose your beneficiary by filling out a form for the Plan Administrator and returning it. For your choice to be effective, the Plan Administrator has to get the form while you are still alive. Each time you file a new beneficiary designation form with the Plan Administrator, you automatically cancel all beneficiary designations you previously filed. If you do not select a beneficiary, or if your beneficiary dies before you die, we will pay the amount to which you are entitled to the following people in the order shown: (1) surviving Spouse; (2) children equally; (3) estate.

When Will I Get My Benefits?

Benefits payable because of your Retirement or Death will be distributed to you (or your beneficiary(ies)) as soon as possible after the Valuation Date at which we value your Account. If you continue working for the Company after age $70\frac{1}{2}$ and you are a 5-percent-or-greater owner of the Company, you must begin to receive your benefits by the April 1 following the year in which you attain age $70\frac{1}{2}$ even if you are still employed at that time.

Benefits payable on account of your Disability or other termination of employment prior to your Retirement Date will be distributed to you as soon as possible after your

Disability or termination and after the Valuation Date at which we value your Account. However, if the vested balance of your Account exceeds $3,500, you must consent in writing to receipt of your distribution if it is payable prior to your Retirement Date.

If your vested Account balance exceeds $3,500 and you do not want to receive your distribution following your Disability or termination of employment prior to your Retirement Date, your Account will be held in the Trust Fund until you attain 65 (or die, if earlier). Your Account will continue to share in earnings, gains, and losses, but it will not receive any further Company contributions or forfeitures.

Benefits payable on account of your Death will be distributed to your beneficiary(ies) as soon as possible following your Death and after the Valuation date at which we value your Account.

How Do You Compute the Value of My Account?

The value of your Account is usually determined by computing the value of your share of the trust as of the Valuation Date coincident with or next following the event that first gives you or your beneficiary(ies) the right to a distribution. If you leave the Company and elect to wait until you reach age 65 (or die before age 65) to get the money in your Account, it will be valued as of the Valuation Date coincident with or next following the event that gives you or your beneficiary(ies) the right to a distribution.

> Example 12: Jim dies on September 2, 1987. The amount to which his beneficiary(ies) is (are) entitled is determined by computing Jim's share of the value of the trust as of _____ [insert last day of Plan Year].

Article XI
Claims Procedure

If you or your beneficiary(ies) feel that you are not getting a Plan benefit that you should receive, you may file a written claim for that benefit with the Plan Administrator or with the individual named by the Plan Administrator to receive claims under the Plan. The Plan Administrator will decide whether to grant or deny your claim. If your claim is denied, you will get, within 90 days after filing your claim, a written notice telling you why it was denied and on what part of the plan the denial is based. The notice will also tell you what, if anything, you can do to have your claim approved. You will have a chance, within 60 days after you get this written notice, to ask for a review of your claim and its denial by the Plan Administrator. You and your representative can review Plan documents that relate to your claim and make written comments to the Plan Administrator. Your claim will then be reviewed by the Plan Administrator, and you will get a written notice of the Plan Administrator's final decision within 60 days after your request for a review.

In some instances the Plan Administrator will not be able to reply to your claim or request for review within the time provided. If this occurs, you will be given written notice of the delay.

APPENDIXES

Article XII
Taxes

Our Plan is tax-qualified under the Internal Revenue Code. In general, this means that the Company gets a tax deduction on its federal income tax return for its contributions to the Plan and that you do not have to pay any tax on those contributions at the time they are made. Also, you do not have to pay taxes on the Trust Fund income or gain at the time it is credited to your Account. As a general rule, you (or your beneficiary(ies)) will pay taxes on any distribution from your Employer Contribution Account when you (or your beneficiary(ies)) receive it. Special rules determine the amount of tax that has to be paid on any distribution. For instance, part of the distribution may be subject to special income-averaging rules. We urge you to consult your tax advisor for details.

If you receive a distribution from the Plan because your employment has been terminated prior to age 55, for any reason other than Death or Disability, there may be an additional 10 percent income tax on the taxable portion of your distribution. The 10 percent tax will not apply if you terminate employment prior to age 55 and start to receive payments that are payable over your life expectancy or the joint life expectancies of you and your beneficiary(ies).

Article XIII
Miscellaneous

What About Amendment or Termination of the Plan?

We intend to continue the Plan indefinitely. However, we specifically reserve the right to amend or terminate the Plan if we must. If we amend the Plan, we cannot reduce the vested amount of your Account. If we terminate the Plan, you will become vested in the entire amount credited to your Employer Contribution Account up to the time of termination. The assets of the Trust Fund must be used to provide benefits under the Plan before the Company may use them for any other purpose.

Is the Plan Insured?

Benefits under this Plan are not insured by the Pension Benefit Guaranty Corporation (PBGC). Money-purchase plans are not covered under the plan termination insurance provisions of the Employee Retirement Income Security Act of 974 (ERISA).

Can I Assign My Benefits?

You cannot assign your rights or interest in your Plan benefits to anyone. Also, you cannot pledge or assign your Plan benefits as security for a loan. There is an exception to this nonassignment rule in the case of certain divorced Participants. If a court issues a "qualified domestic relations order" regarding your Plan benefits, the Plan is required by law to follow such order. Accordingly, the judge or other arbiter of your divorce may assign a portion of your retirement benefits to your Spouse as part of your property settlement or to your children as payment of child support.

Does My Participation in the Plan Affect My Employment Rights?

The Plan is not an employment contract between you and the Company. It does not provide you with the right to continue as an employee with the Company or in any way limit the Company's right to discharge any employee.

Is There a Limit on the Amount That Can Be Credited to My Account?

The total Company Contributions that may be made on your behalf in any one Plan Year may not exceed certain limits established under the Internal Revenue Code. If you reach that limit you will not be entitled to any additional allocations to your Account for that Plan Year.

What Are the Top-Heavy Provisions?

A top-heavy plan is a plan in which 60 percent or more of the account balances held under the plan are attributable to "key employees" as defined in Section 416 of the Internal Revenue Code of 1986. In general, the term "key employee" includes certain highly compensated officers of the Company and certain shareholder-employees. In the event that the Plan becomes top-heavy, the Plan is required to provide for minimum contributions, place a cap of $200,000 on the Compensation considered under the Plan, and provide for faster vesting. If the Plan ever becomes top-heavy, you will be notified by the Plan Administrator of the effect on the Plan and your benefits.

Can I Lose My Benefits Under the Plan?

Not all of your benefits in your Employer Contribution Account under the Plan are fully vested at all times (see Article VI). Once vested, however, your benefits will always be paid to you or, in the event of your death, to your beneficiary, in accordance with the provisions of the Plan.

Please remember, however, that contributions to your Account under the Plan are invested and that some of the investment choices under the Plan may involve the risk of investment loss, which could cause the value of your Account to go down at times.

Article XIV
Your Rights Under ERISA

ERISA gives a Participant in the Plan certain rights and protections. You may:

1. Examine, without charge, at the Plan Administrator's office and at other specified locations such as work sites, all Plan Documents, including the Trust agreement, and copies of all papers filed by the Plan with the U.S. Department of Labor, such as detailed annual reports and Plan descriptions.
2. Get copies of all Plan documents and other Plan information by asking the Plan Administrator in writing. The Plan Administrator may make a reasonable charge for the copies.
3. Get a summary of the Plan's annual financial report. ERISA requires the Plan Administrator to give each Participant a copy of this summary annual report.
4. Get a statement telling you the amount currently in your Employer Contribution Account and the extent to which it is vested. Also, you may get a statement telling you how many more Years of Service you need to become fully vested in your Employer Contribution Account. You have to ask for these statements in writing, and the Plan Administrator does not have to give them

to you more than once a year. The Plan Administrator must provide the statements free of charge.

ERISA also imposes duties upon the people who are responsible for the operation of the Plan. The people who operate the Plan are called "fiduciaries." They have a duty to act prudently and in the interest of you and the other Plan Participants and beneficiaries. No one, including your employer or any other person, may fire you or otherwise discriminate against you in any way, to prevent you from obtaining retirement benefits or exercising your rights under ERISA.

ERISA provides steps you can take to enforce your rights. For instance, if you request materials from the Plan Administrator and do not receive them within 30 days, you may file suit in a federal court. In that case, the court may require the Plan Administrator to provide the materials and pay you up to $100 a day until you receive them, unless the materials were not sent because of reasons beyond the Plan Administrator's control. If you have a claim for benefits that is denied or ignored, in whole or in part, you may file suit in a state or federal court. Of course, we suggest that you follow the claims procedure provided by the Plan (see Article XI) before you sue.

If it should happen that plan fiduciaries misuse the Plan's money, or if you are discriminated against for asserting your rights, you may ask for help from the U.S. Department of Labor, or you may sue in a federal court. The court will decide who has to pay court costs and legal fees. If you win, the court may order the person you have sued to pay these costs and fees. If you lose, the court may order you to pay these costs and fees; for example, if it finds your claim is frivolous. If you have any questions about your Plan, you should contact the Plan Administrator. If you have any questions about this statement or your rights under ERISA, you should contact the nearest Area Office of the U.S. Labor-Management Services Administration, Department of Labor.

Article XV
Definitions

Account means your Employer Contribution Account.

Company means _____ .

Compensation means the total of all money paid to you by the Company during a Plan Year (regardless of whether you were a Participant in the Plan for the entire Plan Year), including bonuses, overtime, commissions, and any pretax contributions made by the Company on behalf of the Participant under the Company's _____ [complete only if Company also maintains a Section 401(k) plan]. However, Compensation shall not include fringe benefits not reported to the U.S. Department of the Treasury as "wages." The amount of compensation used by the Plan will not necessarily be the same amount of compensation shown on the Form W-2 that you receive from the Company.

Disability means a physical or mental condition that, in the judgment of the Plan Administrator, presumably permanently prevents you from performing your job for the Company or such other job made available to you by the Company and for which you are qualified.

APPENDIX C

Employer Contribution Account means the account set up for each Plan Participant that shows the amount of Company contributions made for the Participant and shows the Participant's share of forfeitures and of the income, gain, or loss of the Trust Fund.

Entry Date means _____ and _____ .

Excess Compensation means the amount of your Compensation that exceeds the Taxable Wage Base in any Plan Year.

Hours of Service means:

1. Each hour for which you are paid or entitled to payment for the performance of your employment duties;
2. Each hour for which you are paid or entitled to payment during which no duties are performed due to vacation, holiday, illness, incapacity, layoff, jury duty, military duty, or leave of absence, up to a maximum of 501 hours for any single continuous period during which you perform no duties; and
3. Each hour for which back pay (regardless of mitigation of damages) is awarded or agreed to.

You may be credited under only one of these three categories for each hour.

One-Year Break in Service means a Plan Year during which you have not been credited with more than 500 Hours of Service with the Company. If you otherwise would incur a One-Year Break in Service because you are on a maternity or paternity leave, you will be credited with sufficient Hours of Service (up to 501) for purposes of eligibility to participate or for purposes of vesting to avoid incurring a One-Year Break in Service. If you already have more than 500 Hours of Service in the Plan Year in which your maternity or paternity leave commences, you will receive credit for the leave (up to 501 hours) in the following Plan Year if you otherwise would incur a One-Year Break in Service in the following Plan Year.

Participant means each employee who has met the requirements for participation in the Plan.

Plan Year means a 12-month period commencing on _____ and ending on _____ .

Retire or Retirement means a termination of employment with the Company at or after your Retirement Date.

Retirement Date means the first day of the month coincident with or next following the date on which you attain age 65.

Spouse means the person to whom you are legally married and also a former spouse pursuant to the extent required by a domestic relations order that satisfies the requirements of the Internal Revenue Code and ERISA.

Taxable Wage Base means, with respect to each Plan Year, the maximum amount of Compensation on which social security taxes are imposed.

Valuation Date means the last day of each Plan Year, or more often, as the Trustee determines.

Years of Service means the service credited to a Participant of the Plan for the purpose of determining a Participant's vested interest in his or her Employer Contribution Account.

APPENDIXES

SAMPLE COVER LETTER FOR FORWARDING SUMMARY PLAN DESCRIPTION TO THE DEPARTMENT OF LABOR

SPD
Pension and Welfare Benefit Programs
U.S. Department of Labor
200 Constitution Avenue, N.W.
Washington, D.C. 20216

Dear Sir:

Pursuant to Title I, Sections 102 and 104(a)(1), of ERISA, enclosed herein is the [initial, updated, revised] Summary Plan Description of the XYZ Company Money-Purchase Plan.

Sincerely,

_____
Plan Administrator

PENSION VALUATION VARIETY CHART

Item	A	B	C	D
(1) Benefit date	COMP	COMP	NOW	COMP
(2) Monthly pension accrued for service to (1)	1,000	1,000	1,400	1,000
(3) Valuation date	COMP	NOW	NOW	NOW
(4) Present value of (2) at valuation date (3)	30,000	35,000	50,000	35,000
(5) Marital coverture fraction	90%	90%	70%	70%
(6) Marital present value	27,000	31,500	35,000	24,500
(7) Equivalent marital monthly pension	900	900	980	700
(8) Comment	Value then of benefit then; irrelevant, value in past.	Value now of benefit then; a correct method.	Value now of benefit now; a correct method.	Value now of benefit *when* (?); erroneous value wrong coverture.

Notes: Marital coverture fraction at COMP is 90%, NOW is 70%.
COMP = Date of divorce complaint (or separation)
NOW = Date of current hearing/trial

A&B	10%	90%	100%		
C&D	10%	70%		20%	100%
	Hired	Married	Complaint (Separation)	NOW	Retirement

APPENDIX E

SAMPLE VALUES OF A PENSION AT AGE 65 USING GATT RATES

Set forth here are sample values by interest rate, separate for males and females, for a pension of $1,000 per month at age 65. Please note that these are the values at age 65 when the pension is due to begin, not at any earlier age.

Interest Rate	Male	Female
6.00%	$119,000	$138,000
6.25	$117,000	$135,000
6.50	$115,000	$132,000
6.75	$113,000	$129,500
7.00	$111,000	$127,000
7.25	$109,000	$124,500
7.50	$107,000	$122,000
7.75	$105,500	$120,000
8.00	$103,800	$117,600

These values apply at age 65. For a present value at a younger age, they would have to be discounted for mortality and interest to any particular age. The interest rate used in the discounting to a younger age does not necessarily have to be the same rate as the rate at age 65. That is, the pre-retirement interest rate is often phased in over time, including one or more interest rates over various periods of years prior to retirement. When phased rates are used, the interest rates prior to age 65 are always smaller than the interest rate at age 65. The final or ultimate interest rate is known as the *immediate* or *primary rate*.

APPENDIX F

COVERTURE FRACTION METHOD

WHEN DOES $\frac{1}{2} = \frac{1}{3}$?

EXAMPLE:	AGE:
Hired	35
Married	40
Separated (filed complaint)	50
"Now"	55
Retirement	65

Married plan service: Age 50 − later of age 35 or age 40 = 10 years

All plan service to separation
(complaint):   Age 50 − age 35 = 15 years

All plan service to the present: Age 55 − age 35 = 20 years

Total plan service at retirement: Age 65 − age 35 = 30 years

Projected monthly pension at retirement age 65:   = $1,200

Accrued monthly pension now at age 55 [20/30 × 1,200]:   = $ 800

Coverture fraction #1:

    Married plan service/all plan service to the present: = 10/20

    Marital accrued monthly pension #1: 10/20 × 800:   = $400

Coverture fraction #2:

    Married plan service/total plan service at retirement: = 10/30

    Marital accrued monthly pension #2: 10/30 × 1,200:   = $400

Illustration of Coverture #1
(The Time Rule)

This is an illustration of the coverture fraction method used for the valuation of pensions in divorce under the present value method, to be used in immediate offset to other marital property for equitable distribution. This applies when the benefit is measured at the cutoff date.

3 years	10 years	2 years	20 years
Hired	Married	Cutoff Date	Hearing	Retirement
A	B	C	D	E

(1) The benefit accrual period *while in the plan during the marriage* is the time from Point B to Point C: 10 years.

(2) The *total* actual benefit accrual period is the time from Point A to Point D: 15 years.

(3) The *future* benefit accrual period from Point D to Point E is for information only, not used in benefit calculations in divorce.

(4) The pension benefit accrued for service from A to C is determined as of Point C under the terms of the pension plan. This is the full *accrued benefit* at C, deferred to be payable at maturity Point E. It has been "earned" by the employee, but it is not available for payment until retirement age.

(5) The full accrued benefit is *valued* at Point D. That is, it is actuarially converted to a cash lump-sum equivalent by consideration of the "discount" period from D to E subject to mortality and interest rates over that time period.

(6) The *coverture fraction* is computed as the numerator divided by the denominator, as follows: The numerator is the time from B to C: in this example 10 years. The denominator is the time from A to C: in this example 13 years. This coverture fraction is therefore $10 \div 13 = .76923$.

(7) The actuarial present value of the marital portion of the pension as of date of hearing, Point D, is the product of item (5) $\times$ item (6).

(8) If the parties were *married before the employee spouse was hired,* then the benefit accrual period during the marriage counts from date of hire, as does the total benefit accrual period. The coverture fraction is then equal to unity, or 1.00000.

Illustration of Coverture #2
(The Time Rule)

This is an illustration of the coverture fraction method used for the valuation of pensions in divorce under the present value method, to be used in immediate offset to other marital property for equitable distribution. This applies when the benefit is measured at the date of the hearing.

	3 years		10 years		2 years		20 years	
Hired		Married		Cutoff Date		Hearing		Retirement
A		B		C		D		E

(1) The benefit accrual period *while in the plan during the marriage* is the time from Point B to Point C: 10 years.

(2) The *total* actual benefit accrual period is the time from Point A to Point D: 15 years.

(3) The *future* benefit accrual period from Point D to Point E is for information only, not used in benefit calculations in divorce.

(4) The pension benefit accrued for service from A to D is determined as of Point D under the terms of the pension plan. This is the full *accrued benefit* at D, deferred to be payable at maturity Point E. It has been "earned" by the employee, but it is not available for payment until retirement age.

(5) The full accrued benefit is *valued* at Point D. That is, it is actuarially converted to a cash lump-sum equivalent by consideration of the "discount" period from D to E subject to mortality and interest rates over that time period.

(6) The *coverture fraction* is computed as the numerator divided by the denominator, as follows: The numerator is the time from B to C: in this example 10 years. The denominator is the time from A to D: in this example 15 years. This coverture fraction is therefore $10 \div 15 = .66666$.

(7) The actuarial present value of the marital portion of the pension as of date of hearing, Point D, is the product of item (5) $\times$ item (6). As the benefit is measured further out past the cutoff date, the benefit increases while the coverture fraction decreases. The net result usually is a larger marital benefit.

(8) If the parties were *married before the employee spouse was hired,* then the benefit accrual period during the marriage counts from date of hire, as does the total benefit accrual period.

APPENDIXES

Illustration of Coverture #3
(The Time Rule)

This is an illustration of the coverture fraction method used for the valuation of pensions in divorce under the present value method, to be used in immediate offset to other marital property for equitable distribution. This applies when the benefit is measured at the expected future date of retirement.

	3 years		10 years		2 years		20 years	
Hired		Married		Cutoff Date		Hearing		Retirement
A		B		C		D		E

(1) The benefit accrual period *while in the plan during the marriage* is the time from Point B to Point C: 10 years.

(2) The *total* estimated benefit accrual period is the time from Point A to Point E: 35 years.

(3) The *future* benefit accrual period from Point D to Point E is included as a projection for future benefits.

(4) The pension benefit accrued for service from A to E is estimated as of Point E under the terms of the pension plan. This is the total *accrued benefit* at E, to be payable at maturity Point E. It is presumed to be "earned" by the employee, available for payment at retirement age.

(5) The full accrued benefit is *valued* at Point D. That is, it is actuarially converted to a cash lump-sum equivalent by consideration of the "discount" period from D to E subject to mortality and interest rates over that time period.

(6) The *coverture fraction* is computed as the numerator divided by the denominator, as follows: The numerator is the time from B to C: in this example 10 years. The denominator is the time from A to E: in this example 35 years. This coverture fraction is therefore $10 \div 35 = .28571$.

(7) The actuarial present value of the marital portion of the pension as of date of hearing, Point D, is the product of item (5) $\times$ item (6). As the benefit is measured further out past the cutoff date, the benefit increases while the coverture fraction decreases. The net result usually is a larger marital benefit.

(8) If the parties were *married before the employee spouse was hired,* then the benefit accrual period during the marriage counts from date of hire, as does the total benefit accrual period.

SAMPLE SUMMARY ANNUAL REPORT FORM

[DOL Reg. § 2520.104b-10(d)(3) includes the following sample summary annual report form for pension plans.]

Summary Annual Report for [Name of Plan]

This is a summary of the annual report for [name of Plan and EIN] during [period covered by this report]. The annual report has been filed with the Internal Revenue Service as required under the Employee Retirement Income Security Act of 1974 (ERISA).

Basic Financial Statement

Benefits under the Plan are provided by [indicate funding arrangements]. Plan expenses were $ _____ . These expenses included $ _____ in administrative expenses, $ _____ in benefits paid to Participants and beneficiaries, and $ _____ in other expenses. A total of _____ people were Participants in, or beneficiaries of, the Plan at the end of the Plan Year, although not all of these people had yet earned the right to receive benefts.

[If the Plan is funded in any other manner than solely by allocated insurance contracts:]

The value of Plan assets, after subtracting liabilities of the Plan, was $ _____ as of [date of end of the Plan Year] as compared with $ _____ as of [date of beginning of the Plan Year]. During the Plan Year, the Plan experienced an [increase or decrease] in its net assets of $ _____ . This [increase or decrease] includes unrealized appreciation or depreciation in the value of Plan assets; that is, the difference between the value of the Plan's assets at the end of the year and the value of the assets at the beginning of the year, or the cost of assets acquired during the year. The Plan had a total income of $ _____ , including employer contributions of $ _____ , employee contributions of $ _____ , [gains or losses] of $ _____ from the sale of assets, and earnings realized from investments of $ _____ .

[If any funds are used to purchase allocated insurance contracts:]

The Plan has a contract with [name of insurance carrier(s)] that allocates funds toward [state whether individual policies, group deferred annuities, or other]. The total premiums paid for the Plan Year ending [date] were $ _____ .

APPENDIXES

Minimum Funding Standards

[If the Plan is a Defined Benefit Plan:]

An actuary's statement shows that [not] enough money was contributed to the Plan to keep it funded in accordance with the minimum funding standards of ERISA. [The amount of the deficit was $ _____ .]

[If the Plan is a Defined Contribution Plan Covered by Funding Requirements:]

[Not] enough money was contributed to the Plan to keep it funded in accordance with the minimum funding standards of ERISA. [The amount of the deficit was $ _____ .]

Your Rights to Secure Additional Information

You have the right to receive, upon request, a copy of the full annual report or any part thereof. The items listed below are included in that report [list only those items that are actually included in the latest annual report]:

1. An accountant's report;
2. Assets held for investment;
3. Fiduciary information, including transactions between the Plan and parties-in-interest;
4. Loans or other obligations in default;
5. Leases in default;
6. Transactions in excess of 3 percent of Plan assets;
7. Insurance information, including sales commissions paid by insurance carriers; and
8. Actuarial information regarding the funding of the Plan.

To obtain a copy of the full annual report or any portion thereof, write or call the office of [name], who is [state title of person], at [business address and telephone number]. The charge to cover copying costs will be $ _____ for the full annual report or $ _____ per page for any part thereof.

You also have the right to receive, from the Plan Administrator, upon request and at no charge, a statement of the assets and liabilities of the Plan and accompanying notes, or a statement of income and expenses of the Plan and accompanying notes, or both. If you request a copy of the full annual report from the Plan Administrator, these two statements and accompanying notes will be included as part of that report. The charge to cover copying costs (as indicated above) does not include a charge for copying portions of the report, as these sections are furnished without charge.

You also have the legally protected right to examine the annual report at the main office of the Plan [address(es)] and at the U.S. Department of Labor in Washington, D.C., or to obtain a copy from the U.S. Department of Labor upon payment of copying costs. Requests to the Department should be addressed to:

Public Disclosure Room, N-4677
Pension and Welfare Benefit Programs
Department of Labor
200 Constitution Avenue, N.W.
Washington, D.C. 20216

SAMPLE NOTICE TO INTERESTED PARTIES OF PLAN AMENDMENT

1. Notice to all present employees of XYZ, Inc.
    An application is to be made to the Internal Revenue Service for an advance determination on the qualification of the following employee pension benefit plan.
2. Name of Plan: XYZ, Inc. Retirement Trust (Profit-Sharing)
3. Plan Number: 001
4. Name and Address of Applicant: XYZ, Inc.
    100 Main Street
    New York, NY 10000
5. Applicant EIN: 00-0000001
6. Name and Address of Plan Administrator: (See (4) above.)
7. The application will be filed on [date] with the Key District Director, Internal Revenue Service, at [location], for an advance determination as to whether the Plan, as amended, meets the qualification requirements of Section 401 of the Internal Revenue Code.
8. Employees eligible to participate in the Plan are: all present employees who are or will become eligible to participate.
9. The Internal Revenue Service has previously issued a favorable determination letter with respect to qualifications of this Plan.

Rights of Interested Parties

10. You have the right to submit to the Key District Director, at the above address, either individually or jointly, in conjunction with other interested parties, your comments as to whether this Plan complies with the qualification requirements of the Internal Revenue Code.
    You may, instead, individually or jointly, along with other interested parties, request the Department of Labor to submit, on your behalf, comments to the Key District Director in regard to qualifications of the Plan. If the Department declines to comment on all or some of the matters you raise, you may then, individually or jointly, submit your comments on these matters directly to the Key District Director.

APPENDIXES

Request for Comments by the Department of Labor

11. The Department of Labor may not comment on behalf of interested parties unless requested to do so by the lesser of 10 employees or 10 percent of the employees who qualify as interested parties. The number of persons needed for the Department to comment with respect to this Plan is _____ . If a request to comment is made to the Department, the request must be in writing and must specify the matters upon which the comments are requested and must include:

   - The information contained in items (2) through (4) of this Notice, and
   - The number of persons needed for the Department to comment.

   A request to the Department to comment should be addressed as follows:

   Administrator of Pension and Welfare Benefit Programs
   U.S. Department of Labor
   200 Constitution Avenue, N.W.
   Washington, D.C. 20216
   ATTN: 3001 Comment Request

Comments to the Internal Revenue Service

12. Comments submitted to the Key District Director must be in writing and must be received by [45th day after filing of application]. However, if there are matters that are being sent to the Department of Labor to comment upon on your behalf and the Department declines to comment, then comments on these matters may be presented to the Key District Director if such comments are received by the Key District Director within 15 days from the time the Department of Labor notifies you that it will not comment on a particular matter, or by [45th day after filing the application], whichever is later. A request to the Department to comment on your behalf must be received by the Department by [15th day after filing the application] if you wish to preserve your right to comment on a matter upon which the department declines to comment, or by [25th day after filing the application] if you wish to waive that right.

Additional Information

13. Detailed instructions regarding the requirements for notification of interested parties may be found in Sections 6, 7, and 8 of Revenue Procedure 80-30. Additional information concerning this application (including, where applicable, an updated copy of the Plan and related Trust, the application for determination, any additional documents dealing with the application that has been submitted to the Internal Revenue Service, and copies of Section

6 of Revenue Procedure 80-30) is available at 100 Main Street, New York, NY Room 817, during the hours of 9 a.m. to 5 p.m. for inspection and copying. (There is a nominal charge for copying and/or mailing.)

XYZ, Inc.

Date _____   By _____
President

ENCYCLOPEDIA OF PENSION TERMINOLOGY FOR DIVORCE CASES

A compendium of subjects in alphabetical order for lawyers in family practice who deal with issues of equitable distribution of pension values in marital dissolution.

Accrued Benefit

A participant in every type of pension plan has an accrued benefit. In an individual account plan (defined contribution plan), the accrued benefit is the balance in the participant's account. Once a year, and in some plans more often, the participant receives a statement of his or her account balance. The account balance generally increases every year unless there has been a substantial decline in plan assets due to investment losses. In a defined benefit pension plan, the pension benefit is defined by a formula in the plan. In most plans, the benefit increases each year as pay and years of service increase. The plan records contain the participant's accrued pension benefit for each year, which is determined as of the plan anniversary date. By referring to past records, or by a calculation using prior data for an individual, an accrued benefit can be calculated as of a past date, such as the date of marital separation or filing of the divorce complaint. A plan may not be able to provide the exact accrued benefit as of a specific date, but assuming the benefit changes one year at a time, or ratably by month over a year, the exact date benefit is not essential. If future salary increases are ignored, or if they are projected mathematically, an accrued benefit may be fairly estimated at any desired future date, such as the normal retirement date.

Accrued Benefit Fraction

ERISA requires that a defined benefit pension plan contain a stated method for determining the accrued benefit of a participant at least once a year. The most common method uses the accrued benefit fraction. The numerator of the fraction is the length of credited service in the plan, under the plan's definition of service, up to the date being measured. The denominator is the potential length of credited service in the plan if the individual continues working to normal retirement age. The accrued benefit fraction is then multiplied by the expected pension benefit at normal retirement age. Future pay increases are not included. This is a service-based approach that counts prior pay history as defined in the plan up to the date being measured and assumes that future pay remains unchanged.

Accrued Benefit Reduction

In a qualified ERISA defined benefit plan, a participant's accrued benefits normally may not be reduced. However, with special permission from the IRS and the PBGC, a plan amendment may reduce benefits already accrued. The operation of combined limits for an individual who is a simultaneous participant in two plans sponsored by the same employer can reduce an already accrued benefit in the pension plan. The reduction would depend on the terms of the two plans regarding which plan will suffer a reduction if the participant reaches the combined maximum allowed by pension legislation and IRS regulation.

Actuarial Assumptions

A defined benefit pension plan uses different sets of actuarial assumptions for different purposes. The enrolled actuary for the plan uses these actuarial assumptions to compute the plan's liabilities and to advise the employer on the annual contribution amount. The plan also uses the actuarial assumptions to convert from one form of pension benefit to another, such as from a straight lifetime annuity to a joint-and-survivor annuity. The IRS, the PBGC, and the GATT each requires separate sets of actuarial assumptions for measuring different aspects of benefits and liability for reporting purposes and to determine PBGC premiums. Actuarial assumptions include mortality tables, interest rates, turnover or withdrawal tables, salary scales, disability rates, and expenses. The assumptions in any one plan may vary according to the time frames, before and after retirement. In addition, for purposes of calculating liability and contributions, assumptions may vary by sex, age, and/or employee job classification. Age and sex will affect the conversion from one form of benefit to another in actuarial equivalence.

Actuarial Equivalent Options

A defined benefit pension plan has a standard, normal form of pension payment that allows for no reduction or adjustment to pension amounts calculated under the plan formula. Usually, the normal form of pension payment is a straight lifetime annuity that ends at the death of the retiree, leaving no survivor benefits. Most plans, however, offer a retiring employee a choice among optional forms of benefits. If a plan provides optional forms of benefits, all the forms should be actuarially equivalent (that is, have the same value) so that the plan may remain financially sound and in actuarial balance. For example, if a straight lifetime pension is "traded in" for a pension with benefits guaranteed to be paid over ten years, the actual amount of the pension will be reduced about 10 percent. Similarly, if a 50 percent joint-and-survivor option is elected and the spouse is three years younger than the participant, the actual amount of the pension will be reduced by about 15 percent. Some plans offer subsidized options that are not reduced as much as the actuarial factors would indicate. That is, the benefit option is somewhat higher or better than a true actuarial reduction.

Actuarial Rate

The term *actuarial rate* has different meanings depending on its purpose and the area of actuarial science using it. When a pension plan is valued in a divorce case, the actuarial rate is the factor used to determine the present value of the current accrued pension. The rate is usually stated on the basis of one dollar per year, which requires multiplying the current accrued pension benefit by 12 if the pension is stated as monthly. For example, for a male age 45 with retirement at age 65, the typical actuarial rate would be 2.2516 for one dollar per year. If the individual's current accrued pension is $1,000 per month, its present value is $27,019 ($12 \times 2.2516 \times \$1,000$). Of course, if the pension is stated in annual terms, the actuarial rate may be used directly, as follows: $2.2516 \times \$12,000 = \$27,019$.

Actuarial Soundness

A theoretical mathematical concept that attempts to balance the assets and liabilities of a defined benefit pension plan. If the present value of a plan's current assets and expected future contributions is equal to the plan's liabilities and future expected benefit payouts, then the plan is actuarially sound. Although there is no legal or regulatory requirement that a plan demonstrate such soundness, it is something that an actuary would look for when conducting a thorough valuation of a plan.

Actuary

A professional trained in mathematics and statistics, with an emphasis on probability and the time value of money, who is usually a member of a recognized actuarial organization such as the Society of Actuaries, the American Society of Pension Actuaries, or the American Academy of Actuaries. An actuary who specializes in pensions has usually obtained the federal designation of enrolled actuary, a special status established by ERISA.

Age

The valuation age of the pension plan participant is a vital element needed for determining the present worth of a defined benefit pension plan. There are four generally recognized methods of computing age for this purpose: (1) age last birthday—the person's actual attained age; (2) age next birthday—the age the person will be at the next birthday; (3) age nearest birthday—the person's age within six months, past or future (the age generally used in pension valuations); and (4) exact age—the person's age on the valuation date, in years and fractions of a year or months. The difficulty with the fourth method lies in entering a table of rates by age.

Age Misstatement

An employee's age is a critical element in determining the present value of a pension in a defined benefit pension plan. In one case, an individual who applied for retirement revealed that her true age was 65, not 55 as shown on her employment records. She had misrepresented her age when she was hired. Because the pension plan was small—only 19 participants—the plan actuary contended that the difference between the employee's true age and her reported age was actuarially significant and to the detriment of the plan. The pension plan postponed the commencement of the employee's benefits, relying on the "wrong" age shown on the plan books, and its action was upheld by the court. *Nass v. Local 810 Staff Retirement Plan*, 515 F. Supp. 950 (S.D.N.Y. 1981).

Age Proof

An employee misstatement of age affects the person's eligibility for retirement and the actuary's computations of the person's liabilities and contribution requirements. The following is a standard list of acceptable proofs of age for pension purposes: birth certificate, baptismal certificate or signed statement on church records, United States Census Bureau notification of birth registration, hospital birth record or certificate, foreign church or government record, attending physician's or midwife's signed statement, Bible or family record, certified naturalization record or immigration papers, military records or school records, passport, insurance policy, labor union certified records, voting records, and marriage license or certificate.

Aleatory

Refers to any risk, such as in insurance, or contingency, such as death or disability, that impacts the funding of a pension plan's ancillary benefits.

Alienation or Attachment of Pension

ERISA prohibits attachment, alienation, or garnishment of pensions. However, many states have laws that include pensions as marital property. Thus, when a state court serves an attachment order on a pension plan, ordering the plan trustee to make a payment of plan funds to a spouse, ex-spouse, or anyone who is not a plan participant, the trustee is caught between the requirements of state and federal law. Relief is offered by the Retirement Equity Act of 1984 (REA), which created the concept of a QDRO. A QDRO allows attachment if certain steps are followed, although a general creditor usually cannot attach pension benefits even in the case of bankruptcy. However, a Keogh plan or an IRA may be attachable in bankruptcy in some situations. An ERISA plan that covers only one employee, such as the owner of the company, may be vulnerable to bankruptcy attachment. See also **Collateral, Spendthrift Statute**.

Alimony

Alimony considerations may be taken into account with a pension plan valuation or pension plan deferred distribution if so ordered by the court. The court may wish to consider the need for reduced alimony or none, if the pension's present value is used in immediate offset of other marital assets. For example, if the spouse who would otherwise receive alimony receives substantial property in lieu of a piece of the pension, there may be no need for alimony. If there has been immediate offset of present value plus alimony, the court should distinguish between the spouse's income with and without the pension to avoid a form of double-dipping. That is, once the pension distributions start it may be inequitable to include the pension as income for purposes of affordability of alimony payments if that pension has already been accounted for in an earlier settlement. However, in a Pennsylvania case, the court held that the ex-husband's pension income could be considered when determining alimony even if he was awarded the entire pension in the divorce. *McFadden v. McFadden*, 563 A.2d 180 (Pa. Super Ct. 1989). See **Double-Dipping**.

Aliquot

A fractional part of the whole, such as an aliquot part of a pension, determined by the time rule or by a coverture fraction. See **Coverture Fraction**.

Alternate Payee

The person or persons designated in a QDRO to receive plan benefits incident to a divorce or other marital property settlement or support order. The alternate payee may be the spouse, former spouse, or dependent of the plan participant.

American Academy of Actuaries

A professional organization founded in 1965 as an umbrella group for all actuaries. A member may use the designation "MAAA" after his or her name. The organization's headquarters are located at 1720 I Street, NW, Washington, D.C. 20006.

American Society of Pension Actuaries

A professional organization of actuaries, consultants, and administrators founded in 1966. The categories of membership are: Fellow, Member, Certified, Qualified, Associate, Affiliate, and Government. There are approximately 6,000 members in all categories. The organization's headquarters are located at 4350 N. Fairfax Drive, Arlington, VA 22203.

Annuity

A series of regular payments in equal dollar amounts, payable once a year for a predefined period. Most pension annuities are payable monthly rather than annually. Payments may be at the beginning of each payment period (the first day of each month) or at the end. The period of payments may be for the annuitant's lifetime, over the joint lifetime of two people, for a specific time period regardless of a person's life, or for a person's lifetime with a minimum number of guaranteed payments. An annuity may provide for death benefits with more than one beneficiary or for a death benefit payable only if a specific prenamed beneficiary is the survivor. A straight lifetime annuity is the most common form in a pension plan. It stops at the death of the retiree, with no survivorship benefits.

Annuity Contract

A policy purchased from an insurance company. The policy provides for annuity payments to an individual, with varying terms and conditions, in a certain amount, as stated in the contract. A pension plan may buy an annuity for a retiring participant in lieu of the pension fund making the monthly pension payments. The advantage is that the insurance company takes over all of the paperwork and administration and bears the mortality risk or gain. The disadvantage is that the pension fund must part with a large sum of money to buy the contract. If an annuity has been purchased by a plan for a participant, the annuity retains the tax shelter that the plan had, and the payments are taxable to the beneficiary as received. If a QDRO is in place before the annuity is purchased, the plan may purchase an annuity for the alternate payee as well as for the retiree. If a QDRO is ordered after the annuity is in place, the insurance company's legal department should be consulted to see if the insurer will administer the QDRO directly or if it requires the QDRO to be processed through the plan first. See **Qualified Domestic Relations Order**.

Annuity Investment

The basic purpose of an annuity contract is to provide annuity payments in the future. However, insurance companies may market their annuity products as investment vehicles. A deferred annuity may be sold for a particular cash price today, with the annuity payments to commence at some future date, and with a minimum guarantee of tax-sheltered internal investment growth. The investment growth would increase the eventual annuity payout if such growth amounts to more than the underlying interest assumption of the basic annuity. The selling agent generally will emphasize the potential growth and recommend a lump-sum payout at maturity instead of a series of monthly annuity payments. In the early years, these types of contracts usually have high surrender charges and can be expected to cost more—i.e., have a larger purchase price—than a straight annuity contract. Conversely, a straight annuity contract promises an exact payout at the specified future date, regardless of investment performance. When pension plans use annuities, they are usually straight rather than investment annuities.

Antenuptial Agreement

An antenuptial agreement is presumed valid if it provides that the future husband and wife have fully disclosed to one another the extent of their assets and the extent of possible marital rights. *Cooper v. Oates,* 629 A.2d 944 (Pa. Super. Ct. 1993). The case did not involve a pension, but it raises the question whether potential pension rights and values should be mentioned in an antenuptial agreement. Should the document include references to ERISA if one or both of the prospective spouses are employed and covered by a pension plan? Should an actuarial valuation of prospective pension values be listed in the full and fair disclosure of possible assets? If neither party is covered by a pension plan prior to the marriage, should the agreement mention potential future coverage? Because court cases involving marital agreements leave many questions unanswered, the attorney in family practice should consider the potential pension issues in advising clients.

Assignment of Pension

In most cases, a retiree whose benefits are in pay status may assign or alienate the right to future benefit payments provided that (1) the assignment or alienation is voluntary and revocable; (2) the amount does not exceed 10 percent of any benefit payment; and (3) there is no direct or indirect defraying of plan administration costs. Although for federal purposes the assignment must be revocable, this is not always the case at the state level. For example, a pensioner in a nursing home in Pennsylvania signed over his pension benefits so that payments went to the nursing home. He was married, and his wife, who was also elderly, had no pension of her own. He sued for relief to provide one-half of his pension to the nursing home, preserving one-half as marital property. He argued that in the event of divorce, one-half of his pension would go to his wife. The court denied his request, affirming that the entire pension was available to pay for nursing home care and should be so used; a potential marital property interest that might become an asset in divorce is incidental and does not govern. *Buck v. Commonwealth of Pa.,* 566 A.2d 1269 (Pa. Commw. Ct. 1989). See also **Alienation or Attachment of Pension**.

Back Loading

A benefit formula that gives more weight to later service in a person's career with the employer under the plan in a defined benefit pension plan. For example, the pension benefit may accrue over time at 1 percent of pay for each of the first 10 years of service, plus 1.25 percent for each of the next 10 years, plus 1.5 percent for the balance of years of service in excess of 20 years. In theory, any pay-based defined benefit pension plan may be thought of as being back-loaded under the assumption that a person's pay will increase with time and, therefore, later years of pension benefit will be based on higher pay amounts.

Bankruptcy of the Employee

There is a possibility of the diminution or abrogation of a pension award in a divorce case if the employee-spouse files for bankruptcy. The issue is undecided, however, and is subject to the terms and conditions of a particular case. If a QDRO has been issued and accepted by an ERISA plan, the QDRO would be preserved safely outside of any bankruptcy proceedings. But if the QDRO is not finalized, there may be problems. Two 1990 cases with opposite findings illustrate the potential problems. In *Buccino v. Buccino*, the husband's obligation to pay half the value of his pension fund to his former wife, based on her need for support, was found not to be dischargeable in bankruptcy. The court said it was more than a property division because it was necessary financial support for the wife. *Buccino v. Buccino*, 580 A.2d 13 (Pa. Super. Ct. 1990). In a separate case, a court ruled that a husband's divorce obligation to give his wife half his pension was part of the property division and therefore dischargeable in bankruptcy, although a dissent objected to the wife's loss of her potential property in the husband's pension. *Bush v. Taylor*, 912 F.2d 989 (8th Cir. 1990).

Bankruptcy of the Employer

The bankruptcy of an employer usually will not affect a qualified ERISA plan. If it is a defined benefit pension plan covered by the PBGC, the pension benefits are guaranteed (up to a certain maximum amount) by the federal government. If it is a defined contribution plan, the assets in the plan cannot be reached by creditors. However, caution must be exercised in the case of a Keogh plan, an IRA, and certain aspects of a 401(k) plan in which employee money may be characterized as personal. In the case of the owner of a company—a professional or other one-person entity—the creditors may claim that the plan and the employer are one, which would make the plan assets vulnerable.

Beneficiary

The broad general concept of beneficiary encompasses all employees who are participants in a pension plan, former participants with vested deferred pensions, and retirees in pay status. In practice, however, the term means any person who may be entitled to benefits upon the death of the plan participant, either before or after retirement. The term *beneficiary* is often used interchangeably with the term *survivor*.

Bifurcation of Benefits

If a divorce becomes final before the property settlement has been completed or a court order has been approved as a QDRO and if the employee dies, the nonemployee-spouse may get nothing. If no QDRO exists and the parties are no longer married, the former spouse is entitled to nothing under a pension plan unless the employee has maintained the former spouse as a beneficiary.

Bigamy

In a case of bigamy involving pension death benefits, the second "wife" was denied any benefits as not being the legal spouse. The first and only legal wife received the full amount. In this case there was a marital separation and the husband was paying support to his legal wife under a court order. Some years later, perhaps thinking that the separation was a divorce, the husband changed the beneficiary under his pension plan from his first to his second wife. Upon the husband's death, both wives claimed the death benefits. The pension board initially denied benefits to either wife, but after a hearing awarded the benefits to the current (second) wife. The first (legal) wife appealed and won. *Board of Pensions & Retirement City of Phila. v. Boelter,* No. 1958 C.D. 1989 (Pa. Commw. Ct. Apr. 6, 1990). See **Remarriage**.

Bonds

Bonds are sometimes used as the basis for selecting a particular interest rate to compute the present value of a pension for immediate offset. There are some problems with doing so because the yield of a bond is the actual payment of interest divided by the purchase price. Payment of interest becomes a variable dependent on the price of the bond, although the bond's stated or nominal yield is not indicative of its interest rate. Whatever the yield is, unless each payment can be immediately reinvested at exactly the same rate, it is useless in pension computations. Bonds can also have a negative yield. In 1987, an investor who paid $1,000 for a 30-year Treasury bond in January and sold it in September would have lost $150. The drop in price exceeded the interest paid by that amount, which is a negative return of 15 percent.

Cash-Balance Pension Plan

A special kind of qualified ERISA defined benefit pension plan that reports the value of the current accrued pension to plan participants each year. Upon termination of employment with a vested pension, or retirement, the employee may request a lump-sum payout in lieu of a monthly pension.

Cash or Deferred Arrangement

A cash or deferred arrangement (CODA) is a feature of a qualified 401(k) plan under ERISA. When a plan has this feature, the participant has a choice each year of whether to receive a specified amount in cash as income or to defer the amount into the individual account in the plan as a tax shelter.

Casualty Actuarial Society

A national organization whose members are actuaries working in the fields of property and casualty insurance, workers' compensation, and liability insurance. The organization generally does not handle pension issues. It is located at One Penn Plaza, 250 West 34th Street, New York, NY 10119.

Changed Circumstances

The concept of changed circumstances may be introduced in an attempt to reduce alimony payments when a former spouse retires and begins to receive a pension. If the retiree is the alimony payor, the claim is that his or her income is reduced from a salary to a pension. If the retiree is the alimony payee, the claim is that with pension income, there is less need for alimony.

Cliff Vesting

A plan's vesting schedule is called *cliff vesting* when full vesting is obtained upon the completion of a specified period of service, such as ten years. In ten-year cliff vesting, if an employee leaves with nine years of service, all benefits are forfeited. However, at ten years or more, vesting is 100 percent. Typical cliff vesting is three or five years in single-employer plans and ten years in multiemployer plans.

267

CODA

See **Cash or Deferred Arrangement**.

Cohabitation

It is theoretically possible for a QDRO to cut off benefits to an alternate payee upon that person's cohabitation with a member of the opposite sex, but this would be difficult to police. The plan administrator would most certainly object to any attempt to enforce such a provision. A QDRO may not award benefits that are not in the beneficiary's pension plan, and because no plan has a cohabitation item, it would be proper for the plan to deny such a QDRO provision. See also **Common Law Marriage**.

COLA

See **Cost-of-Living Adjustment**.

Collateral

An interest in a pension plan of any type may not be pledged as collateral, because, if the borrower defaults on the loan, the lender could not collect the collateral. However, in certain complicated divorce situations, it is possible to structure a *standby QDRO* if all parties agree. The standby QDRO would be written to make payments from a plan to the alternate payee only if the employee fails to make agreed-upon payments for support or property distribution. This requires a certain degree of trust among all parties and/or monitoring by counsel to be sure that it is not abused.

Collectively Bargained Plan

A plan established and maintained between one or more employers and one union or collective bargaining unit under a collective bargaining agreement. This type of plan was formerly called a *Taft-Hartley plan*. If more than one employer is involved in the collective bargaining agreement, the plan is called a multiemployer plan. Collectively bargained plans are subject to ERISA (or the PBGC if the plan is a defined benefit plan) and the Multiemployer Pension Plan Amendment Act of 1987. If only one employer (including affiliates) is required to contribute to the plan, the plan is treated in the same way as plans that do not cover union employees are treated.

Commissions

Salespersons, agents, brokers, and others may be compensated in full or in part by commissions. The pension plan will have a definition of compensation for plan purposes that may exclude commissions or include them in whole or in part. In a defined benefit pension plan, it is important to know this in calculating the accrued benefit and also in planning for deferred distribution under a QDRO. Commissions themselves may be included in marital property if they are deferred. In an Alaska case, commissions that a husband had earned before divorce were included in marital property even though he had not yet received payment. *Hartland v. Hartland*, 777 P.2d 636 (Alaska 1989).

Common Law Marriage

Common law marriage may be recognized in some states, but it is difficult to secure pension rights for the putative ''spouse.'' Courts are reluctant to divide a pension as marital property when there has not been a bona fide marriage. The federal government has denied Social Security benefits to a ''widow'' of a common law husband. In a case reported in *The Wall Street Journal* (Dec. 31, 1990), a 74-year-old woman began receiving benefits when her husband died in 1985. However, upon routine paperwork processing, the woman appealed on the basis of a common law marriage, but she lost in federal appeals court. Similarly, a New Jersey court ruled that cohabitation without formal marriage did not give a woman any rights to a man's pension. *Wajda*, 570 A.2d 1308 (N.J. Super. Ct. 1989). In a Pennsylvania case, a woman was denied survivor's benefits from the pension plan of her deceased husband because she was not legally married to him. *Flagg v. Allied Signal Inc.*, as reported in the Pennsylvania Law Journal-Reporter, April 16, 1990.

Community Property

In community property states, pension rights are not subject to the *terminable interest* doctrine, that is, the rights do not stop upon death but remain available for distribution after the death of a spouse. Otherwise, death of either spouse would end the community share of marital property interest in the pension. *Chirmside v. Board of Admin. of Public Employees Retirement System,* 143 Cal. App. 3d 205 (May 20, 1983). The community property states are: Arizona, California, Idaho,

Louisiana, Nevada, New Mexico, Texas, Washington, and Wisconsin. (Mississippi is the only state that distributes property by title.)

Comparison of Pensions

In settling the property in a divorce where both husband and wife have pensions from their respective employers, it is sometimes suggested that each retain his or her own pension with no further investigation. This will almost always be a mistake. The plans may be of different types (e.g., defined benefit, defined contribution) and may have different retirement ages. The spouses' salaries and work histories are usually different, and the benefits provided are probably different. The only correct way to compare pensions is to compare their present values at the same point in time, when all of the variables can be accounted for.

Computation Period

The computation period is a concept introduced by ERISA. There are three computation periods in every ERISA plan: (1) the eligibility computation period, which measures the time required for an employee to fulfill the plan's requirements to become a participant; (2) the benefit computation period, which measures the credited service during which the participant is accruing benefits; and (3) the vesting computation period, which measures the time required to meet the plan's vesting requirements.

Conference of Consulting Actuaries

Formerly known as the Conference of Actuaries in Public Practice, this is a professional organization of actuaries acting as consultants in life, health, property and casualty insurance, and pension benefits. The organization's address is 475 N. Martingale Road, Schaumburg, Illinois 60173.

Contributions

In a defined benefit pension plan, the employer makes contributions for the covered group. Contributions are not made on an individual basis, and a pooled fund of assets provides benefits when they come due. A defined benefit pension plan may allow employee contributions. If so, a separate account is maintained for employee contributions and investment growth thereon. The plan may include the employee contributions (if any) in its funding of benefits, providing no additional benefits, or the employee money may be used to increase benefits. A plan with employee contributions should be reviewed to see if benefits are affected.

In a defined contribution plan, employer contributions are immediately allocated to the individual accounts of the participants. If there are employee contributions, they may go into the same account or into a subaccount earmarked for the person. Contributions to a defined contribution plan result in eventual benefits. In a defined benefit pension plan, there is no direct relationship between contributions and benefits.

Cost-of-Living Adjustment

The cost-of-living adjustment feature (COLA) in a pension plan provides for increases in retirees' pensions to help keep pace with inflation. Not often found in corporate plans, a COLA is standard in federal pension plans and in many state plans and is often a feature in state or municipality pension plans for schoolteachers, police officers, and firefighters. The COLA feature may be equal to inflation as measured by a particular consumer price index or may be a percentage. A QDRO or equivalent order may include a potential COLA but does not have to. A valuation of present value for immediate offset purposes usually does not include a COLA, but it may in some jurisdictions. For example, New Jersey courts recognize a COLA in present values when the plan provides for it. See, e.g., *Moore v. Moore*, 553 A.2d 20 (N.J. Super. Ct. 1989).

COAP

See **Court Order Acceptable for Processing**.

Court Order Acceptable for Processing

A court order acceptable for processing (COAP) is a QDRO-like instrument that attaches a pension in the divorce action of a federal government employee. The COAP applies to civilian employees in the CSRS and FERS, including postal workers. The rules and regulations are set forth in the July 29, 1992, issue of the Federal Register and are codified in 5 C.F.R. Parts 831 *et seq.* A COAP may deal with one or all of the three parts into which the federal government divides the pension system: (1) the pension benefit known as the employee annuity; (2) the refund of employee contributions, if and when applicable; and (3) the death benefits after retirement known as the survivor annuity. These matters are handled by the U.S. Office of Personnel Management, Court Order Benefit Section, P.O. Box 17, Washington, D.C. 20044.

The Office of Personnel Management (OPM) does not offer to review or pre-approve proposed orders, but if a complete order is sent in, lacking only court certification, the OPM may indicate that a preliminary review shows that the order does appear to be qualified. Formal approval requires a certified copy of the divorce decree and/or court-approved property settlement agreement showing the original certification or seal of the court, in addition to the requirements set forth in 5 C.F.R. Part 831 *et seq.*

Coverture Fraction

A coverture fraction is used to determine what portion of a pension value is marital property subject to equitable distribution (usually in a defined benefit pension plan). The fraction is constructed as follows: The numerator is the period of time from the later of (1) date of marriage or (2) date of plan entry to the cutoff date in the applicable jurisdiction. The cutoff date may be the date of marital separation, the date of filing of the divorce complaint, the date of hearing or trial, or the date of the divorce decree. The denominator is the period of time from the date of plan entry to the cutoff date in the applicable jurisdiction. The ending point of the denominator should agree with the date as of which the benefit is being measured. This is also known as *the time rule.* See **Time Rule**.

Credited Service

See **Service**.

Criminal Conduct

Criminal conduct normally does not override vesting rights. The anti-alienation provision of ERISA protects pension rights from being lost even if the individual is convicted of illegal activity. In a decision by the Second Circuit, the court said that the creation of a criminal misconduct exception to vested pension rights would lead to endless legal disputes over its scope. *Ellis Nat'l Bank of Jacksonville v. Irving Trust Co.,* 786 F.2d 466 (2d Cir. 1986). In another case, the profit-sharing benefits of an employee convicted of embezzling company funds were found to be protected by ERISA and could not be garnished. *United Metal Products Corp. v. National Bank of Detroit,* 811 F.2d 297 (6th Cir. 1987). However, in an earlier case, a court allowed the garnishment of an employee's pension account to recapture funds fraudulently obtained from the employer. *St. Paul Fire & Marine Ins. Co. v. Cox,* 583 F. Supp. 122 (N.D. Ala. 1984). See also **Forfeiture**.

Cutoff Date

There is a cutoff date for the measurement of the values of marital property for equitable distribution, and pensions are no exception. In pensions, the cutoff date is the date as of which the accrued benefit will be determined. After that date, no benefit increases due to continuing service or increases in pay will be considered. The cutoff date varies by jurisdiction. It may be the date of marital separation, the date of filing of the complaint, the date of the divorce hearing or trial, the date of the divorce decree, or the date the plan participant retires with benefit commencement. In deferred distribution, the QDRO should clearly specify the cutoff date for benefit determination. In present value computations, it should be understood that the cutoff date refers to the benefit, not its value. That is, the benefit may be the amount of the accrued benefit as it stood five years ago, but its present value is determined by the employee's current age and using current interest rates.

Death Before Divorce

Conflicting court opinions exist from around the country on the effect on a divorce action of the death of one or both of the spouses. In 1983, a divorce action was commenced, and a year later the husband killed the wife and then himself. The court did not end the property distribution that would have flowed from the divorce, because to do so would unjustly enrich the husband's estate at the expense of the wife's estate. The "divorce" action continued by substituting the wife's children as plaintiffs and the husband's estate administrator as defendant. *Drumheller v. Marcello*, 505 A.2d 305 (Pa. Super. Ct. 1986). An opposite Pennsylvania opinion dismissed a divorce action as moot following the death of the husband. The court held that the action was abated, as were the economic claims for equitable distribution. *Myers v. Myers,* 580 A.2d 384 (Pa. Super. Ct. 1990). In a New Jersey case, the wife of a decedent who died during the pendency of divorce proceedings was not entitled to equitable distribution or to take elective share of the estate. *Carr v. Carr,* 551 A.2d 989 (N.J. Super Ct. 1988). However, in Wisconsin, the nonemployee-spouse's share of a pension on an if-as-when basis did not end with the employee-spouse's death. *In re Marriage of Mausing,* 429 N.W.2d 768 (1988). See also **If-as-when**.

Death Benefits

Payments to a beneficiary of a deceased participant may be provided under a qualified plan, but they must be incidental to the retirement benefits, which are the major purpose of the plan.

Decrement

A contingency evaluated by an actuary that reduces the present value of a future monetary event. An example is the probability that an employee will die or become disabled before becoming eligible to retire with a pension.

Deferred Compensation

A general term that encompasses all retirement and savings plans; also the name of a specific type of plan often used for key employees with an employment contract that defers payment of salary or bonus until after termination of employment. See also **401(k) Plans**.

Deferred Distribution

A method of providing pension benefits in equitable distribution of marital assets. The two basic approaches are (1) the court retains jurisdiction and will award benefits of the employee-spouse to the nonemployee-spouse on an if-as-when basis and (2) a QDRO. QDROs are more common because they permit the case to be settled without further involvement of the court. Deferred distribution is in contradistinction to present value for immediate offset. In deferred distribution, it may be helpful to know the present value of the pension, but it is not required. Deferred distribution is used for a defined benefit pension plan, not usually for a defined contribution plan. A favorable aspect of deferred distribution is that both parties share the risk that the pension will ever be payable and both parties have to wait to receive any funds. The disadvantages are the administrative difficulties of drafting a QDRO and obtaining its approval, the continued linkage of ex-husband and ex-wife, and the fact that the alternate payee has to wait to receive a distribution.

Deferred Pension

1. A former employee who was a plan participant and who terminated service with vesting and is waiting to receive a pension upon attainment of a certain age has a deferred pension in the sense that it is delayed until it begins.
2. An employee who is a plan participant and who continues to work beyond normal retirement age without collecting the pension is said to have a deferred pension in that it is deferred past the age at which it was normally expected to begin.

Defined Benefit Plan

A plan designed to provide participants with a definite benefit at retirement (such as a monthly benefit of 20 percent of compensation upon reaching age 65). Contributions under the plan are determined by reference to the benefits provided for the total covered group, not on the basis of an individual's compensation.

Defined Contribution Plan

A plan with individual accounts for participants. The benefits are unknown in advance, as they are provided by the account balance when they become due and payable. Contributions from the employer and/or employee are made into the employee's account. The investment risk is borne by the employee. If investment results are poor, the account balance is low; if results from investment performance are strong, the account grows. The employer is under no obligation to guarantee investment growth. The common defined contribution plans are profit-sharing plans, Keogh plans, 401(k) plans, money-purchase plans, thrift/savings plans, and target plans. Defined contribution plans may be valued for immediate offset or may be set for deferred distribution by use of a QDRO.

Disability Pension

In jurisdictions in which a disability pension is not marital property, it may be possible to determine that the disability pension has two components: a pension for service and compensation for the disability. Thus, if the "pure" pension portion can be split out, it can be valued and considered marital property. For deferred distribution, a QDRO may be designed to pay a portion of the nondisability component of the pension to an alternate payee.

Disability Provision in a QDRO

Assume that after a QDRO has been served on a plan and approved, the employee-spouse becomes disabled before retirement age. If the employee-spouse applies for a disability pension under her company's pension plan long before she would have reached the plan's normal or early retirement age, and if the company accepts her disability application, she would begin to receive a disability pension. But what would happen to the standing QDRO that provided for a payment to the former husband upon the wife's retirement? Did the QDRO provide for the eventuality of a premature retirement due to disability? And if the pension is characterized as a disability award, may the employee-spouse claim that the award is exempt from equitable distribution as it is no longer marital property? A possible solution to this potential problem would be to draft a separate, legally binding agreement, signed by all parties to the divorce, stating that in the event the purpose of the QDRO is thwarted by the employee-spouse's disability, she will make good on the amounts due to the husband, either by direct payments from her to him, or by authorizing the plan to make payments to a third-party bank or other trust arrangement that, in turn, would issue checks to the husband in the amounts envisioned by the QDRO.

Disclosure

In the context of an antenuptial agreement or a property settlement or an inventory and appraisement in contemplation of equitable distribution, it may not always be possible to disclose the exact amount or value of assets, especially a pension. Fair and full disclosure is necessary; it requires a reasonable estimate of the assets' worth so that the general financial resources of the parties are not obscured. *Hess v. Hess,* 580 A.2d 357 (Pa. Super. Ct. 1990). This disclosure is often the result of a *forensic audit* conducted by an impartial expert who provides testimony, if necessary, that verifies the method used to arrive at a particular valuation. The forensic audit is a critical first step in the divorce process because separation agreements have been held invalid because of one spouse's failure to disclose all of his or her income. See, e.g., *Nitkeiwicz v. Nitkeiwicz,* 535 A.2d 664 (Pa. Super. Ct. 1988).

Dissipation

In marital dissolution, some subtle forms of dissipation may occur in pension plans. For example, the employee-husband may make a hardship withdrawal or take out a loan from his plan. In present value, he can claim that such amounts should not be counted. In use of a QDRO, the plan cannot pay funds that are not included and do not exist. At retirement, if the employee-husband selects an expensive option—such as a 100 percent joint-and-survivor annuity with a much younger female as beneficiary—the result will be to reduce the dollar amount of his pension. Therefore, if a QDRO addresses only the pension he actually receives without regard to the effect of its optional form, the alternate payee could receive much less than was anticipated when the original QDRO was drafted.

Double-Dipping

1. If the value of a pension has been included in equitable distribution for immediate offset of marital property, to later count the retired spouse's pension as income for measuring alimony may be considered as a form of double-dipping.

2. In a QDRO, if the alternate payee is receiving a separate independent lifetime pension and is also the beneficiary of the spouse's post-retirement death benefit, such as a joint-and-survivor plan, the alternate payee would receive a "bonus" upon the death after retirement of the participant. The alternate payee's awarded pension continues, and the payee also receives either a lump sum or a survivor pension due to the retiree's death.

DRO

See **Qualified Domestic Relations Order**.

Early Retirement

Early retirement refers to leaving employment with a pension starting before the plan's normal retirement age. A plan may have one stated normal retirement age or several possible ages determined by a combination of age and service. Early retirement does not mean merely before age 65; it depends on the plan. Some rare plans have no early retirement provisions at all. An early retirement pension may start at a particular time even when the employee has terminated service many years earlier. For example, a plan has an early retirement provision of age 55 with 15 years of service. An employee leaves at age 50 with 17 years of service, fully vested. The retiree is a terminated vested participant with a deferred pension. When she reaches age 55, the retiree may ask for her early retirement pension to begin. In a defined benefit pension plan, the early retirement pension will be reduced to allow for its early commencement and for its longer payment period over the person's lifetime. The reduction may be calculated using actuarial factors or using a formula in the plan. If the reduction is less than computed by actuarial factors, it is known as *subsidized early retirement*. See **Subsidized Early Retirement**.

Employee Retirement Income Security Act

The Employee Retirement Income Security Act of 1974 (ERISA), as amended, is the basic federal law governing all qualified retirement plans. It is designed to protect the rights of beneficiaries of employee benefit plans offered by employers, unions, and others. ERISA established the PBGC, set limits on benefits and contributions, created the title of enrolled actuary, and set forth the basic and standard conditions for qualified plans. IRAs are not covered by ERISA, but Keogh plans are covered. See **Keogh Plan**.

Employee Stock Ownership Plan/Trust

An employee stock ownership plan/trust (ESOP/ESOT) is an ERISA defined contribution plan in which the participant's account consists primarily of the employer's stock. Valuation of an individual's interest at any particular time may be difficult because it would depend on the market value of the employer's stock at that time. Nevertheless, such plans may be valued for equitable distribution, and they are subject to a QDRO.

Employer-Sponsored IRA

An IRA that is sponsored by the employer to help its employees make a tax-deductible contribution to an IRA and to invest the funds in a particular type of investment. The employer-sponsored IRA should be distinguished from a simplified employee pension plan (SEP), which requires employer contributions and must meet certain requirements with respect to participation, discrimination, withdrawals, and contributions. However, both are subject to the requirements of a QDRO, as they are considered marital assets.

Enrolled Actuary

A title established by ERISA, under the Joint Board for Enrollment of Actuaries. The Joint Board consists of the Secretaries of the Department of Labor and the Treasury. Every qualified defined benefit pension plan covered by ERISA must be certified once a year by an enrolled actuary. Plans covered by the PBGC that terminate must be certified by an enrolled actuary. A person becomes an enrolled actuary by the successful completion of examinations jointly sponsored by the federal government and the professional actuarial societies. There are approximately 5,000 persons holding this designation in 1999. An enrolled actuary must meet continuing education requirements to remain in good standing. See **Qualified Opinion**.

Equal Pensions

Identical pension amounts payable to two different individuals do not have equal values. The following factors make the values different even if the monthly dollar payment is the same: sex, age, time when payments begin, source of payments, form of payments (lifetime only or with survivor benefits), adjustments for Social Security, adjustments for cost-of-living increases, subsidies or supplements, guarantees, and financial stability of the payor.

Equitable Distribution

The concept of marital property that attempts to allocate a fair division of the marital assets not based on community property or titled property alone. A pension that accrues during the marriage, which is neither vested nor measured, is still subject to equitable distribution. *Whitfield v. Whitfield,* 535 A.2d 986 (N.J. Super. Ct. App. Div. 1987).

ERISA

See **Employee Retirement Income Security Act of 1974**.

ERISA Plan Types

ERISA divides plans into two broad categories: pension plans and welfare plans. Under the rubric of pension plan fall both pension plans and profit-sharing plans of all types. Welfare plans include medical, health, hospital, disability, and life insurance coverage plans. Pension plans are subdivided into defined benefit plans and defined contribution plans. Defined contribution plans include money-purchase pension plans, Keogh plans, target benefit plans, thrift/savings plans, profit-sharing plans, and 401(k) plans. Defined benefit plans, in addition to the traditional defined benefit pension plan, include cash-balance pension plans and defined benefit Keogh plans (the latter are rare). Defined benefit plans are distinguished in that they all require an annual certification by an enrolled actuary. Defined benefit plans may be single- or multiple-employer or multiemployer, and they may or may not be covered by the PBGC. Plans of professional corporations with fewer than 25 participants are exempt from PBGC coverage, as are plans covering only one employee or only a husband and wife.

ESOP/ESOT

See **Employee Stock Ownership Plan/Trust**.

Expert Witness

A certified public accountant's appearance as an expert witness regarding the method of valuing a pension in a divorce case was disallowed because he had limited experience with pensions, did not understand PBGC tables, and could not explain the source of the figures he presented. His sole function was to perform the mathematical calculations, and this was considered insufficient to qualify him as an expert. *Hegerfeld v. Hegerfeld*, 555 N.E.2d 853 (Ind. Ct. App. 1990).

Extra Effort

The use of the time rule or coverture fraction is sometimes departed from when the employee-spouse has engaged in extra effort that increased the pension to a degree that exempted the increase from marital property. The employee-spouse would have to demonstrate that remarkable effort not connected to the marriage served to increase the nonmarital portion of the pension. In one case, a candidate standing for election argued that, if elected, he would get a bigger pension, and the extraordinary effort required in a political campaign precluded the pension increase from being considered marital property. The court disagreed. No spectacular effort is required to be a politician. *Fondi v. Fondi*, 802 P.2d 1264 (Nev. 1990).

Federal Pensions

Civilian employees of the federal government are covered by one of two retirement programs, depending on the date of employment. The older program is the Civil Service Retirement System (CSRS); the newer is the Federal Employees Retirement System (FERS). Employees in service before January 1, 1983, were in CSRS and continue in it unless they voluntarily transfer to FERS. Employees hired after January 1, 1983, are in FERS. Employees in CSRS are not covered by Social Security. The CSRS pension benefit is considered generous in comparison to nongovernmental pension plans, in theory to make up in part for the absence of Social Security benefits. Participants in FERS are covered by Social Security, and the pension benefits in the defined benefit portion of FERS are relatively modest. There is a thrift plan available to FERS participants. CSRS members are in a good defined benefit pension plan and may participate in a modest thrift plan. FERS members are in a small defined benefit pension plan, may participate in a good thrift plan, and are covered by Social Security. The federal pension systems will accept a form of QDRO on the defined benefit pension plans and will accept an order on the thrift savings plan known as a retirement benefits court order. See **Court Order Acceptable for Processing.**

Final Pay Plan

A defined benefit pension plan in which the benefit formula uses the pay from the last year or average of a fixed number of years before retirement. An example is the average of the highest five consecutive years' pay in the last ten years immediately preceding age 65. A final pay plan is in contrast to a *career average pay plan* in which 20 or 30 years of pay would be averaged in the pension benefit formula.

Floor Plan

A plan that serves to provide a minimum benefit if a second designated plan's benefit would otherwise be smaller. For example, a profit-sharing plan may provide that if the person's account when converted to a monthly pension would be less than the pension generated by a benefit formula, then the larger pension will be paid. The underlying benefit formula would be contained in the floor plan. If the floor plan benefit is smaller than the companion plan's benefit, then the floor plan benefit is ignored. This type of plan is also known as a *floor-offset plan* or an *offset-floor plan*. It should not be confused with an *offset plan*, which subtracts Social Security benefits and which has nothing to do with a floor plan. See **Offset Plan**.

Forfeiture

In a defined contribution plan, such as a profit-sharing plan, employees who leave without full vesting forfeit the nonvested portions of their individual accounts. These forfeitures are reallocated among the accounts of the remaining participants. However, the forfeitures may be held in a suspense account pending a formal break-in-service of the departing employee. If the employee returns to work within a specified time period, the account balance is restored. Otherwise, the forfeiture is imposed and redistributed. In a defined benefit pension plan, nonvested amounts are not specifically identified. Forfeitures of employees who leave with less than full vesting are benefits not paid, so the funds remain invested in the pool of plan assets. Remaining participants do not benefit from forfeitures in a defined benefit plan. Vested amounts in any type of plan are usually nonforfeitable with special exceptions. In a non-ERISA plan, otherwise vested benefits may be forfeited for various reasons. Forfeitures of vested benefits in an ERISA plan are quite rare. See also **Criminal Conduct**.

Forms of Pension Annuity

A qualified defined benefit pension plan generally offers several forms of pension annuity to a retiring employee. In actuarial mathematics, the forms of payment are equivalent to each other, but for any particular employee one form of payment may be preferable to the others. Examples of the dollar amounts of optional forms of pension benefits are set forth below for a typical male employee retiring at age 65 with a wife age 60.

1. Straight life or life only—The retiree's pension is paid in full according to the plan's benefit formula. The pension stops when the retiree dies and there are no death or survivor benefits. The pension benefit is $1,000 per month.

2. Life with ten years certain or life with 120 monthly payments guaranteed—The retiree receives a reduced pension payable as long as he lives. If the retiree dies within the first ten years of retirement, before 120 monthly pension payments have been made, the balance of the ten years' worth of payments is paid to his beneficiary or beneficiaries. If the retiree lives more than ten years after retirement, his pension ceases at death with no further benefits due. Note that the employee may have named any number of beneficiaries or contingent beneficiaries. The pension benefit is $910 per month.

3. Ten-year certain only—The retiree's pension is increased, and the pension benefit is paid for exactly ten years. The plan guarantees 120 monthly pension payments, whether the retiree is alive or dead. Any number of beneficiaries may be named. The pension benefit is $1,200 per month, greater than the monthly straight life pension because the same value is paid out in ten years instead of being stretched out over the retiree's lifetime.

4. 100 Percent Joint-and-Survivor—The retiree's pension is reduced, based on the age of the beneficiary (survivor), a specific individual named to receive pension payments after the death of the retiree. Upon the death of the retiree, the survivor beneficiary receives the same (reduced) amount (100 percent) that the retiree was receiving. If the beneficiary dies first, there is no replacement. In some plans, a "pop-up" version allows the retiree's pension to be restored to its full amount if the beneficiary dies first. The pension benefit is $800 per month.

5. 50 Percent Joint-and-Survivor—The retiree's pension is reduced, based on the age of the beneficiary (survivor). The same conditions apply as in the 100 percent J&S annuity described above. Upon the death of the retiree, the survivor beneficiary receives one-half (50 percent) of the reduced amount that the retiree was receiving. A smaller reduction in the retiree's benefit is required because only one-half of the pension is paid to the beneficiary. The pension benefit is $850 per month.

The examples given above are illustrative only. The amounts (exact and relative to each other) will vary with the particular pension plan and with differences in the ages of the individuals, as well as with the sex of the retiree.

401(k) Plan

Section 401of the Internal Revenue Code deals with qualified plans. This section has numerous subsections, such as 401(a), which defines the basic structure for qualified plans, and 401(k), which defines the cash and deferred salary reduction profit-sharing plans. When a plan is qualified it is known generally as a "401 plan."

Front Loading

A benefit formula that gives more weight to early service in a person's career with the employer under the plan in a defined benefit pension plan. For example, the pension benefit may accrue over time at 1.5 percent pay for each of the first 10 years of service, plus 1.25 percent for each of the next 10 years, plus 1.0 percent for the balance of years of service in excess of 20 years. Thus, the percentage decreases with time even though in most cases a person's pay will increase with time, so there is a balancing out between earlier and later years. Compare **Back Loading.**

Garnishment

ERISA prohibits the alienation, assignment, or attachment of pensions in a qualified plan. Nevertheless, this did not stop the Internal Revenue Service from garnishing a taxpayer's vested pension benefits to satisfy an IRS judgment for unpaid taxes, according to a ruling of the Sixth Circuit Court of Appeals in *United States v. Sawaf,* No. 94-1236 (6th Cir. 1996). The bank trustee of the individual's profit-sharing plan followed the order of garnishment of the federal district court and withdrew approximately $200,000 from his account (which had a balance of approximately $300,000) and remitted the funds to the IRS. The employee filed an appeal with the Sixth Circuit. The court found that IRS regulations contained special exceptions to the general anti-alienation rule, one of which is the collection by the United States on a judgment resulting from an unpaid tax assessment. Thus, the bank and the IRS were correct in garnishing the individual's profit-sharing funds to the extent of the amount due the government.

The law in many states includes pensions as marital property. If a state court serves a garnishment order on a pension plan to make a payment of plan funds to a spouse, ex-spouse, or anyone who is not the plan participant, the plan trustee is caught between state law and federal law. The Retirement Equity Act of 1984 created the concept of a QDRO, which allows garnishment of pensions if the details are correctly followed. However, a creditor cannot garnish pension benefits, nor can pension benefits be reached in bankruptcy, except in unusual cases. note that a Keogh plan or an IRA may in some situations be attachable in bankruptcy. An ERISA plan that covers only one employee, the owner of the company, also may be vulnerable to bankruptcy attachment.

GATT

See **General Agreement on Tariffs and Trade**.

General Agreement on Tariffs and Trade

The international negotiations concerning the General Agreement on Tariffs and Trade (GATT) were conducted in a series of meetings and agreements known as "rounds." In December 1994 Congress passed H.R. 5110 as Pub. L. No. 103-465 to implement the Uruguay Round. When Congress passed the Uruguay Round, the bill included pension provisions that originally had been drafted as a separate bill. These pension provisions were included in GATT, applicable to United States pension plans only, under the theory that they would produce a net revenue gain that would offset anticipated losses from GATT's trade provisions. The pension bill embedded in GATT became law under a congressional "fast track" allowing no chance for alteration.

The pension provisions are found in Title VII, Subtitle F, Part I of Subpart C, Section 767. The embedded pension provisions are labeled "The Retirement Protection Act of 1994." The mortality table prescribed therein is the 1983 Group Annuity Mortality (GAM) Table, as spelled out in Revenue Ruling 95-6.

The pension provisions in GATT prescribe the interest rates to be used in defined benefit pension plans as the smoothed average of 30-year U.S. Treasury bonds. In technical detail, that means the 30-year constant maturity rate that is interpolated from the daily yield curve, which relates the yield on a security to its time to maturity and which is based on the closing market bid yields on actively traded Treasury securities in the over-the-counter market.

The rates thus derived are reported weekly in a Federal Reserve Statistical Release known as "Selected Interest Rates," with yields shown in percent per annum. Each release lists 39 different interest rates, of which only the 30-year constant maturity rate is of concern to pension practitioners.

Hardship Withdrawal

A qualified ERISA profit-sharing plan or 401(k) plan is permitted to offer a hardship withdrawal provision. This allows for a distribution of the individual's account balance, in full or in part, while still employed. The IRS has strict requirements for what constitutes a hardship for this purpose. There must be immediate, heavy financial need for medical expenses of the participant, spouse, or dependent, or tuition and related educational fees, for example. The distribution is taxable as personal ordinary income and is subject to the premature distribution penalty if the employee is under age $59\frac{1}{2}$. The amount of the distribution may be computed by the plan to allow for taxes. For example, the employee may obtain 125 percent of the amount needed, so that after all taxes it nets out to the needed sum.

Husband-and-Wife Annuity

A form of pension offered in collectively bargained union or multiemployer plans for a participant who is married when he or she retires. Such plans are subsidized joint-and-survivor pension plans, but there is little or no actuarial reduction to provide for the added benefit to the survivor. The beneficiary can only be the spouse at the time of retirement. If the parties are divorced before retirement, this form of annuity will not apply. A QDRO cannot order this form of pension, because the parties must be married at the time it commences. However, routine joint-and-survivor pension options are available with actuarial reduction if the parties agree.

If-as-when

A court order awarding benefits to the former nonemployee-spouse if, as, and when the employee-spouse receives the pension is a limited form of deferred distribution. A proper QDRO awarding benefits to an alternate payee would take into account the contingency of the employee-spouse's death either before or after retirement and would allow for the alternate payee to elect commencement of an early retirement pension whether or not the participant takes early retirement. The availability of an early retirement pension conflicts with the need to wait for the participant's pension to start, as would be the case in the literal meaning of if-as-when.

Improper Payout

A pension plan, knowing that a participant's divorce was pending and that pension benefits would be involved, nevertheless paid a full lump-sum distribution to the participant upon his application for retirement. When a DRO was served on the plan, the plan responded that the participant had no benefits to act upon, because he had been paid in full. The court ordered the plan to pay the participant's spouse the amount awarded to her as alternate payee under the QDRO. The court ruled that the plan would have to take an action against the participant if it wished to recoup the payment that had been paid to him improperly. *In re Marriage of Baker*, 251 Cal. Rptr. 126 (1988).

Inflation

Inflation may be accounted for in retirement plans in a number of ways, or it may simply be ignored. In a defined benefit pension plan, when the pension is based on final pay or an average of pay in a short number of years before retirement, that in a sense allows for inflation by using that presumably higher pay in the formula. In a defined contribution plan, the investment returns in the individual's account will reflect inflation depending on the investment mix. A defined benefit pension plan may allow for the effects of inflation after retirement by adding a cost-of-living adjustment so that a retiree's pensions may keep pace with inflation. Occasionally a company will beef up its pension plan by granting ad hoc increases to pensioners in recognition of inflation. A QDRO may, but does not have to, recognize the possibility of inflationary increases in benefits by awarding the alternate payee a share of any such increases.

Individual Retirement Account

An individual retirement account (IRA) is not a pension, but it may be marital property subject to equitable distribution in a divorce. An IRA may be transferred to a former spouse following a divorce with no tax consequences. It cannot be paid in cash. A QDRO is not needed for such transfer. The financial institution holding the IRA of one divorced spouse will have the paperwork to effect a transfer to the IRA of the other spouse. The new IRA may be in the same or a different financial institution.

Integrated Plan

A plan that recognizes either benefits or contributions under Social Security. Taking into account Social Security benefits results in more benefits for the higher paid and reduced benefits for the lower paid in an allowable difference. A plan with this feature is said to be integrated or to contain a *permitted disparity*.

Interest Rates

In a defined contribution plan, the interest or investment gains earned are credited to the individual account. In a defined benefit pension plan, the pension benefit is determined by a formula in the plan without regard to the investment earnings of the plan assets. To compute the present value of a pension in a defined benefit pension plan, it is necessary to use a set of interest rates to discount future potential payments to their present worth. This does not affect the benefit as a payment; it concerns its value or what it would cost to purchase an annuity. In actuarial mathematics, the present value of a future financial obligation is very sensitive to interest rates. A standard inverse relationship exists: The interest rates and the present values move in opposite directions. A lower interest rate produces a higher present value, and a higher interest rate produces a lower present value. Standard interest rate assumptions are available on a current basis, updated monthly, from the Federal Reserve Board. See **Bonds**.

Internal Revenue Code

The Internal Revenue Code (Code; IRC) covers qualified ERISA plans in Section 401(a), tax-sheltered annuities in Section 403(b), profit-sharing plans that have a salary reduction feature and are with or without matching employer contributions in Section 401(k). Section 401(k) also covers thrift and savings plans that have pretax employee contributions. All Section 401(k) plans are defined contribution plans.

Investment Gain and Loss

Individual accounts in a defined contribution plan are credited or debited with investment gains and losses usually once a year, but sometimes quarterly or even monthly. The investment results posted to the accounts include realized and unrealized performance. In other words, so-called paper gains and losses are included even though they are not actual in the absence of a transaction. When a QDRO is served on a defined contribution plan, it should indicate whether unrealized performance is to be taken into account in the award to the alternate payee.

Investment Risk

Investment risk in a pension plan means who benefits and who loses when investments of the plan perform more or less well. Investment risk depends on the type of plan. In a defined benefit pension plan, the employer bears the investment risk. If the plan's assets perform very well, the employer may reduce its annual contributions to the plan. If the plan's investments fare poorly, the employer must make up the investment losses with larger contributions. It is not an exact dollar-for-dollar match in the year of occurrence. The enrolled actuary for the plan measures the investment gain or loss and advises the employer on contribution levels to spread out the adjustment over several years. In a defined contribution plan, the employee bears the investment risk. If the investments of a profit-sharing plan, target benefit plan, or money-purchase pension plan suffer, so does the employee's individual account.

IRA

See **Individual Retirement Account**.

Joinder Agreement

See **Master Plan**.

Joint-and-Survivor Annuity

See **Qualified Joint-and-Survivor Annuity**.

Joint-and-Survivor Option

One of the most popular optional forms of an actuarially equivalent pension payment that is mathematically computed in relation to a straight lifetime pension. In most plans, the retiree's pension is reduced to provide the annuity. Occasionally, a plan will fully subsidize the amount, so that it is a "free option." A joint-and-survivor (J&S) annuity can have only one specific named beneficiary. When the retiree dies, the beneficiary, if then living, receives the survivor portion of the retiree's reduced pension. In a 100 percent J&S option, the beneficiary receives for the rest of his or her life the same pension amount that the retiree was receiving. In a 50 percent J&S option, the beneficiary receives one-half of the retiree's pension. The larger the percentage chosen, the more the retiree's pension is reduced originally. Thus, although a 50 percent J&S option does not reduce the retiree's pension as much as would a 100 percent J&S option, if the beneficiary should die first, the retiree who selected either J&S option would continue to receive the reduced pension after the beneficiary's death. That is part of the actuarial tradeoff. Some plans, however, have a "pop-up" feature that restores the retiree's full pension if the beneficiary should die first. See **Pop-up Pension Benefit**.

Joint-and-Survivor Option Factors

The factors that would reduce a retiree's pension to provide for a joint-and-survivor form of pension vary by the age and sex of the retiree and the beneficiary, as shown in the following example:

Retiree: Male, age 65   Beneficiary: Female, age 60
100 percent option   50 percent option
Factor = .71   Factor = .83

Under the 100 percent option, if the retiree's full pension is $1,000 per month, it will be reduced to $710 per month. Upon the retiree's death, the beneficiary will receive $710 per month for life. Under the 50 percent option, if the retiree's full pension is $1,000 per month, it will be reduced to $830 per month. Upon the retiree's death, the beneficiary will receive $415 per month ($1,000 × .83 ÷ 2) for life.

Keogh Plan

Named for late Congressman Eugene Keogh (D-NY), Keogh plans are retirement plans for self-employed persons. Keogh plans are sometimes called "H.R. 10 plans" because Congressman Keogh's bill was the tenth bill introduced in the House of Representatives in 1962. ERISA and its amendments and other federal laws, rules, and regulations now make no distinction between Keogh plans and any other qualified plan. Most Keogh plans were profit-sharing plans, although there were a few defined benefit Keogh plans. Many Keogh plans were frozen as the laws changed, accepting no additional contributions but remaining invested as tax shelters. If a party in a divorce case has ever been self-employed or a member of a partnership, it should be determined whether there is an old Keogh plan with funds still in it. Such a plan is subject to valuation for equitable distribution and is also subject to a QDRO.

Leased Employee

When leasing company X provides employees to work on the premises of company Y, company Y pays fees to company X, and company X pays wages to its employees. If company Y has a pension plan, the leased employees cannot participate in the plan, because they are not employees of Y. Company X may have a plan for its employees no matter where they work. In the discovery phase of a divorce case, it is advisable to find out who each party's legal employer is and whether there are any leasing or independent contractor arrangements that may be involved in pension plans.

Level Income Option

At retirement, a participant in a defined benefit pension plan who is covered by Social Security but not yet eligible to receive Social Security benefits may elect a leveling option. The plan would pay the retiree an increased monthly pension until he or she is eligible by age for the Social Security benefits to start, and then the plan's pension would decrease. The actuarial value of the pension with this step-down feature is designed to be the same as the actuarial value of a fixed-amount lifetime pension for the same person.

Life Expectancy

Life expectancy is both a concept and a mathematical function. In general, all defined benefit pension plans must take into account the probability of death before or after retirement. Although sometimes loosely called life expectancy, the mathematics involves the calculus of probabilities, which is not merely looking up in a table the number of years of a person's expected remaining lifetime. Published life expectancy figures are byproducts of actuarial mortality tables. For example, a standard table for white males would list the average number of years of life remaining to a white male age 40 as 34. Taken literally, this would mean the subject dies at age 74. However, the mathematical probability that a white male age 40 dies at age 74 is only 53.8 percent. That is, more than one-half of all white males who are currently age 40 will die at age 74. The rest will die either before or after they reach that age. Life expectancy is not an accurate means for developing the present value of a pension. It is an interesting mathematical concept, but it is too gross a function to be used with any precision.

Life Insurance

A pension plan may provide death benefits by the use of life insurance. Usually, a plan that does so is a small, defined benefit pension plan; however, some profit-sharing plans may have life insurance as well. The insurance is provided for active participants only. In a defined benefit pension plan, the insurance premiums are paid from plan assets. In an individual account type plan, premiums are deducted from the person's account. The insurance may be term or whole life. If whole life insurance is offered, in a defined benefit plan the cash values are the property of the plan, not the employee. In an individual account plan, the cash value of life insurance, if any, accrues to the benefit of the particular account. In either type of plan, if a lump sum is payable upon termination of employment or the employee's retirement, it is possible for the life insurance policy to be distributed as a benefit to the individual. In that case, the cash value, if any, counts as part of the distribution and is taxable. Note that a distributed life insurance policy cannot be rolled over into the person's IRA.

Liquidity of Assets

When a plan is served with a QDRO requiring payment of a monthly pension, liquidity of plan assets is generally not a concern. If the QDRO requires a lump-sum distribution, however, then the nature and liquidity of plan assets must be considered. For example, a profit-sharing plan may be ordered to pay $50,000 as a lump sum to the alternate payee from the participant's account. The account may have more than enough in value, but it may be invested in equities that have to be sold or in certificates of deposit that have a penalty for early cashout. It should be made clear exactly what the settlement or award is, either in percentages or dollars, and whether it is affected by the net amount distributable.

Loans

A qualified ERISA plan may permit loans to participants but is not required to make loans available. If loans are available, they must be nondiscriminatory. To apply for a plan loan, a married participant must have the written consent of the spouse, witnessed by a plan representative or notarized. If a QDRO is involved, it should be made clear whether the order applies to benefits or account values net of any loans. Receipt of a loan from one's pension plan is not a taxable event unless the participant defaults on the loan or otherwise fails to repay the plan, in which case the loan will be recharacterized as a lump-sum distribution.

Loss of Pension

An elected or appointed official, a member of the armed forces, a police officer, or a firefighter may lose or forfeit a non-ERISA pension, either prospective or in pay status, because of a felony offense. With rare exceptions, a crime cannot cause the loss of a vested or matured pension in an ERISA plan. See also **Criminal Conduct, Forfeiture**.

Lump-Sum Award or Distribution

A divorce settlement may include a provision for a QDRO to award a lump-sum amount from an employee's pension to the alternate payee. If the employee-spouse is a participant in a defined benefit pension plan, it is difficult, if not impossible, for the QDRO to be implemented as intended because a typical defined benefit pension plan is established and maintained to pay monthly annuity type pensions to retirees, not lump sums. The solution is to convert the designated lump sum into equivalent monthly pension payments. The computation may be done by a consulting actuary or, by the plan, if it is willing. Assumptions have to be made as to mortality, interest rates, and retirement age. Then calculations are made to convert the awarded lump sum into the form of pension benefit that the pension plan is able to accept. Some plans may allow lump-sum distributions of small amounts ($5,000 or less, for example) or a refund of employee contributions, if any.

Malpractice

The failure of an attorney to protect a nonemployee-spouse's pension rights may result in a malpractice award against the attorney. In 1987, a Maryland jury awarded a wife more than $75,000 in damages against her divorce attorney. *Pickett, Honlon & Berman v. Haislip,* 533 A.2d 287 (Md. Ct. Spec. App. 1987). The lawyer was found negligent, in part, for failing to employ experts to evaluate the husband's assets. In 1990, the failure of a Missouri attorney to protect a wife's rights to a share of the husband's military pension resulted in a malpractice award of over $100,000. The attorney had originally advised his client correctly that a military pension was not considered marital property, but the law changed before the case was over, and the attorney was found negligent for ignorance of the new law that recharacterized military pensions as marital property.

Marital Property

Contributions made to a pension fund after the cutoff date for measuring marital property are the separate property of the employee-spouse, not available for equitable distribution in marital dissolution. The value of the pension at the cutoff date may be credited with passive increases, but not contributions, up to the date of trial or other settlement of the property issues in the divorce case. (Depending on the jurisdiction, the cutoff date may be the date of marital separation, the date of filing of the divorce complaint, or the date of the divorce.) In a defined benefit pension plan, the employer's contributions to the general pension fund are for all employees covered by the plan, not earmarked for individuals. The continuation or the absence of contributions in such a plan has no bearing on the employee's pension benefits. The proper value for marital property purposes is determined in a two-step process, reflecting two time frames. First, the pension benefit is determined that has accrued for pay and service up to the cutoff date. No increase in the pension benefit is counted after the cutoff date. Second, the value of that pension is determined currently by actuarial factors using the employee's current age and current interest rates. The result is the current present value of the cutoff date pension benefit.

Marital Property Distribution

See **Equitable Distribution**.

Master Plan

A master plan is a pension or profit-sharing plan in a standardized format that has been pre-approved by the IRS and meets the requirements of ERISA. A master plan always appears in two parts: the basic document and the adoption agreement. The adoption agreement specifies the particular provisions for the employer that are available in the basic plan. When a master plan is involved in a divorce settlement, counsel should obtain both the basic document and the adoption agreement (sometimes known as the *joinder agreement*). In all other respects, a master plan is an ERISA plan with a summary plan description, benefits statements, and all of the other features found in qualified plans. An alternate version of a master plan is a prototype plan for which the adopting employer specifies the trustees of the plan assets. A prototype plan is different from a master plan in which the organization issuing the plan holds and invests the plan assets.

Matured Pension

A pension matures when all the conditions for its payment have been fulfilled, but payment has not yet begun. An example of a matured pension is the pension of an employee who has reached the plan's retirement age but continues to work.

Military Pensions

The Armed Forces Retirement System provides generous pensions to its members who retire with 20 or more years of active duty service. There is no vesting as such, so if a member never completes 20 years' service, there will never be a pension under this system. From time to time, however, the system makes available special limited programs for retirement with fewer than 20 years of service. Military service credits may count in other pension systems to increase a pension, such as in plans for civilian employees of the federal government, certain teachers' retirement plans, or pension programs for police officers and firefighters. In a divorce, such plans will accept a form of QDRO, but the order applies only when the pension enters pay status. The retirement age in the Armed Forces Retirement System is the age at which the person retires after 20 years of service. For participants in the military reserves there is a different pension system, with retirement at age 60.

Modification of Judgment

A husband's pension was not considered in a Florida divorce case. Some years later, the wife asked for equitable distribution of the ex-husband's pension because it had been overlooked. The court chose not to reach back to modify a judgment to redistribute the assets in the divorce, including the pension. *Lapinta,* 13 Fla. L. Weekly 1969 (1988). However, a 1990 case in West Virginia allowed the decree of final judgment to be reopened because the parties had misunderstood the value of the pension. The schoolteacher husband had received a statement from the retirement system stating the amount he would receive if he left employment at that time. Later, he realized that the stated amount represented only the return on his contributions and that the actuarial pension value was much greater. The court allowed the mistake to be corrected. *Langdon v. Langdon,* 391 S.E.2d 627 (W. Va. 1990).

Money-Purchase Pension Plan

A defined contribution plan under which the employer's contributions are mandatory and are based on each participant's compensation. Retirement benefits under the plan are based on the amount in the participant's individual account at retirement.

Mortality

The probability of mortality is a vital element in the computation of the present value of a pension. In pricing an annuity, the probability of the death of the annuitant at any future time must be included in the calculations. Several standard mortality tables, which fall into two broad categories, are available for use. Within a particular category there is not much significant variation unless it is a very old table—say, 50 years old. However, the categories are important. There are mortality tables for life insurance that are dramatically different from pension or annuity mortality tables. Mortality rates in life insurance tables are higher because they anticipate more deaths. In annuity or pension tables, mortality rates are lower because they anticipate fewer deaths and longer lives with more payouts. This structure allows for variations among the covered population and has proved to be a financially stable arrangement over many years. See also **Life Expectancy**.

Multiemployer Plan

A pension plan, maintained under a collective bargaining agreement, that covers the employees of more than one employer. Generally, the employers are in the same industry but are not financially related.

Multiple-Employer Plan

A single-employer plan is an ERISA plan sponsored and maintained by one employer entity. When additional employers join the plan to save the administrative costs of covering their employees, the plan is known as a multiple-employer plan. Usually, the employers are related in ownership in some way or are cooperating in a business venture.

Murder

If divorce ends an entitlement, the murder of a spouse by the other is deemed equivalent to an entitlement-ending incident just as if a divorce had occurred. For example, if a QDRO or some form of structured settlement awards benefits that cease in the event of a divorce, murder would serve in place of a divorce. See also **Criminal Conduct**.

Need for Attorney

In a 1990 California case, the parties to the divorce agreed on property distribution without the knowledge of their respective attorneys. As part of their agreement, each party would keep his/her own pension plan. At trial three years later, the attorneys first learned of the agreement. There was no evidence of the value of the pension plans and no proof that the wife's pension was equal to the husband's. The court decided that whenever a party is represented by counsel, a stipulation or agreement affecting the party should not be accepted without the knowledge and consent of the attorney. *In re Marriage of Maricle,* 269 Cal. Rptr. 204 (Cal. App. Dist. 1990).

Net/Gross Pension

In determining the present value of a pension in pay status, it is important to distinguish between the net and the gross pension. The gross pension is the amount of the payment the retiree is entitled to receive from the pension plan. The net pension is the actual amount of each pension check after deductions. The deductions may be mandatory or voluntary. They may include union dues, health insurance premiums, life insurance premiums, withheld taxes, charitable contributions, and other miscellaneous items. Deductions from the gross pension may include loan amounts being repaid, missed employee contributions being made up, and purchase of prior service credits. For valuation purposes, it is usually appropriate to focus on the amount of the gross pension, although taxation may be taken into account in some venues. In deferred distribution by use of a QDRO, it is essential for the order to clearly specify whether the net or gross pension is involved.

Normal Form

Every plan establishes benefits on the basis of a "normal form." In a defined contribution plan, it is to be expected that the normal form will be a lump-sum distribution. In a defined benefit pension plan, it is usually a straight lifetime annuity, ceasing at the death of the retiree. A typical plan will offer, at retirement, options to convert the normal form into some other form. The conversion may be determined as the actuarial equivalent of the normal form, or it may be somewhat better than the mathematical adjustment so that the pension is subsidized. A defined benefit pension plan covered by ERISA must provide for a qualified joint-and-survivor annuity (QJSA) if the participant is married. However, a QJSA need not be the normal form, because it may be reduced by the plan to adjust for the coverage of two lives. The normal form is one of the determinants of the present value of a pension. If a QDRO is served on the plan, the form of pension should be addressed. See **Lump-Sum Distribution**.

Normal Retirement Age

The normal retirement age (NRA) in a plan is the age that, when attained, permits the participant to voluntarily cease employment and receive a full, unreduced benefit, whether a lump-sum distribution or an annuity. NRA is also the measuring point for vesting. For example, if a participant has not attained full vesting under the plan's vesting schedule for years of service, upon reaching NRA, full vesting becomes automatic. The NRA may be a fixed age (such as 65) or may be derived from a formula or from a combination of age and service. Some examples are (1) age 60 with 10 years of service, (2) age 55 with 20 years of service, (3) any age with 35 years of service, (4) a "magic number" (such as 85) consisting of the total of the employee's age (58) and years of service (27 years).

Offset Plan

A plan that reduces participants' benefits by an amount specified (by formula) in the plan. A defined benefit pension plan may dovetail its benefits with Social Security by subtracting a percentage of the Social Security benefit from the plan's formula benefit. This is a method of integrating the plan with Social Security, using the IRS rules for permitted disparity. The concept of permitted disparity allows for higher-paid employees to receive larger benefits than lower-paid employees by recognizing the curve over which Social Security benefits are constructed. See **Integrated Plan, Social Security Integration**.

Offsets to Pension

A plan may provide that pension benefits are decreased or offset by disability benefits, unemployment compensation, or worker's compensation. In valuing a spouse's plan benefits for equitable distribution or for deferred distribution, these possibilities should be considered. If offsets exist in the plan, then the individual facts and circumstances should be considered to see if these items are applicable. In some cases, if a retiree returns to work for the same employer or in the same industry, his or her pension may be reduced or suspended. If there is any possibility of such reduction or suspension, it should be examined in detail.

Overlooked Pension

See **Modification of Judgment**.

Partners Unfunded Pension Plan

Special discovery and valuation methods apply when an individual in a divorce action is a partner in a professional firm—for example, an accountant or an attorney. A partnership may have a special arrangement to provide superannuation benefits to retired partners, in a program separate and apart from any regular pension plan. The ''plan'' would be exempt from ERISA, as an unfunded, nonqualified plan with benefits to be paid from the general assets of the partnership. The plan is considered a contractual agreement between the partnership and selected individual partners. Such an arrangement is not subject to any of the rules and regulations of the IRS, the PBGC, or any other federal agency and is not within the ambit of ERISA. Nevertheless, there is a value to these potential promised benefits, and such a value is subject to actuarial determination and may be set forth as a property item in divorce. Further, at the option of the partnership, such a plan may accept a court order similar in many respects to a QDRO. The QDRO-like order may take the form of a legal agreement between the partnership and the partner undergoing the divorce. The partnership would agree to pay to the former spouse a portion of the benefits otherwise due to the retired partner. The tax treatment of such an arrangement has to be structured carefully so that each party is properly responsible for the payments received.

Pay Definition

A plan must define the pay status of the participant and define the pay basis for benefits or contributions. The 12-month period over which the pay is measured need not be the same as the plan year as long as they overlap by at least one day. The following items may be included or excluded by the plan definition of pay: regular or base salary or wages or the annual rate; pay as reported on IRS Form W-2 (problem: which block item on the form?); commissions; tips; overtime; premium pay; bonuses; reimbursements; expense allowances; moving expenses; deferred compensation; welfare benefits; awards for back pay; jury duty; sick pay; shift differentials; credit during leave of absence; credit for temporary military service; and amounts deferred in 401(k) plans.

Pay Status

When an employee retires and starts receiving monthly pension payments, he or she is said to be in pay status. (In rare cases, a plan participant may be in pay status while still employed.) Such payments have a present value, actuarially determined as the present worth of the future stream of expected payments taking into account mortality and interest. If a retiree in pay status is divorcing and a QDRO is served on the plan, the QDRO may order a portion of the retiree's pension benefits be paid to the alternate payee. Usually, a QDRO is thought of as a form of deferred distribution, but a pension in pay status is immediate, not deferred, and it may be subject to a QDRO-ordered division of the amounts being paid. Whether pension payments should be counted as income for purposes of measuring alimony is an issue to be settled by the facts and circumstances of the particular case.

PBGC

See **Pension Benefit Guaranty Corporation**.

Pension Benefit Guaranty Corporation

The Pension Benefit Guaranty Corporation (PBGC) is a federal government corporation chartered under ERISA to insure certain defined benefit pension plans. A plan covered by the PBGC files annual returns and pays a premium required by federal law and regulations. If such a plan should terminate with insufficient assets to provide promised pension benefits, the PBGC will take over the plan and pay the pensions, up to stated maximum amounts.

Pension Valuation Formula

The formula for computing the present value of a person's benefits in a defined benefit pension plan is: Benefit × Rate × Fraction. "Benefit" is the individual's accrued benefit under the plan, based on pay and service and any other plan features up to the cutoff date in the applicable jurisdiction, stated as a monthly pension payable at normal retirement age. "Rate" is the GATT rate at the time of the valuation, using the person's current age and the normal retirement age. "Fraction" denotes the portion of the present value that is marital property, and it is calculated by dividing the years of service while married and in the plan by the total years of plan service to the cutoff date.

Pension Worth

Most legal jurisdictions accept a spouse's interest in a pension plan as marital property for equitable distribution in divorce. When the pension plan is a defined contribution plan with individual accounts (e.g., a 401(k) plan, a thrift or savings plan), a participant's pension is equal to the amount in his or her account.

Defined benefit pension plans pose more of a conceptual problem because the promised pension benefit is usually due many years in the future, when the employee retires. The actuarial answer is that the appropriate present value does indeed equal the worth of the pension, whether it is a future pension to be paid or a pension now being received. The only difference is that there is a discount period for the active employee to represent the chance of death before retirement while also discounting the future prospective pension for interest during the period before payments begin. A pension of any kind always has a calculable value. In some cases, the court may wish to modify the pure actuarial result by increasing or decreasing the present value based on the particular facts and circumstances of the case. The starting point should always be the pension value mathematically computed using standard methods and reasonable actuarial assumptions of mortality and interest.

The actuarial answer often seems frustratingly unsatisfactory to the family practice lawyer who knows that if the client—the employee—dies before retirement, then there is no pension. Nonetheless, the divorce settlement may award the pension's present value to the nonemployee-spouse.

The actuary has included in the computations of present value the probability of death either before or after retirement, but the actuarial assumptions are not predictions. The employee-spouse may die the day after the present value of his pension has been distributed in a divorce settlement. Alternatively, he may live a long time. No one can say, but an actuary can provide a value that takes potential longevity into account.

299

Period Certain

A period certain is a form of pension sometimes offered by a defined benefit pension plan as an option at retirement. This form of pension pays the retiree a fixed monthly amount for an exact period of time, regardless of when the retiree dies. For example, assume a period certain pension of $1,000 per month will be paid for exactly ten years. If the retiree continues to live beyond the ten-year period, there is no further pension, as it was payable only for ten years. If the retiree dies before receiving ten years' worth of pension payments, the balance is payable to the retiree's beneficiaries or estate. There is, by contrast, the *certain and life pension*, a form of pension that continues to be paid beyond the original guaranteed time period as long as the pensioner lives.

Permitted Disparity

See **Integrated Plan, Social Security Integration**.

Plan Administrator

A title created by ERISA for qualified plans. Every ERISA plan must designate a plan administrator in the plan document and in the summary plan description. The plan administrator may be an individual, a committee, or the employer entity. Generally, the plan administrator is not the consulting, administrative, or actuarial firm that provides services for the plan, nor is it the trustees that hold plan assets, unless specifically named as such. The plan administrator is responsible for operating the plan, making decisions concerning eligibility, vesting, benefits, and all other details. It is the plan administrator who reviews a DRO and decides if it is a QDRO.

Plan Amendment

Plans are often amended to keep up with changing laws and regulations, or as a result of a change in the employer's circumstances. A plan amendment would not reduce participants' accrued benefits, but it may well increase them. An amendment may increase future benefits only or may have a retroactive effect increasing all benefits, past and future. An amendment may change the future terms and conditions of benefits, such as the normal form or early retirement age. The possibility of a future plan amendment is ignored in the computation of present value; however, in deferred distribution using a QDRO, the parties should consider whether or not to include potential future changes in the plan.

Plan Booklet

A summary plan description (SPD) is often in the form of a booklet, so it is commonly referred to as the plan booklet. However, there is no required size, shape, or form of printing; thus, even if an SPD is called a booklet, it may not appear to be one.

Plan Document

The formal plan text of an employer-sponsored qualified retirement plan. This is the binding legal contract under which a plan is established and maintained. A copy must be available for inspection by a participant at no cost. A reasonable charge may be imposed for a participant to keep a copy.

Plan Year

Every pension plan runs on an accounting year or fiscal year, known as the plan year, which is any 12-consecutive-month period that has been chosen by the plan for keeping its records. Common plan years are the calendar year, January 1 to December 31, and the June 30 year, July 1 to June 30. However, a plan may use whatever 12-month period was selected when the plan was established; for example, March 1 to the last day of February, or October 31 to October 30, or April 1 to March 31. If the plan routinely issues benefit or account statements, they will be determined as of the last day of the plan year and may be expected to be available from three to six months after the plan year has ended. All of the forms for governmental reporting will be based on the plan year. If the plan does not routinely issue benefit or account statements and one is being requested for property valuation in divorce, it is usually administratively more convenient for the plan to provide benefit or account information as of a plan year-end date rather than some specific date that may be the date of marital separation or divorce complaint. This is also true for QDRO purposes.

Pop-Up Pension Benefit

A defined benefit pension plan may allow for the death of a named beneficiary during the life of the pensioner who has elected a joint-and-survivor (J&S) annuity. By that election, the retiree's pension was actuarially reduced to allow for the survivor annuity. If the potential survivor dies first, the retiree's pension in most arrangements would remain reduced. In a "pop-up" situation, however, the pension is restored to the retiree for future payments as if the J&S option had never been selected. See also **Qualified Joint-and-Survivor Annuity**.

Postponed Retirement

An employee working beyond normal retirement age in a defined benefit pension plan is on postponed retirement, also known as *deferred retirement*. Some plans may allow the pension to start at normal retirement age even though the participant is still employed. If so, the pension is in pay status and not postponed. If the pension is postponed, the plan must increase benefits in one or both of the following ways: (1) Pension benefit accruals increase as pay and service continues, or (2) the pension benefit may no longer grow with pay and service but will be increased by actuarial factors to recognize its postponement. The most generous plan will increase the late pension for continuing pay and service and by actuarial factors.

Present Value Update

The current worth of a pension is as of a given date (the valuation date). All pensions have present value, whether the pension is vested, deferred, matured, or in pay status to a retiree. In a divorce case, some time may pass between the time the valuation was made and the date the case is ready to be adjudicated. Sometimes, months or even years will go by until the case is heard. Counsel for the divorcing couple may attempt to bring the pension value up to date by adding interest to the previously determined pension value. Updating the pension's present value, however, creates problems for the following reasons:

1. The present value of the pension was initially determined using mortality and interest discounts. The participant is still alive, so the mortality decrement would have to be factored back into the value.
2. Interest rates change over time. The interest rate that might be used to update a prior value may well lead to controversy over what rate is appropriate and reasonable.
3. The pension plan may have been amended, the employee-spouse's status may have changed (active, terminated, disabled, retired), and changes in statute and/or case law that would affect current results may have occurred.

The proper way to update an existing valuation is to perform a new, current valuation.

Professional Serving as Own Trustee

A professional person—doctor, lawyer, actuary, or accountant—may establish and maintain a pension plan and be the plan trustee. If state law allows a sole trustee with one person as both trustee and beneficiary, federal pension law will accept it. It is possible for one person to be the owner-employer, the employee, the participant, the plan administrator, and the trustee. Sometimes a husband and wife serve as the trustees. In a divorce, counsel should scrutinize the duties and responsibilities of co-trustees toward each other in order to protect the interests of all involved and the assets in the pension trust fund.

Professional's Pension Plan Assets

When a professional person has incorporated and established a pension or profit-sharing plan for the corporation, the professional often wears many hats: employee, 100 percent stockholder, an officer, and the trustee of the plan. If such a professional is the respondent in a divorce case involving equitable distribution, his or her control over the plan's total assets may have to be considered, along with the present value of accrued benefits in the plan. For example, assume a doctor who has no full-time employees establishes a pension plan and a profit-sharing plan for herself. She decides the amount of the annual contribution to the profit-sharing plan, deposits the amount required for the pension plan, and controls the investments of both plans. What happens if the doctor's account in the profit-sharing plan starts losing value because her plan investments perform poorly? It could be argued that the decline in value was caused by the doctor's actions as plan trustee and that she unilaterally dissipated marital assets. In the case of a defined benefit pension plan, the plan assets are generally not a concern, because the actuarial present value of the participant's's accrued benefit is determined. However, what if the invested funds exceed the present value of the pension benefit? Can the surplus plan assets be considered marital assets?

Projected Benefit

In a defined benefit pension plan, the plan formula is used to estimate the future pension benefit of a participant. Using current pay information, assuming that the person continues to work until normal retirement age and that pay remains level, the ultimate pension benefit may be calculated. The future benefit can be projected taking into account future pay increases. This projected benefit is an estimate, not guaranteed, because the plan may be amended before the participant retires or the participant may terminate service with the employer. The projected benefit may be illustrated in a benefit statement to the employee. Sometimes only the projected benefit is shown, not the accrued benefit. In computing present value, care should be taken as to the benefit being used. In deferred distribution, it should not be assumed automatically that a projected benefit will be exactly what is currently estimated.

Prototype Plan

A pension or profit-sharing plan in a standardized format that has been pre-approved by the Internal Revenue Service. This type of plan always appears in two parts: the basic document and the adoption agreement. It is a variation of a Master Plan. See also **Master Plan**.

QDRO

See **Qualified Domestic Relations Order**.

QDRO Annuity Contract

In the case of an existing annuity contract that will pay a pension at a future date, it is possible to use a QDRO to have the contract pay a part of the future pension to the former spouse, the alternate payee. This applies only when the annuity contract is part of, or has been purchased by, a qualified pension plan.

QDRO as Collateral

When the parties to the divorce agree, it may be possible to have a QDRO drafted to serve as a form of security or collateral. The terms of the QDRO would not become effective unless and until the primary issue was in default. If the plan refuses to accept such an order, it may be possible to settle the case with an order written but not served on the plan until conditions so require.

QDRO at Imminent Retirement

When an employee near retirement is involved in a divorce that is not yet final and a QDRO is used to award the employee's spouse a pension from the employee's defined benefit pension, some important decisions have to made quickly. One of the most important issues is whether the nonemployee-spouse should sign a waiver of the otherwise mandated joint-and-survivor (J&S) form of pension benefit. In defined benefit pension plans covered by ERISA, and in certain other plans as well, a J&S form of benefit is mandatory unless waived by both spouses. If the waiver is not signed, witnessed, and properly notarized before the divorce is final and the employee retires, the employee-spouse's pension benefits will be reduced to reflect the J&S feature. It may be possible for the employee-spouse to ask the employer to defer commencement of pension payments until the spouses have thought through the advantages and disadvantages of the J&S form of pension before it becomes locked in place. During this period, the nonemployee-spouse is protected in the event of the death of the retiring employee, so a survivorship benefit may not be important. Counsel for the employee-spouse should be aware of the potential pension benefit reduction for J&S coverage and advise the client accordingly.

QDRO for a Defined Contribution Plan

It may be deemed straightforward to have a QDRO award a portion of the account balance in a defined contribution plan. However, the following issues should be considered:

1. As of what date is the account to be divided? Date of marital separation, date of filing of the divorce complaint, date the case was settled, date the order was drafted or signed, or date the order is approved by the plan?

2. Is interest on the account to be credited to the new subdivided account? If so, at what rate and from what date?

3. Is the new subdivided account to be credited with plan investment gains? If so, is unrealized appreciation to be included?

4. If the plan allows participants to make investment choices for individual accounts, does the alternate payee have the same rights as the participant?

QDRO for Life

The intent behind a QDRO served on a defined benefit pension plan is usually to ensure that the alternate payee receives a monthly pension payment for life. The order must be drafted properly for this to happen; otherwise, payments to the alternate payee will stop after retirement following the death of the participant.

There are two ways to protect the benefits of the alternate payee after retirement. First, the QDRO may award a separate, independent lifetime pension to the alternate payee almost as if that person had been an employee. This approach has an actuarial cost attached, which the plan will determine and which will reduce the amount of the monthly pension benefit. Second, the QDRO may require that the participant, at retirement, elect a J&S form of pension, naming the alternate payee as the beneficiary. The second approach also requires an actuarial reduction. Both approaches reduce the pension benefit as the price of providing post-retirement lifetime benefits to the alternate payee. Estimates of the possible benefit reductions should be requested from the plan before a decision is made. Note that it is possible for a QDRO to cover both kinds of pension for the alternate payee. This may be considered a form of *double-dipping*. The alternate payee is receiving a lifetime pension and, after the death of the participant, an additional J&S benefit. Thus, the alternate payee receives two pensions for the rest of his life.

QDRO Future Value

In a divorce settlement that uses a QDRO to pay a former spouse a future pension from a defined benefit pension plan, the purchasing power of the dollar as well as the amount of the monthly pension are issues to be considered. For example, David and Judith, both age 45, divorced in 1998. Judith was awarded 50 percent of David's current accrued pension benefit. David's then current accrued pension benefit was $2,000 per month, payable at age 65. By the time David reaches age 65, assuming he still works for the same employer and that the pension benefit formula is based on pay and service, his retirement pension may be in the vicinity of $4,000 per month. Judith's share of the pension, however, is fixed at 50 percent of the accrued pension at the time the case was settled: $1,000. Twenty years hence, would $1,000 per month have the same purchasing power as it does today? It is assumed that while David continues with the same employer, his pay keeps rough pace with inflation and his ultimate pension benefit will reflect increases in the cost of living by routine operation of the pension benefit formula. A possible solution to the perceived problem is for Judith to be awarded a percentage of David's actual pension benefit when he retires, instead of the accrued pension at settlement, taking into account the length of the marriage.

QDRO Multiple Plans

An individual may be covered by more than one plan simultaneously. A common situation is a defined benefit pension plan and a profit-sharing plan. Or, a union official may be covered by plans of the local and the national union, or by the employer's plan as well as by a union plan. In railroad work an employee covered by the Railroad Retirement Board may also be in a plan of his employer, say for example, the CONRAIL supplemental plan. When a QDRO is to be used in these situations, there should be only one per plan; each plan should have a separate order served on it. In some cases it may be possible to combine the benefits that would be awarded to save time and fees by focusing only on one plan in an amount equal to that which would also come from the second plan.

QDRO Signatures

In order for an order to become a QDRO, only one signature is needed: the signature of the court so that it is a valid order. There is no requirement that the attorneys or the parties must sign it. In many cases it may be advisable for all parties and their lawyers to sign it for the record, but it is not required. The Plan Administrator makes the determination as to whether the order is qualified, but he or she does not actually sign the order itself.

QJSA

See **Qualified Joint-and-Survivor Annuity**.

QPSA

See **Qualified Pre-Retirement Survivor Annuity**.

Qualified Domestic Relations Order

A qualified domestic relations order (QDRO) is an order of a court of competent jurisdiction relating to family practice, which order has been submitted to the plan administrator of an ERISA plan who has determined that the order is qualified. Before its qualification, the QDRO is a DRO, a domestic relations order. Federal law permits a court to order a DRO to be qualified, but this is a situation to be avoided. The court should sign the DRO but should not attempt to have a plan approve it in the absence of exceptional circumstances.

Qualified Joint-and-Survivor Annuity

A form of pension benefit mandated by ERISA for all defined benefit pension plans. Unless properly waived, the QJSA is the form of pension that a married participant must elect. The percentage of the survivor portion may vary from 50 percent to 100 percent, as set forth in the plan or as selected by the retiree.

Qualified Opinion

An opinion of an enrolled actuary pertaining to a defined benefit pension plan under ERISA that expresses some reservations or mentions some departure from standard principles or practices. A qualified opinion is generally considered to have a negative connotation.

Qualified Plan

An ERISA plan that has met the federal statutory and regulatory requirements, has received a favorable determination letter from the IRS, and maintains its qualified status by amendments to comply with changes in laws and regulations as they occur from time to time. Every qualified plan is an ERISA plan, but not vice versa, as it is possible for an ERISA plan to lose its qualification. Being qualified ensures the tax-sheltered status of the plan's investments and defers taxation of plan participants on accruing benefits and/or account values until these are actually paid out.

Qualified Pre-Retirement Survivor Annuity

All ERISA pension plans are required to provide death benefits payable to the spouses of employees who die while employed as "active" participants. The required death benefit is a qualified pre-retirement survivor annuity (QPSA). The requirement applies only to spouses and to persons who are divorced with a valid QDRO in place that extends QPSA benefits to a former spouse.

Railroad Retirement System

A non-ERISA plan managed by the Railroad Retirement Board (RRB). Railroad workers' pensions consist of two parts, known as "tiers." Tier I is equivalent to Social Security, is not included in valuations of marital property for equitable distribution in divorce, and is not subject to attachment by QDRO. Tier II, however, is a regular type of defined benefit pension plan; it is subject to valuation and attachment as if it were an ERISA plan.

REA

See **Retirement Equity Act.**

Real Estate

When a defined benefit pension plan has been valued for immediate offset, the value has been accepted by all parties, and the value happens to equal the net value of the real estate owned by the parties, it is common for the parties to agree to a settlement whereby the employee-spouse keeps the pension and the nonemployee-spouse gets title to real estate. The title transfer should be handled carefully. If title is transferred too soon, the recipient (nonemployee-spouse) may sell the property before the divorce is final or might lose a prospective buyer if the title is transferred while real estate negotiations are proceeding.

Reconciliation

A marital separation may be followed by a reconciliation that does not work, followed by a divorce. If a QDRO was executed in conjunction with the first separation, and not revoked, it still applies regardless of the intervening reconciliation. If the QDRO was canceled because of the reconciliation, it cannot be reinstated as is, but a new one is required. *Crawford v. Crawford,* 392 S.E.2d 675 (S.C. Ct. App. 1990).

Remarriage

It is theoretically possible for a QDRO to cut off benefits to an alternate payee upon that person's remarriage, but it would be difficult to administer. The plan administrator is likely to object to such a provision. The plan would not have a provision ending benefits at remarriage, and a QDRO cannot require benefits that are not in the plan. Even in the absence of a QDRO, the alternate payee's remarriage usually does not cut off benefits. For example, after divorcing his first wife, but before the equitable distribution of property—including a pension—was settled, a man remarried another woman and then died. The trial court nevertheless proceeded to award certain marital property and pension rights to the first wife. The second wife appealed the decision and lost. The appeals court decided that the first wife was entitled to the award based on her needs, length of marriage, and the parties' standard of living during the marriage. *Dunn v. Dunn,* 544 A.2d 448 (Pa. Super. Ct. 1988).

Reopening Divorce

In a case from Maryland, a divorce that did not consider a military pension because federal law at that time did not allow such could not be reopened merely because the federal law changed. There was no mistake, irregularity, or clerical error in the divorce. *Andresen v. Andresen,* 564 A.2d 399 (Md. 1989). See also **Alimony, Modification of Judgment**.

Retiree Data

When a party in a divorce action is retired and receiving pension payments, the data required for the pension valuation is somewhat different from what is needed in the case of an active employee. In addition to name, date of birth, and so forth, the following information is needed:

1. Date of retirement and the last day worked
2. Date of commencement of pension payments
3. Type of retirement with respect to timing (Normal, Early, Special Early, Late, Deferred)
4. Form of pension (straight life, fixed number of years certain, life with a guaranteed payment period, joint-and-survivor (percentage), or a combination of more than one form)
5. Whether the pension is a fixed, level amount or subject to change at a certain future date or upon attainment of a stated future age
6. Whether the pension is subject to cost-of-living increases
7. The gross amount of the pension
8. The net amount received
9. The named beneficiary(ies) if there are any post-retirement death benefits

Retirement

For purposes of a pension plan or profit-sharing plan, a participant may "retire" yet remain in active employment. If the plan so provides, a participant who reaches the plan's retirement (e.g., age 65) may start receiving benefits whether or not he or she ceases to work. Therefore, a participant may work beyond retirement age and receive both a salary and a pension. Termination of employment without commencement of pension payments may be loosely called "retirement," but it is not considered retirement in the pension sense. The concept of retirement is usually reserved for those cases in which pension payments are made either as a lump sum or as an annuity in pay status.

Retirement Equity Act

The Retirement Equity Act of 1984 (REA), as amended. The REA established the concept of and the requirements for a QDRO.

Revised Valuation

When some time has passed after a valuation of a defined benefit pension plan in a divorce case, a new valuation may need to be done. Whether to do a revised valuation depends on how much time has passed and how much interest rates have changed, if any. If the person's age has changed by one year or more, the present value will change. If interest rates have changed by more than one-half of a percentage point, revision of valuation would be warranted. However, an increase in interest rates resulting in a decrease in present value may offset the increase in present value due to increased age. In actuarial present value, values are inverse to interest rates: the higher the rate, the lower the present value. Another consideration is case law. If there has been a significant change in local case law that would affect the results, the valuation should be revised.

Salary Projection

For purposes of estimating employer contributions that fund a defined benefit pension plan, an actuary will often use a salary scale table to project future pay increases for the covered group of plan participants. Some employers may show estimated future pension benefits with illustrated future pay increases in annual benefit statements to participants. There are three general methods used in salary projections:

1. Use a fixed annual interest rate to calculate the average annual pay increase for future years (e.g., 3 percent or 5 percent per year).
2. Use salary scale tables that have been developed by actuaries. There are 15 to 20 such tables available.
3. Develop the pay history from the experience of the covered group for a particular employer or by industry.

Salary projections are generally not used for valuations of pensions in divorce except in New Jersey, where family courts allow their use.

Salary Reduction Plan

See **401(k) Plan**.

Schedule B

A qualified defined benefit pension plan under ERISA must file annual returns with the IRS using a form in the Form 5500 series. One of the attachments is Schedule B, a form that provides actuarial information on the plan and must be signed by an enrolled actuary. There may be an attachment to Schedule B, prepared by the actuary, summarizing the terms of the plan. In a divorce case involving a small pension plan, counsel may find it helpful to obtain a copy of such attachment for review.

Schedule SSA

A qualified defined benefit pension plan under ERISA must file annual returns with the IRS using a form in the Form 5500 series. One of the attachments is Schedule SSA, which is filed only to report that a participant has terminated service and has a vested right to a deferred pension benefit. Upon receipt of Schedule SSA, the IRS forwards the form to the Social Security Administration. When the retiree applies for Social Security, he or she is notified that there is a pension benefit waiting from that prior employment.

Second Wife

See **Remarriage**.

Separation Date

The cutoff date in some jurisdictions for measuring marital property, also known as the marital separation date. The separation date has significance in the valuation of pensions in two respects: (1) The monthly pension benefit accrued for service and pay may be valued up to the separation date, and (2) the separation date may be used in the denominator of the marital coverture fraction to measure the marital portion of the pension benefit or value. See **Coverture Fraction**.

Note that spouses sharing a house may be legally separated. The date that one spouse moved out of the bedroom into a separate bedroom on a different floor of the house may mark the separation date. Living in separate areas of the same house, not socializing, not eating meals together, and virtually not speaking to each other constitutes living separated and apart.

Service

Retirement plans measure an employee's length of service in three ways:

1. *Continuous service* represents the actual length of employment.
2. *Credited service* represents the period of time during which the employee is earning pension credits.

3. *Vesting service* is the period of time that is counted in the plan's vesting schedule to obtain partial or full nonforfeiture rights to a benefit. Each service may have its own definition in the plan, when it starts, when it ends, how absences are counted, conditions of minimum and maximum time periods, and so on.

Service Purchase

Some plans offer this option, also known as *buy-back*, which allows an employee who terminated service and was subsequently reemployed to recoup prior service credits. A service purchase provision may also be found in governmental pension plans for obtaining credit for military service.

Severance Pay

There are conflicting opinions on whether severance pay should be considered marital property. Two cases in California dealt with whether a spouse's employment severance benefits are community property when they are received when the marriage is ending. The rulings in both cases affirmed that severance payments are not community property, because, unlike pensions, they are made in lieu of future service, not as a reward for past service and not as deferred wages. *In re Marriage of De Shurley*, 207 Cal. App. 3d 992 (1989); *In re Marriage of Lawson*, 208 Cal. App. 3d 446 (1989). However, in Arkansas, a nonemployee-spouse was awarded one-half of the employee-spouse's severance pay when the court decided that the benefit was earned by years of service during the marriage. *Dillard v. Dillard*, 772 S.W.2d 355 (Ark. Ct. App. 1989).

Sex-Based Rates

ERISA prohibits discrimination by sex in pension benefits and values. However, the GATT and the PBGC publish sex-based mortality tables for use in computing the pension liabilities of defined benefit pension plans under their coverage. If retirement age is 65, present values of pensions for female employees whose current age is about 35 to 50 run some 20 percent higher than the present values of pensions for male employees of the same current age.

An actuary may use different mortality tables by sex of the employee as long as doing so does not affect an individual's benefits. In advising the employer on the annual contribution to a defined benefit pension plan, one of the components used in the actuarial valuation may be sex-based mortality. The pension formula in the plan does not vary by sex and will not be affected. The use of sex-based mortality tables to value life estates for inheritance tax liability does not violate equal protection even though males and females will be treated differently. The substantial increase in accuracy by using sex-based tables was required in the valuation of life estates by a New Jersey tax court in *Estate of Darrin,* 11 NJ Tax 482 (1991).

Simplified Employee Pension Plan (SEP)

A retirement program that takes the form of individual retirement accounts for all eligible employees subject to special rules on contributions and eligibility. See also **Individual Retirement Account**.

Single-Employer Plan

An ERISA plan sponsored and maintained by one employer entity. If additional employers join the plan, it is known as a multiple-employer plan. Banding together is usually done by employers who are related in ownership in some way or who are cooperating in a business venture. See **Multiemployer Plan**, **Multiple-Employer Plan**.

Social Security Benefits

Social Security benefits are not subject to equitable distribution, so present values are not computed and a QDRO cannot be used. A court may, if it wishes, recognize that a person will or will not receive Social Security benefits for purposes of measuring income. In occupations not covered by Social Security, there may be a generous defined benefit pension plan that presumably makes up for the absence of Social Security benefits. In such a case, it is possible to compute a theoretical Social Security pension and then subtract its present value from the actual pension present value to arrive at a net value for the basis of equitable distribution. It is also possible to make such an adjustment in deferred distribution. See also **Integrated Plan, Social Security Integration**.

Social Security Integration

Social Security benefits and taxes are structured upon a wage base established by federal law. The wage base changes from time to time, generally increasing every year by a cost-of-living measure. An individual whose annual income exceeds the wage base in a particular year pays taxes and eventually will receive a benefit conditioned only on the wage base. The pay in excess of the base is not counted for Social Security. An individual whose pay is always below the wage base receives benefits based on entire pay. This disparity leads to an allowance for a pension plan to provide higher benefits in a formula using pay above the wage base. A plan is said to be integrated with Social Security when it recognizes Social Security either in terms of benefits or the taxable wage base, which results in more benefits for the higher-paid participants and less for the lower-paid participants. This differential is known as a *permitted disparity*. Another approach is to subtract from the pension formula benefit a percentage of the Social Security benefit. In all cases, Social Security itself is not affected. The person receives the Social Security benefits to which he or she is entitled. It is the pension plan that works around Social Security.

Social Security Offset

A defined benefit pension plan may be integrated with Social Security in that the plan benefit formula subtracts a percentage of a computed Social Security benefit. Social Security itself is not affected, only the pension from the plan is modified. Some individuals are not covered by Social Security by virtue of their employment. For example, civilian employees of the federal government in the Civil Service Retirement System are not in Social Security. In most of these cases, and in the Civil Service especially, the employer provides a pension benefit that is larger than would be available in comparable jobs. The theory is that the pension benefit subsumes Social Security. If this reasoning is followed, then in valuing such a pension as marital property a theoretical value representing imputed Social Security would be subtracted out of the pension value. *Cornbleth v. Cornbleth*, 580 A.2d 369 (Pa. Super. Ct. 1990).

Social Security Retirement Age

The age at which an individual may apply for and receive full, unreduced Social Security benefits, known as the primary insurance amount (PIA), depends on the individual's year of birth according to the following table:

Born 1937 or earlier	Age 65
Born 1938–1954	Age 66
Born 1955 or later	Age 67

Society of Actuaries

The Society of Actuaries is a professional organization founded in 1949 with two categories of members: associates and fellows. An associate uses the designation

ASA and a fellow uses FSA. The society's address is 475 N. Martingale Road, Schaumburg, IL 60173-2226.

Sole Distribution to One Spouse

The present value of a spouse's pension, determined as a value and found to be marital property, may nevertheless be awarded solely to that spouse. *Malseed v. Malseed,* 565 A.2d 453 (Pa. Super. Ct. 1989).

Speculative Nature of Pension

The uncertainty as to whether a pension will ever be received does not preclude determination of the pension's present value or its award in equitable distribution. A pension that was accrued during the marriage but was not vested and not matured is subject to equitable distribution. *Whitfield v. Whitfield,* 535 A.2d 986 (N.J. Super. App. Div. 1987).

Spendthrift Statute

Spendthrift provisions contained in the state laws of Wisconsin prohibited a city pension plan from honoring a qualified domestic relations order. The court could order the employee-spouse to make a specific option selection under the plan, but it could not order the plan to pay a benefit directly to the nonemployee-spouse. *Lindsey v. Lindsey,* 412 N.W.2d 132 (Wis. Ct. App. 1987). See also **Alienation or Attachment of Pension, Collateral**.

Status

The status of an employee in a pension plan or profit-sharing plan varies with time and the internal plan definitions, which in general progress through the following stages:

1. Employee not eligible for membership in the plan due to status—for example, a union member or an hourly paid employee when the plan covers only salaried employees.
2. Employee not yet eligible pending attainment of age 21 and/or completion of one year of service, or transfer from an ineligible to an eligible category.
3. Eligible employee (participant) with no accrued benefits—e.g., with less than two years of credited service.

4. Participant with accrued benefits, zero vested.
5. Participant with accrued benefits, partially vested.
6. Participant with accrued benefits, fully vested.
7. Participant with matured benefits, eligible for retirement (early or normal).
8. Participant working beyond normal retirement age.
9. Retired participant in pay status receiving a pension.
10. Former participant who terminated service with partial or full vesting, waiting for age to receive deferred pension.

Statute of Limitations

A former husband had retired and was making monthly payments to his former wife from his pension, not by means of a QDRO. He stopped paying, but his former wife did nothing for 12 years. When she eventually asked the court to order her ex-husband to make current and back payments, his defense was that she was barred by the ten-year statute of limitations for enforcing judgments. Both the trial court and the appeals court ruled for the former wife. Pension payments are similar to child support; each due payment starts its own time period. The statute of limitations barred only payments that were due more than ten years earlier. *In re Ward,* 806 S.W.2d 276 (Tex. Ct. App. 1991).

Stipulation of Value

In the interest of saving time and expense, and with the perception that pension values are difficult to ascertain and to understand, the parties to a divorce may stipulate the equitable distribution of pension values. Before the stipulation is made, however, counsel for the spouse whose pension is at issue should obtain a reasonable estimate of the pension value. Occasionally, circumstances are such that the court will reject a stipulation. A change in pension value after the stipulation may or may not be considered depending on the situation. If a stipulation is a reasonable compromise, it may be accepted even though it is not as precisely accurate as possible. *In re Marriage of Hahn,* 273 Cal. Rptr. 516, 517 (Cal. Ct. App. 1990); *In re Marriage of Norris,* 302 Or. 123, 727 P.2d 113 (1986); *Wayda v. Wayda,* 576 A.2d 1060 (Pa. Super. Ct. 1990); *Negrotti v. Negrotti,* 98 N.J. 428, 487 A.2d 328 (1985).

Strike

What happens to the pension of a striking worker is not definitively established. Conflicting results in two cases involving strikes and pension benefits still stand because the United States Supreme Court refused to hear them, allowing the Circuit Court of Appeals' decisions to stand. Newspaper workers in Wilkes-Barre, Pennsylvania, incurred reductions in their pensions for the period on strike. The Third Circuit allowed the reductions because the employees were not at work and earned no pay during the strike. *Wilkes-Barre Publ'g Co. v. Newspaper Guild,* 647 F.2d 372 (3d Cir. 1981). However, the same circuit court disallowed reductions in Teamsters' pensions due to a strike for different reasons. If the time the Teamsters were on strike had been subtracted out of the Teamsters' pensions, it would have affected the pension benefit accrual rate, not just its service component. That would have been the same as an amendment reducing benefit accruals, which is prohibited by ERISA. *Hoover v. Cumberland Area Teamsters Pension Fund,* 756 F.2d 977 (3d Cir. 1985).

Structured Settlements

Structured settlement offers are common in personal injury and wrongful death cases, and they arise once in a while in pension settlement situations as well. A structured settlement offer takes many forms, but it usually follows a pattern: payment of $X now, followed by a payment of $Y five years hence, then $Z five years after that, followed by a final payment of $W ten years later. The offer may or may not continue for the stated numbers of years whether or not the recipient dies. To decide whether to accept such an offer and how to prepare a counter request, it is necessary to reduce the future promised stream of payments to one lump-sum present value. This is a mathematical problem solved with actuarial techniques. The actuary can evaluate any set of payment times, amounts, and conditions, using various interest rate assumptions and introducing a mortality factor if any of the payments depends on the recipient's survival.

Subsidized Early Retirement

A defined benefit pension plan has a normal retirement age. Pension payments that begin at a younger age cost more, so they are reduced to reflect the actuarial difference. A true actuarial reduction takes into account sex, age, mortality, and interest rates and keeps the plan in actuarial balance. Many plans provide reduced early retirement benefits under a more favorable system than true actuarial reduction. The system may be adopted for administrative convenience as well as the plan's and the employees' ease of understanding. Early retirement factors in the plan may be subsidized in order not to penalize employees who retire early. Such subsidization may be due to the employer's generosity or to its corporate policy to encourage employees to leave early. Any reduction factors that produce early retirement benefits greater than true actuarial are considered subsidies. The subsidized early retirement is paid from the employer's annual contributions as determined by the plan's enrolled actuary in general for the whole group.

Subsidized Joint-and-Survivor Pension

Pension payments that cover two lives cost more, so they are reduced to reflect the actuarial difference. A true actuarial reduction takes into account sex, age, mortality, and interest rates and keeps the plan in actuarial balance. Many plans provide joint-and-survivor reductions under a more favorable system than the true actuarial reduction. This may be done for administrative convenience or for the plan's and the employees' ease of understanding. Any reduction factors that produce joint-and-survivor benefits greater than true actuarial factors would warrant are considered subsidies. The subsidized feature is paid for from the employer's annual contributions as determined by the plan's enrolled actuary in general for the whole group. See **Qualified Joint-and Survivor Annuity**.

Summary Annual Report

A report that a qualified plan is required to furnish to participants annually, giving a summary of the highlights of the plan's overall financial transactions.

Summary of Material Modifications

A qualified ERISA plan is required to update its summary plan description (SPD) whenever there is a significant plan amendment. Rather than reprint the SPD in total each time, the plan may issue a summary of material modifications (SMM) as an update. When gathering information on a plan, counsel should always request the SMM.

Summary Plan Description

Every qualified ERISA plan is required to have a summary plan description (SPD) that summarizes the terms and conditions of the plan in language designed to be understood by the typical plan participant. Because it is usually printed in the format of a booklet, the SPD has come to be known as the *plan booklet* even if it is not in the size or shape of a booklet. The plan administrator must keep a supply of SPDs available and must give one to every employee, whether or not the employee is a plan participant (with certain exceptions for nonunion members).

Note that the SPD is not the same as the governing plan document. The plan document must be made available for inspection at no cost at the main office of the plan administrator, and a reasonable fee may be charged for making a copy for a plan participant.

Survivor Benefits

A post-retirement death benefit in a defined benefit pension plan is a common form of survivor benefit. The provision for a beneficiary to receive a payment upon the death of a pensioner is not free. Normally, the retiree's pension is reduced to allow for the potential death benefit. In an immediate offset valuation for equitable distribution of a pension, the present value of the pension automatically includes survivor benefits without any special calculations. This is because the retiree's pension for life, without a survivor feature, has a certain value. When the pension is reduced to provide survivor benefits, the pensioner gets a smaller pension, but the value of the combined benefits is the same as the value of the lifetime benefit before reduction. See also **Qualified Joint-and Survivor Annuity**.

Suspense Account

A bookkeeping account in a defined contribution plan that records amounts forfeited by employees who left employment before they were fully vested. Eventually the amounts held in suspense are reallocated among the accounts of the remaining participants in the plan.

Taft-Hartley Plan

See **Collectively Bargained Plan**.

Target Plan

A defined contribution plan with individual accounts that is also known as a target benefit plan or an assumed benefit plan. The plan contains a benefit formula that sets forth the theoretical retirement pension. The employer makes actuarially determined contributions to fund the targeted pension. The employee will not receive that pension, however. The employee receives the balance in his or her account. The individual account consists of employer contributions and investment gains and sometimes employee contributions. A target plan is subject to valuation for equitable distribution and to a QDRO. If a QDRO is served on the plan, it should award a percentage of the account rather than a lump-sum amount or a monthly pension.

Taxation

Pension payouts are taxed first to the recipient as personal ordinary income in the year in which received. If paid as an annuity, the total amount received each year is subject to personal ordinary income tax. If paid in a lump sum, the pension may be eligible to be rolled over into an IRA to defer taxes. Annuity payments are not permitted to be rolled over. If there have been employee contributions, the taxable portion of the received benefits is adjusted. Payments to a former spouse (alternate payee) pursuant to a QDRO are taxable to the recipient, not to the participant. If a lump sum is paid by the QDRO, it is not subject to the premature distribution 10 percent excise tax penalty, regardless of the age of the alternate payee. This is true whether or not the lump sum is rolled over into an IRA.

TIAA-CREF

The Teachers Insurance Annuity Association and College Retirement Equities Fund is a special kind of insurance company for the use of Section 501(3)(c) institutions such as universities, colleges, teaching hospitals, and museums. It receives contributions, holds and invests the monies, and then makes annuity payments to retired employees. TIAA-CREF is a voluntary program on two levels: The employer has the option of participating, and each eligible employee of a participating employer has the option of joining. TIAA-CREF itself is not a pension plan; it is a funding vehicle. It will accept the equivalent of a QDRO upon proper processing and set up a separate account for the divorced spouse. The TIAA portion of a participant's account is invested in fixed-income investments, whereas the CREF portion is in equity securities like a mutual fund. Each participant has the choice of allocating his or her account among TIAA and CREF in varying percentages. TIAA-CREF accounts are subject to valuation as well as to deferred distribution.

Time Rule

Used to determine what portion of a pension value is marital property subject to equitable distribution by use of a fraction (usually in a defined benefit pension plan). The numerator of the fraction is the period of time from the later of (a) date of marriage or (b) date of plan entry to the cutoff date in the applicable jurisdiction. The cutoff date may be the date of marital separation, the date of filing of the divorce complaint, the date of hearing or trial, or the date of the divorce decree. The denominator is the period of time from the date of plan entry to the cutoff date in the applicable jurisdiction. The ending point of the denominator should agree with the date as of which the benefit is being measured.

Top-Heavy Plan

An ERISA plan in which either the benefits or contributions are weighted more for higher-paid employees than for lower-paid employees, within permissible limits. When a plan is considered top-heavy, it is required to have faster vesting than a plan that is not top-heavy. The status of being top-heavy may vary from year to year. In general, a plan is top-heavy if more than 60 percent of the benefits or contributions are attributable to key employees. In a top-heavy plan, there are minimum requirements for benefits and/or contributions for the non-key employees. See **Key Employee**.

Total Offset

There are two entirely different meanings to this phrase: (1) The use of the present value of the pension as an immediate offset compared to other marital property in equitable distribution may be considered to be a total offset of the pension, and (2) the computation of the present value of a pension discounts future amounts to the present by taking interest and mortality into account. If it is supposed that the future rate of inflation is exactly equal to the interest rate, then it could be argued that they offset each other in a total offset. This concept is rarely used in valuation of pensions in divorce.

Tracing

A method of attempting to identify marital property in the assets of a pension plan, usually a defined contribution plan. Every contribution made by the employer and by the employee is accounted for, with the separate investment results attributed to each activity. This is a very difficult and time consuming process that is rarely used.

Transfer/Rollover

A *transfer* occurs when, pursuant to a QDRO, the trustee of a qualified plan in which the employee-spouse is a participant writes a check for an amount of money directly to the trustee of the alternate payee's IRA. The check is made payable to the IRA, not to the alternate payee. The transfer is thus exempt from the 20 percent withholding for federal income tax and, regardless of the alternate payee's age, exempt from the 10 percent excise tax for early withdrawal.

A *rollover* occurs after a person has received a distribution paid out from a qualified plan or from an IRA. The recipient of the funds from the plan or the IRA has a 60-day period in which to roll over all or part of the money into an IRA. If the rollover is done within 60 days, there is no immediate tax consequence. However, if the payment comes from a qualified plan as a lump-sum distribution, it is subject to 20 percent withholding for federal income taxes whether or not it is rolled over into an IRA. The age of the person has no bearing on the availability of a rollover or on the 20 percent withholding.

Trust

The assets of a qualified ERISA plan are held in trust. The funds must be kept separate from the employer's funds. The trust is tax sheltered. The document establishing the trust may be a separate item known as the trust agreement, or it may be included in the plan document, which would be called the plan and trust. A QDRO would not be served on the trust, but on the plan administrator. In some cases, it would be helpful for the trust to be informed if a QDRO is being considered. See **Wasting Trust**.

Trustee

The entity that holds and invests the plan funds. The trustee's fiduciary responsibility may be held by an individual, a committee, a bank, or a trust company. A corporate employer normally would not be its own plan trustee; however, a bank that has a plan for its employees may have the bank trust department serve as trustee. Although in a small plan the same person may be the plan administrator and trustee, procedurally the trustee is not the plan administrator. For example, a QDRO would be served on the plan administrator, not the trustee. A professional person, such as a doctor, lawyer, actuary, or accountant who forms a professional corporation, may establish and maintain a pension plan and be its trustee. If state law allows a sole trustee with one person as both trustee and beneficiary, then federal pension law will accept it. It is possible for one person to be the owner-employer, the employee, the participant, the plan administrator, and the trustee. Sometimes a husband and wife may serve as plan trustees. In case of a divorce, the situation must be carefully examined to protect the interests of all involved, especially the duties and responsibilities of the co-trustees toward each other and the assets in the pension trust fund.

Underfunded

A defined benefit pension plan undergoes regular actuarial valuations, usually every year, that measure the plan's assets and liabilities and guide the employer in the amount of contributions to be made to keep the plan funded. Each plan valuation includes a "snapshot" of the total of the present value of all of the accrued benefits to date for all of the participants. If this total value exceeds the value of plan assets, the plan is said to be underfunded on that basis. This is not an unusual situation, nor is it a cause for concern in most cases. However, in a divorce involving a person who is the owner of a small professional practice and who may be the only participant in the plan, the amount of plan funding should be examined. Assume, for example, the husband controls the plan and the value of his accrued pension is $100,000. The marital portion is $80,000, and the wife is awarded $40,000. However, the plan is underfunded: It does not have $100,000 or even $80,000 in assets, so the husband claims his wife's share should be reduced. The counter argument is that if the plan has enough funding to meet the wife's share, it can be awarded to her on the presumption that eventually the husband's share will catch up with future contributions and investment results.

Union Member

A union member is a person who belongs to a union in connection with his employment with an employer who has a collective bargaining agreement with the union. The person would be covered by a multiemployer pension plan. If the person is an officer or office staff employee of the union and the union has its own pension plan, the person would be a participant in two plans: the multiemployer plan and the union's own plan. If the person is a high-level union official he or she may also be an officer or employee of the national union and a participant in the union's national pension plan and, therefore, a simultaneous participant in three pension plans. See **Multiemployer Plan**.

Unisex Tables

Actuaries have constructed mortality tables that blend together the separate statistics for male and female mortality so that the tables' use would be based on the age of the person only, regardless of gender. Unisex tables should be used with care because different tables have been constructed for different reasons with varying blends of male and female components. For example, a mortality table for nurses or clerical workers or other occupations in which female employees traditionally outnumber male employees would be a unisex table with a combination of more females than males. A unisex table for traditional male occupations, on the other hand, would have a combination that is predominantly male. All unisex tables are not equal. The PBGC starts its mortality table as a unisex table and then adjusts it separately by sex so that males and females have different rates and factors. Female factors are higher, so the present value of the same pension for a man and for a woman of the same age would be higher for the woman. The pension itself is not affected, so there is no discrimination in the pension plan. See **Sex-Based Rates**.

Unit Benefit Plan

A defined benefit pension plan in which the benefit formula is based on a small unit multiplied by the number of years of credited service. The unit may be a dollar amount or a percentage of pay. An example would be $25 of monthly pension per year of service, so that with 30 years the pension is $750 a month. Or, the formula could be one percent of pay per year of service (pay having its own definition, varying by plan), so that with 30 years of service and average monthly pay of $2,000 the pension is $600 a month.

Updating Valuation

If the present value of an individual's pension in a defined benefit pension plan was computed more than one year before the case is due to be heard or settled, the present value must be updated. It is not correct to merely add interest to the prior value, because the old value was computed using the interest rates of a year ago. Because interest rates generally change over time, the value would have to be recomputed as of the prior date using current interest rates before it can serve as a basis for updating. Furthermore, the old value was computed using a mortality discount, and the person is still alive; so the mortality component would have to be added back. The preferred method for updating is to do a new, current valuation based on current age and current interest rates.

Valuation Date

To determine the present value of a defined benefit pension plan for immediate offset for equitable distribution, it is necessary to have a specific valuation date. The "present" in present value refers to the valuation date. On a given valuation date, the person's age, length of service, and eligibility for benefits will be determined. The valuation date also will determine what assumptions the actuary makes as to mortality tables and interest rates. Some jurisdictions require that the valuation date be as close as possible to the date the divorce is settled, the date of distribution. In this context, distribution does not mean that the pension plan makes a payment, but rather that the marital property is distributed.

Vesting and Vesting Schedules

Vesting bestows on an employee a nonforfeitable right to a pension. All ERISA plans must contain an approved vesting schedule by which a plan participant attains the rights to a pension. There are standard schedules from which a plan may choose and one required schedule if the plan is top-heavy. Union plans, known as multiemployer plans, have a different set of rules. A plan may have a vesting schedule that is more generous, but not one that is more strict. Some non-ERISA plans have no vesting as such, in that an employee must qualify for retirement to receive a benefit; termination of service at a time the employee is not eligible for a pension results in loss of all benefits. The Armed Forces Retirement System, for example, has no vesting prior to retirement eligibility. See **Cliff Vesting**.

Veteran's Pension

Retired military personnel receive a pension if they are eligible. This is called a military or armed forces pension or a veteran's pension. If it is a regular pension for service, then it is treated routinely in a divorce case. The pension has a present value, and it may be the subject of a court order equivalent in effect to a QDRO. A medical or disability pension is different. In most jurisdictions, a disability pension will not be included as marital property. The exact description and details of any such pension should be obtained. See **Disability Pension**.

Waiver of Benefits

In certain special cases, usually involving a small defined benefit pension plan, the key executive or owner of the company may have waived a portion of potential pension benefits to stay within plan limits or under government-mandated maximums. It may be a *moving waiver* that automatically adjusts upward as limits or maximums increase by law or regulation. In appraising the pension value as marital property or in drafting a QDRO, care should be taken to see if any such waiver exists.

Waiver of Joint-and-Survivor Annuity

Every qualified ERISA defined benefit pension plan must provide that if the recipient of benefits is married, the benefits must be payable in the form of a qualified joint-and-survivor (J&S) annuity with the spouse as the beneficiary. This requirement applies to certain defined contribution plans, also depending on the terms and provisions of the particular plan. The waiver of a J&S annuity is applicable only at the time of benefits payments, with no bearing if benefits are not yet being paid. If the marriage is dissolved by divorce before benefits begin, this feature does not apply. In most plans, this benefit is not free of cost. For the participant and spouse to receive a J&S pension, the basic monthly pension would be reduced by actuarial factors recognizing the age of the spouse. To avoid the benefit reduction or to request a different form of optional pension, the nonemployee-spouse must sign a waiver of J&S annuity, and the waiver must be witnessed by a designated plan officer or notarized.

Waiver of Withholding

An individual receiving benefits from a pension plan must have personal ordinary income tax withheld unless a waiver of withholding has been signed. This would apply as well to an alternate payee receiving benefits under a QDRO. It is up to the individual recipient to sign the waiver before receiving benefits. If a pension has started and is in pay status, it may be possible for the recipient to ask the plan to stop tax withholding. The plan should be willing to comply if the proper paperwork is done. Note that the waiver is applicable to annuity payments, not a lump-sum distribution.

Wasting Trust

When a defined benefit plan has terminated but not distributed plan assets, the funds are held in a so-called wasting trust. No contributions are made, but there are investment gains. As benefits will be paid out eventually, the assets in trust will be used up "wasting" away to zero. Even though the plan has terminated, it is still subject to valuation and available for QDRO because its assets are in a tax shelter.

Windfall

A pension award to the nonemployee-spouse may be considered to be a windfall because of the size or the percentage awarded. Depending on the facts and circumstances of a particular case, the court may award far more than 50 percent of a pension to the nonemployee-spouse for various reasons. Sometimes the death of the employee-spouse under a QDRO may produce a larger than expected benefit for the nonemployee-spouse, or a windfall. If a QDRO is such that the alternate payee continues to receive a pension after the retiree dies and in addition receives a survivor benefit, the alternate payee may be considered to have received a windfall or a death bonus.

Wrongful Discharge

In a case of wrongful discharge from employment, or wrongful termination of service, damages should include not only lost wages, but also the loss of potential pension benefits as marital property. It is possible for an actuary to compute the pension's present value and a lump sum for damages.

Year of Service

The concept of year of service, introduced by ERISA, is important in the determination of a participant's accrued benefit account balance at any time. A plan may define a year to be a consecutive period of 12 months in which the participant has attained at least 1,000 hours of service, or it may define a year as the period between the first day and the last day of the particular plan year. When the measure of a year is the completion of 1,000 hours of service, the employee will receive credit for a year of vesting and benefit accrual about halfway through a particular year. Attention should be paid to the timing if a person otherwise appears to be about six months short of attaining eligibility, vesting, or benefit accrual.

Zero-Coupon Bonds

Bonds sold at deep discount. The word "coupon" in connection with a bond refers to its nominal yield. For example, a 6 percent coupon on a bond with a par value of $1,000 pays $60 interest per year. A zero-coupon bond pays no interest, but its original issue purchase price is very low compared to its par value. For example, a $1,000 zero-coupon bond may sell at issue for $200 or $300. At maturity, the bond is redeemed at its face value of $1,000. The difference between the bond's redemption value at maturity and its purchase price is the realized gain or profit.

Zero-coupon bonds are created by "stripping" bonds of their coupons. The coupons are bundled and sold as separate investment items to purchasers who desire income but receive no interest. The purchaser of the bond holds it in expectation of receiving a realized gain as the bond increases in market value on its way to maturity. If a person who is entitled to full and true ownership of zero-coupon bonds sells the bonds, he or she would have a realized gain. If the person's entitlement is limited only to interest, dividends, and realized gains on sales, and the bonds are not sold, that person would receive nothing from holding the zero-coupon bonds. The bonds pay no interest or dividends, and there is no actual profit from them until they are sold. While the bonds are held, their investment growth is measured as unrealized appreciation.

INDEX

INDEX

INDEX